The al-Baqara Crescendo

Advancing Studies in Religion

SERIES EDITOR: CHRISTINE MITCHELL

Advancing Studies in Religion catalyzes and provokes original research in the study of religion with a critical edge. The series advances the study of religion in method and theory, textual interpretation, theological studies, and the understanding of lived religious experience. Rooted in the long and diverse traditions of the study of religion in Canada, the series demonstrates awareness of the complex genealogy of religion as a category and as a discipline. ASR welcomes submissions from authors researching religion in varied contexts and with diverse methodologies.

The series is sponsored by the Canadian Corporation for Studies in Religion whose constituent societies include the Canadian Society of Biblical Studies, Canadian Society for the Study of Religion, Canadian Society of Patristic Studies, Canadian Theological Society, Société canadienne de théologie, and Société québécoise pour l'étude de la religion.

1 The al-Baqara Crescendo
Understanding the Qur'an's Style, Narrative Structure, and Running Themes
Nevin Reda

The al-Baqara Crescendo

Understanding the Qur'an's Style, Narrative Structure, and Running Themes

Nevin Reda

McGill-Queen's University Press
Montreal & Kingston • London • Chicago

© McGill-Queen's University Press 2017

ISBN 978-0-7735-4885-5 (cloth)
ISBN 978-0-7735-4886-2 (paper)
ISBN 978-0-7735-4887-9 (ePDF)
ISBN 978-0-7735-4888-6 (ePUB)

Legal deposit first quarter 2017
Bibliothèque nationale du Québec

Printed in Canada on acid-free paper that is 100% ancient forest
free (100% post-consumer recycled), processed chlorine free

This book has been published with the help of a grant from the
Canadian Federation for the Humanities and Social Sciences,
through the Awards to Scholarly Publications Program, using funds
provided by the Social Sciences and Humanities Research Council
of Canada.

McGill-Queen's University Press acknowledges the support of the
Canada Council for the Arts for our publishing program. We also
acknowledge the financial support of the Government of Canada
through the Canada Book Fund for our publishing activities.

Library and Archives Canada Cataloguing in Publication

Reda, Nevin, 1965–, author
The al-Baqara crescendo : understanding the Qur'an's style,
narrative structure, and running themes / Nevin Reda.

(Advancing studies in religion ; 1)
Includes bibliographical references and index.
Issued in print and electronic formats.
ISBN 978-0-7735-4885-5 (cloth).
– ISBN 978-0-7735-4886-2 (paper).
– ISBN 978-0-7735-4887-9 (ePDF).
– ISBN 978-0-7735-4888-6 (ePUB)

1. Qur'an. Sūrat al-Baqarah – Commentaries. I. Title. II. Series:
Advancing studies in religion ; 1

BP128.17.R43 2017   297.1'22721   C2016-905747-X
                                        C2016-905748-8

For my daughters,
Naila, Malak, Lenah, and Jasmin Zeinab El-Tahry;
my nieces, Hedayat and Zein Reda; and
my nephews, Ismail, Hussein, and Ali Reda

Contents

Tables

Acknowledgments

Surat al-Baqara has been a wellspring of discovery and inspiration for me: first, when writing my doctoral dissertation, entitled "Coherence in the Qurʾan: Repetition and Narrative Structure in Surat al-Baqara"; and second, when rewriting it for this monograph. In addition to the thought-provoking qualities of this extraordinary text, many outstanding individuals have contributed to the successful completion of this monograph, and to them I express my heartfelt appreciation. I begin by recognizing the contributions of Malak Ḥifni Nāṣif (d. 1918), Hudā Shaʿrāwī (d. 1947), Nabawiyya Mūsā (d. 1951), Durriyya Shafīq (d. 1975), and all the pioneers of the Islamic feminist movement in Egypt, without whose struggle to bring education to girls, I may never have learned to read. I also acknowledge their contemporary counterparts whose scholarship has helped to develop the field of Islamic studies, particularly in the areas of hermeneutics and Islamic feminism. The ones who have inspired me, befriended me, and/or helped to shape my thinking the most include Amina Wadud, Laleh Bakhtiar, Ziba Mir-Hosseini, Jasmin Zine, Ayesha Siddiqua Chaudhry, Aisha Geissinger, Maliha Chishti, Omaima Abu Bakr, Mulki al-Sharmani, Asma Afsaruddin, and Laury Silvers.

With regard to my dissertation, which prefigured this book, I thank my many teachers, friends, and colleagues in the Department of Near and Middle Eastern Civilizations at the University of Toronto. Foremost in this group is my thesis supervisor, Todd Lawson, who offered me excellent advice and academic guidance at every stage of my work. He also shared with me his expertise on the Qurʾan and on Islamic thought during my years of graduate studies. It is he who first drew my attention to the word "crescendo," which figures so strongly in this heavily revised monograph.

I owe a special thanks to my committee members for their painstaking review of my dissertation and for being such excellent teachers over the years. Walid Saleh taught me how to approach the classical *tafsīr* commentaries and brought me to an appreciation of the breadth and sophistication of this tradition. Sebastian Günther shared with me some of his extensive knowledge of the classical Arabic sources of Islamic thought, particularly those related to education. On the Biblical side of my education, I am deeply indebted to R. Theodore Lutz for teaching me almost everything I know about the Biblical Hebrew language and how to analyze its poetry. It was during my study of the Psalms that I first came across inclusios and realized their importance for the study of Surat al-Baqara. I am also profoundly grateful to my external examiner, Angelika Neuwirth, for her valuable insights, particularly in relation to the diachronic approaches. My dissertation was made possible by a University of Toronto doctoral fellowship. I am also indebted to my school in Cairo, the Deutsche Evangelische Oberschule, where I learned the German language at an early age, without which I would not have had access to some of the ground-breaking scholarship upon which my work is founded.

The journey of turning my dissertation into a book and the numerous revisions, additions, and deletions that it entailed also received support. I owe a special thank you to Katherine Bullock for her thorough reading and invaluable feedback in the final stages of the manuscript's editing. She has come to my aid at a critical juncture of my academic life on more than one occasion. I also owe thanks to my friends and colleagues at Emmanuel College of Victoria University at the University of Toronto, who contribute to a working environment of colleagiality and scholarly excellence that is conducive to intellectual dynamism. I am particularly grateful to Pamela Couture, who went out of her way to support this work, giving me valuable feedback on my initial book proposal to McGill-Queen's University Press. I also owe thanks to Mark Toulouse and Terence Donaldson for introducing me to Christine Mitchell, who made publication of this volume possible, and to my excellent editorial team at McGill-Queen's, led by Kyla Madden, Ryan Van Huijstee, and

Robert Lewis. My daughter Malak El-Tahry spent many hours indexing the book. Two anonymous reviewers for the press also provided me with superb feedback, which has helped me to fine-tune this manuscript.

Without an audience, no author can see her work come alive and touch the hearts and minds of people. I take this opportunity to thank the Noor Cultural Centre, its president, Samira Kanji, and its young coordinators, Azeezah and Khadijah Kanji, for allowing me a platform to disseminate my work outside of the purely academic milieu, and the Canadian Council of Muslim Women and its executive director, Alia Hogben, who have always had my back in my many endeavours. I also express my appreciation to Shari Golberg and Susan Harrison, with whom I have worked across faith traditions on various occasions for more than a decade, reading texts and bringing them to a larger audience. Surat al-Baqara has often featured in these diverse initiatives.

Finally, I express my deepest gratitude to my mother, Zeinab Hanem Aboul Fetouh, and my sister, Jehan Reda, for their unwavering support of me and my children, as well as to my brother, Omar Reda, and my late father, Ismail Reda, for their encouragement and belief in me. My sister and my brother were my first nonspecialist readers, providing me with pointers to make the book more comprehensible to the general public. Their spouses, Akram Reda and Laila Marei, also lent valuable support throughout my al-Baqara venture. Last but not least, I owe a very special thank you to my husband, Yehia El-Tahry, for his constant support and many sacrifices, as well as to our beloved daughters, Naila, Malak, Lenah, and Jasmin Zeinab, for forgoing many precious hours of family time and motherly care. Also in my thoughts are my nieces, Hedayat and Zein Reda, and my nephews, Ismail, Hussein, and Ali Reda, who are always in my heart, even though they are an ocean away. This book is dedicated to my daughters, nieces, and nephews with the hope that their generation may find delight in the radiant Surat al-Baqara.

The al-Baqara Crescendo

Introduction

The notion of crescendo stems from the world of music, which recalls the chanting of the Qur'an, with its melodious rhythms and rhymes. The performance, aesthetic reception, and emotive qualities of the sacred text have the ephemerality and elusiveness of the experience of music. Like song, the chanted Qur'an can evoke feelings of sadness and joy, apprehension and calm, mounting exhilaration and abrupt culmination. It comes to life in the soundscape, a virtual kaleidoscope of auditory artistic expression, even while it can be trapped in the pages of a book and transmitted through the visual dimension alone. When captured in the written word, the Qur'an gains a more solid, tangible dimension that is conducive to visual scrutiny and minute scholarly analysis. This form enables the seeker to explore the text's vast landscape of literary figures and artistic qualities that help to explain the emotive experience. The scholar is able to marshal theories, methodologies, and cross-disciplinary insights in order to illuminate the unique blend of characteristics and constituents that make up the sacred text. Understanding these features can enhance the aural experience, when the words are set free in the acoustic realm.

Like many scholars before me, I keep track of the aural dimension of the Qur'an while examining the written word at leisure and applying theories from various disciplines that can greatly contribute to understanding its style, narrative structure, and running themes. In the world of Qur'an scholarship, East and West come together, each bringing its unique strengths and preoccupations to the study of the scripture and thereby enriching the field with a plethora of provocative ideas and interdisciplinary insights. Within this cornucopia of intellectual treasures, holistic approaches have emerged that treat the Qur'an and its individual suras as whole coherent units, as opposed to employing the more traditional, atomistic, verse-by-verse treatments. They are based on the assumption that disjointed methods of interpretation lead to a fragmented grasp of the sacred text, whereas holistic ones produce a more comprehensive understanding. Islamic feminists in particular are taking a decided interest in this emerging trend and are searching for readings that are more conducive to contemporary aspirations of social justice and women's rights. Such reformists explore the Qur'an's compositional schema because they think that it will produce new understandings that will change the way the text has been interpreted across the ages. These creative thinkers imagine a Qur'an that consistently makes sense and that elevates human thinking into new realms for the benefit of all of humanity. But where does one begin this journey? For some, it must start at the very beginning of the scripture with a structural analysis of Surat al-Baqara, the first major hurdle in unlocking the mysteries of the Qur'an's unusual configuration.

Not all suras currently pose a significant challenge to structural analysis, at least from the perspective of the Western academy, where the composition of Qur'anic suras has received considerable, if somewhat haphazard, attention. Early Orientalists who pioneered the study of the Qur'an in the West were of the opinion that it is a disjointed assortment of pericopes. For example, Richard Bell (d. 1952) argued that the unit of composition was not the sura but rather the short piece.[1] For him, these short pieces did not display organizational consistency and could not be considered strophes, contrary to the argument of his somewhat older, ingenious contemporary David Heinrich Müller (d. 1912). Rather, for Bell, disconnectedness was a major characteristic of the Qur'an's general style.[2] Reynold Alleyne Nicholson's (d. 1945) appraisal was probably the harshest (and hastiest) in expressing early Orientalist difficulties with understanding the Qur'an's organization: "The preposterous arrangement of the Koran … is mainly responsible for the opinion almost unanimously held by European readers that it is obscure, tiresome, uninteresting; a farrago of long-winded narratives and prosaic exhortations, quite unworthy to be named in the same breath with the Prophetic Books of the Old Testament."[3] Nonetheless, as the discipline evolved, scholars were able to identify structural outlines for some of the smaller suras, particularly Meccan ones, which are associated with the first years of the prophet's mission in the city of Mecca. In particular, the work of Angelika Neuwirth on their structure and composition has led to the widely promulgated notion that these suras form coherent units.[4] She follows in the tradition of Theodor Nöldeke (d. 1930), who explored the Qurʾan's historical development by connecting it to its immediate, ancient Arabian context.[5] However, like Nöldeke, most scholars were unable to identify a compositional schema for the longer Medinan suras, which are associated with the later years of the prophet's mission in the city of Medina. These suras can often appear confusing and disjointed due to their considerable length and multiple topics. Bell's assessment of the Qurʾan's style still holds traction here, scholars not being in agreement on whether Medinan suras display a tangible, identifiable structure or whether they are a disorganized jumble of verses without rhyme or reason.

There are many challenges associated with approaching al-Baqara and the rest of the long Medinan suras as whole, cohesive units, not the least of which are length and disparity of contents. Their difficulties are exacerbated by the Qurʾan's history since it emerged piecemeal, not as a single unit. Thus, although some of its passages are associated with certain events, the tradition often relates others to different sets of events, even within the same sura, thereby strengthening the case for the longer suras being "collection baskets for isolated verse groups."[6] There is also no consensus among scholars as to when the Qurʾan took its final form; whereas some attribute its internal arrangement to the time of Muḥammad (d. 9/632), others locate it in the reign of the third caliph ʿUthmān ibn ʿAffān (d. 34/656). Last but not least is the problem of chronology: the Qurʾan's organization in its present-day form differs from the order of revelation, so it is not possible to assume a historically chronological schema of composition.

Surat al-Baqara is the longest of the Medinan suras and, in fact, the longest sura in the Qurʾan; it spans 286 verses and comprises more than two of the thirty parts into which contemporary editions of the Qurʾan are divided. Its size is commensurate with the number of topics it treats, so it epitomizes the textual and literary challenges of the Medinan suras. Moreover, it has a foremost position in the canon since it is the first sura a reader or listener is faced with after the short, simple, seven-verse Surat al-Fātiḥa. Al-Baqara thereby almost invites readers to take up its challenges first and to bridge this hurdle before attempting to proceed further into the Qurʾan.

In spite of the challenges, one thing about Surat al-Baqara – and indeed the entire Qurʾan – remains clear: at some point in early Islamic history, it took its final shape and position in the canon; recent manuscript evidence from the mosque Al-Jāmiʿ al-Kabīr in the city of Ṣanʿāʾ suggests a likely *terminus ante quem* of 671 CE.[7] It has remained more or less unchanged ever since and has functioned in Muslim life and liturgy in this form. The question is whether Surat al-Baqara followed some sort of compositional schema when this final form took shape? Irrespective of who composed it or when it materialized, did the sura follow a preconceived plan? In other words, does al-Baqara have a clearly defined structure and a unifying factor indicating that it is a coherent composition, even one imbued with organizational aesthetics?

In the following pages, I answer this question using insights gained from literary theory and from the study of the Bible, particularly the notion of orality. It is the contention here that approaching al-Baqara as an *oral* text by paying attention to its *oral* structural markers can help to provide answers. Although we are now used to reading texts that use visual forms of typesetting to highlight and organize them, there was a stronger focus on orality in pre-Islamic Arabia and the early centuries of Islam. Even today, the Qurʾan has not lost its oral dimension; it is recited out loud in the liturgy and elsewhere and has not lost its aural appeal, even while it has acquired a substantial visual dimension. Beginning to comprehend the oral/aural dimension of this text requires a shift in thinking that transposes one into an auditory mind frame, where oral/aural methods of organizing text are dominant.

The notion of orality – and also its related aurality – is not new in the study of the Qurʾan; for example, Michael Sells has pointed to aural intertextuality as a feature of some of the hymnic suras.[8] Here, I use orality and aurality more or less interchangibly since my concern is with the distinction between the auditory and visual realms, not with the finer nuances of giving and receiving verbal communication. The general topic of orality/aurality is in need of further research, and addressing it in full is beyond the scope of this work. Rather, the concern here is with specific oral structural markers and how they systematically identify al-Baqara's compositional subunits and contribute to our understanding of the sura. It is the contention here that these primarily oral organizational features help to identify the sura's general layout and distinctive characteristics. Moreover, when the sura is viewed as a totality, it becomes evident that these rhetorical devices and literary figures contribute to a gradual increase in intensity, culminating in a peak. Whereas in a musical crescendo this feat is accomplished through the medium of volume, in Surat al-Baqara such an artistic phenomenon is embedded in its compositional schema. Rather than employing decibels, the al-Baqara crescendo is composed of narrative, themes, and above all repetitions, which take very distinct forms. Like a musical crescendo, it can be visually discerned in the captured word but cannot be fully appreciated unless released into the auditory realm and aurally experienced.

Some of the concepts and terminology employed here are more commonly used in the study of the Bible, including terms such as "holistic," "inclusio," "*Leitwort*," "concatenation," "divine self-revelation," "poetics," "synchronic," and "diachronic." They need to be qualified for use in the Qurʾanic context, and the subtle differences between their meanings in the various discourses need to be clarified, whether these discourses are Muslim, Christian, or Jewish. This endeavour highlights the connections between the discourses and anchors this study within the larger context of the Abrahamic scriptural heritage, thereby situating the Qurʾan within its "Biblical" literary tradition, as previously advocated by Andrew Rippin.[9]

For example, in Biblical studies, both synchronic and diachronic approaches are used to study the Biblical text, the former treating the text "as is" and the latter examining its development over time. Yet despite this difference or because of it, the contributions of each approach are well recognized within the discipline. In Qur'anic studies, diachronic approaches have a history but have so far failed to solve the riddle of al-Baqara's structure. Here, I use a synchronic approach when positing answers to this riddle. Although I do not deny the valuable contributions of diachronic approaches, some questions are best answered using a synchronic approach, which can provide different and equally valuable insights. Viewing the two approaches together within the broader Biblical context shows the history and significance of both kinds of approaches and how both can enrich the discipline.

The intellectual straddling of Qur'anic and Biblical fields of study is not unusual but has a longstanding history in the West. Particularly in the early burgeoning of Islamic scholarship, some of the foremost scholars of Islam were prominent Biblical scholars who produced worthy publications in both fields, such as Abraham Geiger (d. 1874), Julius Wellhausen (d. 1918), and Theodor Nöldeke (d. 1930).[10] Today, even though the growth of scholarship has made it increasingly difficult to combine expertise in both fields, there is a growing desire among academics to connect the reading traditions of the two scriptures. This objective can be noted in a number of recent articles and books, such as Sebastian Günther's "O People of the Scripture! Come to a Word Common to You and Us (Q. 3:64): The Ten Commandments and the Qur'an" and Brian Arthur Brown's edited volume *Three Testaments: Torah, Gospel, and Quran*.[11] It can also be observed in other avenues of inter-academic communication and human interaction, such as the emerging practice of "scriptural reasoning."[12]

Marshalling interdisciplinary and cross-disciplinary insights into the study of the Qur'an is a way of invigorating the discipline and acknowledging the contributions of many to the field. It allows scholars from various academic backgrounds, both Muslims and those of different persuasions, to come together in an exchange of knowledge that is centred on the Islamic revelation. Insights from the study of the Bible, which permeate our collective culture in Western academia, not only facilitate the communication process but also help us to explain the Qur'an and answer questions using familiar terms, shared concepts, and a common language. Such interpretive endeavours enable cross-cultural interaction and enlightened encounters between faith traditions in their various expressions. Although this work is centred on the Islamic scripture, it is not inconceivable that such bridges might invigorate and enrich the study of the Bible in different ways.[13]

This work is a study of the poetics of Qur'anic narrative, specifically the poetics of Surat al-Baqara's narrative structure. The term "poetics" in connection with "Qur'anic narrative" or "narrative structure" is new in Qur'anic studies but has an established history in relation to Biblical narrative. In the world of literature, "poetics" refers to the concern with literary figures, rhetorical devices, and how a text comes together in established norms and creative structures that the reader can appreciate aesthetically. It applies to prose as well as poetry. Poetics can sometimes overlap with hermeneutics, the theory concerned with interpretation, since understanding the poetics of structure can also affect the meaning a reader assigns to a text. Using the term "poetics" to describe this work locates it within a broader context and thereby helps to clarify its subject matter for those well versed in literary criticism or Biblical studies.

However, the study of the poetics and hermeneutics of sacred texts is located within a *social* context, engaging discourses within the Islamic intellectual milieu and the surrounding world. This work is not devoid of such innerconnections, particularly in relation to feminist theory, social reform, and power dynamics as they revolve around exegetical and hermeneutical authority. For example, this monograph, by the novelty of its approach, engages the question of who gets to lay down the rules of Qur'an interpretation, a question that has social ramifications. As a result, this work is located within a broader context of socio-rhetorical interpretation, an exegetical trend that seeks to integrate the rich resources of sociology and anthropology into the study of rhetorics. To be sure, this work is more narrowly focused on *poetics* and does not address the *logic* of the poetic structures in the language of syllogisms, major premises, and minor premises. Rhetorics is a much broader field of study that includes the poetics of narrative structure. Nevertheless, as

Vernon Robbins has pointed out, no single work in the area of socio-rhetorical interpretation integrates all the resources of rhetorics and the social sciences.[14] Such an endeavour is not humanly possible. Rather, a scholar will energetically work on one or two aspects of the text interactively with modern concerns, bringing practices of interpretation together. As its hyphenated name implies, socio-rhetorical analysis is therefore invariably interdisciplinary, but it also attempts to address the social responsibility of dealing with sacred texts.[15]

This monograph has seven chapters. Chapter 1 provides a rationale for Surat al-Baqara's unusual organization and establishes a reading framework within which to demonstrate how the sura's contents revolve around a central theme. Using essentially literary methods, it posits assumptions about scripture as a literary genre that form the basis for the readings. It postulates that a distinctive feature of this genre is its portrayal of the divine, which leads to two complementary readings. The first is termed a "divine self-revelatory" reading, which this chapter develops using literary theory, rather than theology, positing "God" as a central protagonist within the narrative. The second, derived from the assumption that scripture as a genre has an instructional dimension, is termed a "pedagogical" reading. Each reading is elucidated with reference to its theoretical background in the history of scholarship, showing relevant parallels in Biblical studies. Together, they provide a rationale for the Qurʾan's odd organization – suggesting that it is constructed in ways that best meet the suggested objectives of scripture as a genre. This chapter also shows the connections between this hermeneutical framework and emerging feminist hermeneutics, thereby locating it within its broader intellectual context and the search for alternatives to traditionalist methods of interpreting the Qurʾan.

Chapter 2 establishes the format of Surat al-Baqara as a divine response to a supplication for guidance in Surat al-Fātiḥa, the brief, prayer-like sura that immediately precedes al-Baqara and acts as an introduction to it and, as it happens, to the entire Qurʾan. To give substance to this claim and establish a more tangible foundation for it, the chapter introduces the first of a series of literary devices: *iqtiṣāṣ*. This figure is a special kind of repetition, one that makes it possible to knit together the disparate elements that form a distinctive compositional style. The chapter also illustrates concatenation, which it frames as a special kind of *iqtiṣāṣ* that produces smooth transitions. It describes the concatenation between al-Fātiḥa and the beginning of al-Baqara, showing how concatenation highlights the connections between the two suras. The framing of al-Baqara as a divine response to a human supplication underlines both the pedagogical and the divine self-revelatory dimensions of the sura, adding substance to the notion that Surat al-Baqara is organized in ways that meet these two objectives. The chapter therefore shows how concatenation functions as a rhetorical device that brings into relief the rationale for al-Baqara's organization. The chapter also contains a divine self-revelatory reading and a pedagogical reading of Surat al-Fātiḥa, showing how they set the stage for similar readings of al-Baqara.

In Biblical scholarship, the notion of orality is intricately tied to the study of repetition since it is one of few available means of organizing oral texts. Repetitions can function both as cohesive elements that tie a text together and as structural dividers that indicate compositional subunits. In addition, they can emphasize certain segments of text, often through a broken or uneven pattern, such as the ones that display progression, gradation, and a peak of sorts. Chapters 3–6 explore this phenomenon more fully, taking al-Baqara's compositional schema onto firmer ground by clarifying how repetitions can pinpoint the sura's structure and common themes. The book's first two chapters begin this line of inquiry by identifying special figures that outline the sura's structure, whereas the next two chapters explain the special devices that indicate the sura's common themes.

Accordingly, chapter 3 introduces the inclusio, a framing device that systematically encloses the sura's main sections. The chapter describes seven of these creative figures in minute detail, showing how they follow one after the other and segment the sura in a quasi-symmetrical fashion. It also shows how these lexical repetitions consistently coincide with the sura's internal thematic borders, thereby providing a rhetorical, tangible means of outlining the sura's thematic subunits. The chapter also illustrates the special, incremental character of the al-Baqara inclusios, their mounting intensities, and their culmination in a finale, like narrative versions of musical crescendos. It thereby introduces the notion of a dynamics of rising and falling emphasis, similar to the dynamics in musical compositions, which generally consist of rising and falling volume. Although dynamics is an established and well-studied phenomenon within the field of music, the notion is new in Qur'anic studies and worthy of analysis.

Whereas chapter 3 deals with *verbatim* repetitions, which repeat the exact same word, phrase, or sentence, chapter 4 examines *thematic* repetitions, which consist of alternating topics. It surveys various types of alternations and chiasms, including the uneven, broken chiasm, the chiastic structure, and the ring construction. It thoroughly describes the al-Baqara figures, showing how they organize this sura's contents and pinpoint its structure. This exposition affirms the structural outline painted by the inclusios, forming a second, independent line of investigation. It also demonstrates how al-Baqara's thematic figures relay emphasis to the end, reinforcing their crescendo-like, mounting emphasis. Al-Baqara's structure is thus sketched twice: once by its verbatim repetitions and a second time by its thematic ones. Its mounting, crescendo-like dynamic is also illustrated twice: once in the verbatim devices and once in their thematic counterparts. The convergence of the structural outlines painted by the two different kinds of rhetorical devices suggests that they are not haphazard but worthy of close attention. Moreover, the way that the rhetorical devices consistently coincide with the sura's thematic organization affirms their importance as oral structural markers.

Chapters 5 and 6 are concerned with the notion of running themes and with examining how Surat al-Baqara's contents are intimately connected to them and revolve around them. Whereas chapter 5 addresses lexical figures, chapter 6 examines thematic ones, in each case showing how the figures bind the sura's different parts together as a unit. Chapter 5 begins by briefly exploring various common themes suggested by scholars across the ages, moving the notion of a central theme onto more tangible ground by introducing the *Leitwort*, a term and concept better known from the study of the Bible. In Surat al-Baqara, this special keyword is identified as the term "guidance," distinguished by its special location in the first inclusio and its high concentration throughout the text. The chapter illustrates how this keyword becomes "God as Guide" in the divine self-revelatory reading, functioning as the spine around which the narrative flows. Each of the sura's various sections progressively develop this theme and push the narrative forward, modifying and elaborating it in three different contexts: humanity as a whole, the Children of Israel, and the nascent Muslim community. The image of God that emerges in this reading is that of a universal, transcendent, systematic guide, a sender of prophets whose substantive guidance ultimately leads to success or failure.

Chapter 6 offers a second running theme of Surat al-Baqara, the notion of "responsibility," which is made evident by examining its thematic repetitions from a pedagogical perspective. The chapter also introduces the progressive structure – yet another figure that is better studied in the Bible. Surat al-Baqara displays progression since its three panels progress chronologically in time, portraying the election first of humanity as a whole, then of the Children of Israel, and finally of the Muslim community. This chapter illustrates how these panels revolve around the central idea of responsibility by systematically linking election to incumbent expectations and performance reviews within their compositional schema. The chapter thereby demonstrates that in a pedagogical reading, the patterns of changing themes and how they are organized within the sura as a whole suggest that al-Baqara revolves around the idea of responsibility. The chapter also explores the finer nuances of this pedagogy, showing how the sura's internal structures layer it with notions of pluralism, social memory, monotheism, and error.

The analysis in this monograph relies on sophisticated techniques that were not available throughout much of Islamic history. Yet is it possible to fully comprehend al-Baqara without them? Or even with them? Although these questions may never be adequately answered, to convey something of the sura's exegetical possibilities and the way it can be interpreted without modern literary theory and rhetorical analysis, chapter

7 introduces the work of two of the Islamic tradition's best-known exegetes: Burhān al-Dīn al-Biqāʿī (d. 885/1480) and Muḥammad Ḥusayn al-Ṭabāṭabāʾī (d. 1981). Al-Biqāʿī is a classical exegete who stands out in the tradition for his unabashed defence of using the Bible to interpret the Qurʾan, an approach that found support within his intellectual milieu. He also happens to have written the most outstanding work the classical tradition has to offer on approaching suras as whole units. This chapter locates his commentary within his intellectual milieu, showing the sectarian tensions that made holistic approaches to the Qurʾan so difficult and how al-Biqāʿī surmounted these challenges. This history explains why holistic approaches were so rare in the tradition until the twentieth century. Al-Ṭabāṭabāʾī is a modern exegete who also stands out for his exceptional contributions to the Islamic tradition. As this chapter clarifies his context, it explains the factors that led to the twentieth-century rise in the popularity of regarding suras as whole units. Both scholars have provided treatments of Surat al-Baqara as a whole in their monumental commentaries, the relevant excerpts being translated here. The chapter shows parallels between the conclusions drawn here and the analyses of these sages, providing windows into the Islamic exegetical tradition.

The book's conclusion briefly summarizes the structure and central themes of al-Baqara and recapitulates the poetics of the sura's unique configuration. This interpretive framework can potentially change some of the disjointed, atomistic meanings that exegetes have traditionally assigned to individual verses and passages. Visualizing the sura's general layout may also help today's listeners to better follow its recitation and to experience its flow of meanings and changing dynamics when it is released into the soundscape of oral performance.

Notes on Translation

All translations from Arabic and German are my own unless otherwise stated. Qurʾanic passages are translated in consultation with the work of Laleh Bakhtiar and ʿAbdullah Yūsuf ʿAlī.[16] I have followed Bakhtiar's translation of derivatives of the root *k-f-r* as "to be ungrateful" rather than "to disbelieve" or "to be an infidel."[17]

I have used no transliteration for words such as Qurʾan, sura, hadith, Sufi, Sunni, Shiʿi, and Shia, which are now prevalent in the English language. I have transliterated less common Arabic words in accordance with the following table.

TABLE 0.1
Transliteration of Arabic letters

Arabic	Transliteration	Arabic	Transliteration	Arabic	Transliteration
ء	ʾ	خ	kh	ط	ṭ
ا	ā	ذ	dh	ظ	ẓ
ي	ī, y	ز	z	ع	ʿ
و	ū, w	ش	sh	غ	gh
ث	th	ص	ṣ	ق	q
ج	j	ض	ḍ	ة	a
ح	ḥ				

1

How to Read the Qur'an Holistically

Understanding the Rationale

When the first revelation commanded the prophet Muḥammad to "read" (Q. 96:1), he experienced some initial confusion before responding with a recitation of the relevant verses.[1] Today, we recognize that the act of reading encompasses a lot more than a simple enunciation of the text. Rather, it is a complex cognitive process that involves using the knowledge and skills one has at one's disposal to decipher the meanings that lie dormant within the text. As a result, every reading is also inherently an interpretation, one that takes place within the readers' minds as they first silently form the words and then voice them out loud. All readers bring a unique lens to their interpretation of the text, composed of their individual history, questions, and presuppositions, which give each reading its singular character. Like a camera, viewers can focus on a certain aspect of the text, zoom in on the minute details of a single verse, or pull back to a wide angle, taking a snapshot of the sura in its entirety. Readers must carefully choose the lens through which they view the sura, adjusting the focus and aligning the frame before taking the interpretive snapshot. Each step in this preparation process shapes the final reading and helps to define and explain its intricacies.

Like the proverbial forest, the Qur'an has a rich landscape of symbols and allegories, stories and laws, with which readers can become engrossed, causing them to lose sight of the bigger picture. For this reason, in order to understand Surat al-Baqara as a whole, a holistic lens becomes necessary, one that casts a wide angle and views the sura in its entirety. As a result, it does not zoom in on the minute details of small passages, such as those on fasting, pilgrimage, or Abraham, which can distract one from the bigger picture. Rather, these passages are viewed as building blocks, which are of interest for the way they are arranged within the sura's general design, not for their discrete, detached meanings. Such an approach highlights the underlying patterns of the sura's overall structure that allow one to uncover meanings that are uniquely conveyed by the way its contents are organized. The study of methods of interpretation to derive meaning is termed "hermeneutics," so this lens is in some ways a hermeneutics of structure. However, this lens can also pick up on the artistic qualities that are embedded in the sura's design. This area of investigation is relatively new in Qur'anic studies, as is its related terminology. But it is known from other disciplines, such as Biblical studies, where it is termed "poetics" or even "poetics of narrative structure" and denotes the theoretical study of the literary structures of a text. It is not reserved for poetry alone but can apply to prose and other texts,[2] where it can often intertwine with hermeneutics. A special, holistic lens addresses both of these intertwined dimensions, giving depth to the aesthetics of a sura by exploring how its artistic beauty resonates with meaning.

Holistic Approaches to the Qur'an: A Brief Overview

The word "holistic" is well established in a variety of disciplines, but it is relatively new in Qur'anic studies and therefore needs some clarification. It has occurred in the work of Mustansir Mir, Amina Wadud, and Asma Barlas, who have provided brief explanations.[3] Mir is well known for bringing several works that treat suras as unities to the attention of a wider scholarly audience, using the expression "sura as a unity" to describe this phenomenon. He does not equate the two terms, explaining "holistic" as "predicated on the assumption that the Qur'an is a well-integrated book and ought to be studied as such."[4] Wadud does not define exactly what she means by "holistic," but it is understood in the context to refer to a category of exegesis that approaches the Qur'an as a whole. She places her own work within this category, describing it as based on analyzing each verse in its context and "within the context of the Qur'anic Weltanschauung, or world-view," among other things.[5]

Barlas offers a similar explanation, using the words of Paul Ricoeur (d. 2005), "a whole, a totality," in connection with reading the Qur'an as "a cumulative, holistic process."[6] Wadud and Barlas are therefore the earliest scholars to consciously identify their work as "holistic" since Mir does not apply it to his own creation but uses it to describe the work of Amīn Aḥsan Iṣlāḥī (d. 1997).[7] Wadud and Barlas are better known for pioneering Islamic feminist hermeneutics, their books' major contributions to the field. Their work is based on the assumption that patriarchal interpretations are not generally holistic and that holistic readings are more advantageous to women. This assumption is given substance in the recent work of Aisha Geissinger, who has explored classical Qur'an commentary in relation to gender and has demonstrated how depreciatory understandings of gender are reflected in traditionalist exegesis.[8]

Linguistically, "holistic" is related to holism and is used in various disciplines to denote the idea that the properties of a given system – in this case, the Qur'an – cannot be fully determined or explained by the sum of its component parts alone – in this case, the individual verses. It assumes that there is value gained in viewing all of its components together and is concerned with uncovering this added value.

It is noteworthy that the term "holistic" is sometimes linked to New Age spirituality, which may explain the reluctance of some scholars to use it. Due to its association with this contemporary cluster of variegated heterogeneous phenomena, it may be initially less confusing to use only Mir's phrase "as a unity" and entirely avoid any reference to "holistic." However, "as a unity" does not necessarily indicate examining how a sura's contents relate to a central theme. Indeed, not all the exegetes whose approach Mir has described as reading "as a unity" have been successful in identifying a central theme for al-Baqara. In addition, "holistic" has a well-established history in related disciplines, particularly Biblical studies, where it similarly conveys textual integrity.[9] The related expression, "as a whole," is also quite popular in Biblical studies. Therefore, there are well-established precedents for using "holistic" in its literary, text-based sense, without evoking the experiential, spiritual dimension it acquires in connection with New Age religion.

An advantage of this term is that it facilitates clarifying the distinction between two sets of approaches that address the Qur'an's coherence in some form or other. The first set comprises linear approaches, such as in the work of Salwa El-Awa, who uses relevance theory from the field of linguistics to establish coherence. She has applied her method to two suras, dividing them into sections and exploring the contextual impact of each passage on preceding and subsequent passages. El-Awa's approach is the most current in a group of modern and classical approaches that share a focus on the textual relations of the various parts to each other, as opposed to analyzing their relationship to an abstract notion, such as a central theme. The second set comprises holistic approaches, and although they are similar to their more linear counterparts, they move a step beyond coherence, often identifying a central theme or other feature that ties the text together and imbues it with an organizational logic of some kind. Coherence-related approaches, whether linear or holistic, contrast with the traditional "atomistic" methods, which generally approach the Qur'an on a verse-by-verse basis, treating each passage as virtually independent of its literary context.

Thus the term "holistic" is useful in describing and referring to this special quality, which moves beyond coherence and the passages' immediate, linear connections. It can be defined as referring to analytic or exegetical approaches, which are concerned with coherence and consistently move beyond the boundaries of a verse or its immediate vicinity to treat either suras as a whole or the entire Qur'an as a whole. In effect, suras are divided into sections or pericopes, and the relationships between the various parts are studied and viewed together as a totality with the intent of finding a central idea, to which the entire sura's contents relate and which ties the sura together as a unit.

An added advantage to using the term "holistic" is in the methodological bridges it builds between the disciplines of Qur'anic studies and Biblical studies, where the term is well established. This common methodological dimension of "holistic" is evident in the work of Barlas, who uses the word in conversation with the intellectual contributions of Paul Ricoeur, a well-known Biblical scholar.[10] In contrast, Mir's phrase "as a unity" is absent in Biblical studies and thus separates the Qur᾿an from its broader intellectual context. Therefore, as one can see, there are several advantages to using the term "holistic" that make up for any confusion arising from its possible association with New Age religion.

The works of Wadud, Barlas, and Iṣlāḥī are part of a larger umbrella – that of modern Qur᾿an interpretation, which often looks for connections within the Qur᾿an and establishes common themes. In addition to Iṣlāḥī, examples of scholars of this genre include ʿAbd al-Mutaʿāl al-Ṣaʿīdī (d. 1971), Ashraf ʿAlī Thanwī (d. 1943), Muḥammad ʿIzzat Darwaza (d. 1964), Sayyid Quṭb (d. 1966), Muḥammad Ḥusayn al-Ṭabāṭabāʾī (d. 1981), Muḥammad al-Ghazālī (d. 1996), and Muḥammad Fārūq al-Zayn.[11] Authors who have specifically explored Surat al-Baqara include Muḥammad ʿAbd Allāh Drāz (d. 1958), David Smith, and Raymond Farrin.[12]

Within the general framework of traditionalist Qur᾿an hermeneutics, this method can be placed under "interpreting the Qur᾿an by means of the Qur᾿an" (*tafsīr al-Qur᾿ān bi'l-Qur᾿ān*), which has been widely accepted as the most desirable method, as can be noted in the hermeneutics of Taqī al-Dīn Aḥmad ibn Taymiyya (d. 728/1328), who was followed by Badr al-Dīn al-Zarkashī (d. 794/1391), Jalāl al-Dīn al-Suyūṭī (d. 911/1505), Muḥammad Ḥusayn al-Dhahabī (d. 1977), and others.[13] In some of its permutations today, this method involves interpreting obscure or unclear passages intertextually by means of other, clearer passages within the same scripture. Of course, if one accepts the theories of Abdol Karim Soroush, all readings are also inherently of the category "interpretation by means of personal judgment/opinion/reason" (*tafsīr bi'l-ra᾿y*),[14] which Ibn Taymiyya and others find blameworthy. It is sometimes difficult to distinguish between these two categories, except that the latter carries pejorative undertones and is used to establish a polemic. Since there are many possibilities of reading the Qur᾿an intertextually, personal judgment is undeniably a factor in any reading – not only in the choice of texts but also in the way one imagines the relationship between the texts.

Holistic approaches contrast with the more traditional, atomistic approaches, which generally fall under the category of exegesis by transmission (*tafsīr bi'l-ma'thūr*) and thus restrict the authority to interpret the Qur'an to exegetes living in the first and early second centuries of Islam, such as ʿĀ'isha bint Abī Bakr (d. 58/678), Abd Allāh Ibn ʿAbbās (d. 68/687), and Ismāʿīl ibn ʿAbd al-Raḥmān al-Suddī (d. 127/746). The work of Ibn Jarīr al-Ṭabarī (d. 310/923) is foundational for this genre, and is organized in a verse-by-verse, seriatim manner.[15] For each verse, he provides a number of different interpretations, replete with chains of transmission, going back to such early authorities. The interpretations are not always congruent with each other and can conflict. They also do not always fit either the literal meaning of the text or the literary context, which can necessitate harmonizing between text and interpretation.[16] Al-Ṭabarī makes no claim that these traditions go back to the prophet but bases the authority of these early interpreters on their presumed superior understanding of the Arabic language.[17] The bulk of these traditions should therefore technically not be classified as hadith – reports with chains of transmission that go back to the prophet. Rather, such traditions can be termed *āthār* (singular *athar*) – similar reports that go back to a companion of the prophet or an immediate successor, not to the prophet himself. The term *ma'thūr* derives from this latter term. Over the centuries, other commentators have added and discussed relevant aspects of the verses, such as legal issues, but the verse-by-verse sequential organization has usually been adhered to.

Whereas al-Ṭabarī bases his argument for transmitted traditions on the presumed superior understanding of these early exegetes of the Arabic language as it was spoken and understood at the time of the prophet, not so Ibn Taymiyya. This thinker suggests that the prophet *explained* the Qur'an to his companions, who in turn communicated this explanation to their immediate successors; thus these *āthār* carry prophetic authority and function as exegetical hadith in his four-tiered hermeneutical framework. Even though the method that Ibn Taymiyya ranks above all others is that of "interpreting the Qur'an by means of the Qur'an," he does not seem to set much store by it but directs the budding exegete to use transmitted interpretations if the first-ranked method should prove too tiresome (*fa'in aʿyāka dhālika*).[18] These reports make up the remaining three epistemological categories of his hermeneutical framework, the second using hadith to interpret the Qur'an, the third using reports that go back to the prophet's companions, and the fourth using reports that go back to their immediate successors. Thus Ibn Taymiyya's theory combines the seemingly irreconcilable – innovative holistic approaches and atomistic traditionalist ones – into a single hermeneutical framework. To be sure, he may never even have envisioned the usages to which modernists would put his notion of "interpreting the Qur'an by means of the Qur'an." Nevertheless, this ability to harmonize opposing methodologies may explain the popularity of his theory in both modernist and traditionalist circles today. One can note its popularity in traditionalist circles in the proliferation of the commentary of Ibn Taymiyya's student Ismāʿīl ibn ʿUmar ibn Kathīr (d. 774/1373), which has been summarized by no less than three modern authors.[19] Then again, his four-tiered classification allows modernist exegetes to locate their exegetical projects in the first-ranking category and thereby to claim methodological and epistemological superiority over patriarchal, traditionalist ones. Ibn Taymiyya's hermeneutics thereby caters to both modernist and traditionalist circles.

In light of the above, holistic treatments of the Qur'an are often modern compositions that fall under the epistemological category of "interpreting the Qur'an by means of the Qur'an." Some are feminist exegetical works since the earliest authors to consciously identify their approach as "holistic" were incidentally also the first feminist exegetes to address the Qur'an from a woman's perspective. One should note that feminist works that identify as holistic are not generally sura-centric. That is, they do not focus on suras, their running themes, and how they are organized but instead typically address content that is directly related to women's lives – topics such as marriage, divorce, inheritance, and testimony, all of which occur in Surat al-Baqara. Rather than focusing on an individual sura, they cut across sura boundaries when examining this woman-related content. Thus there are different kinds of holistic approaches, some that focus on individual suras and others that approach the Qur'an as a whole. However, in keeping with the work of ʿĀʾisha

ʿAbd al-Raḥmān (d. 1998), who was the first woman exegete after a centuries-long hiatus, holistic treatments are often located within the literary approaches to the Qurʾan.

The Qurʾan as Literature

Literary investigations into the Qurʾan have a long history; they include many medieval works, such as those of ʿAmr ibn Baḥr al-Jāḥiẓ (d. 254/868), ʿAbd al-Qāhir al-Jurjānī (d. 471/1078), and Jār Allāh Abū al-Qāsim al-Zamakhsharī (d. 538/1144).[20] However, they differ from literary approaches today in the sense that there was little consciousness of literature as an independent, academic discipline. Rather, it was a preoccupation with the Qurʾan that stimulated literary discoveries and led to the development of Arabic literary theory. Conversely, in modern universities today, literature has lost its umbilical connection to religious doctrine, developing profane (i.e., nonsacred, nontheological, worldly) tools and methods with which to study any text. It is this characteristic that gives literary approaches a special significance in today's intellectual environment; even though they are not necessarily devoid of religious undertones, their conscious application of profane treatments makes them imminently suitable as common ground for scholars of various faith orientations. A literary approach is therefore an appropriate choice for this study, which engages a variety of discourses not only from the domain of Qurʾanic studies but also from Biblical scholarship.

Like many women exegetes, ʿĀʾisha ʿAbd al-Raḥmān developed her skills in a modern university, which created the space for studying the Qurʾan as "literature." ʿAbd al-Raḥmān's commentary is a particularly good example of this phenomenon, even though she addresses only the shorter Meccan suras.[21] She adopts the literary method of her teacher, Amīn al-Khūlī (d. 1967), and treats each sura as a unit, taking an interest in internal structure and the relationship of various pericopes to each other. She argues that the Qurʾan is the most significant Arabic literary achievement and should be studied as such.[22] She locates her work squarely in the literary realm, giving precedence to literary context over inherited traditions. Conversely, these arguably "profane" literary treatments of the Qur'an have met with some resistance since their inception, particularly from the religious establishment, which occasionally takes exception to some of these innovative methods and treatments.[23] Literary approaches also have advocates outside of the Egyptian academic milieu in which they first appeared, such as Mustansir Mir and A.J. Johns, who seem to have arrived at them independently of each other and of al-Khūlī.[24] Johns has pointed to their potential as "common grounds" since they can provide a joint framework for scholars from various cultural backgrounds and persuasions. For example, this potential can be noted in the parallels between the work of ʿAbd al-Raḥmān and Angelika Neuwirth, which shares a similar treatment of oaths in the Meccan suras.[25]

Can one regard the Qur'an as "literature," or even as "world literature,"[26] as ʿAbd al-Raḥmān seems to imply? Her statement is echoed in the words of Northrup Frye: "If one is attempting a serious study of Islamic literature, one has to begin with the Koran as a piece of literature."[27] Nevertheless, this Biblical critic was unable to see a special something, or "kerygma" (proclamation), in the Qur'an, as he did in the Bible, partly because the Qur'an is not in the form of a continuous story-like narrative. So although Frye toyed with the notion of the Qur'an as literature, he was unable to come up with a hermeneutical method in order to study its "discontinuous kerygma," or proclamatory voice – if one can so describe the Qur'an. Limited as he was by his embeddedness in a cultural context in which the Bible figured very strongly – whether directly or indirectly – his critique of the Qur'an, however secondary it may seem, is an example of the difficulties of approaching the Qur'an as literature in a North American or European context, mediated as it is by its distinctive language, figures of speech, and poetic imagination. Indeed, approaching the Qur'an as literature is not without its problems, for as Ayman El-Desouky so eloquently expresses when he speaks of texts that resist cultural transfer and thus the norms and analytical tools of certain disciplinary methods, "The history of the reception of the Qur'an's unique language styles and textual arrangement in the West is one such history of resistance, and as such can present a powerful modality for the dilemmas of approaching other cultures' literatures."[28] Even in countries with an "Islamic" cultural context, where the Islamic tradition is dominant and where the question of what makes the Qur'an distinctive as scripture was settled in the tenth century in favour of the literary side, approaching the Qur'an as literature is not without its problems since this approach has forever remained entangled with theological postulates.[29] As El-Desouky points out, "Beyond its status as scripture, the Qur'an and its textual and literary features present strongly the need for a conceptual language that is able to cross the borders of discourses of knowledge production, local and localized provenance of voice, and differing histories of reception and literary practice."[30]

Literary Devices and the Oral Dimension

Yet how are we to come up with this conceptual language when our imagination is forever permeated with Biblical ideas and structures? Even the term "kerygma" is better suited to analyzing the Bible, whose Gospels proclaim the "good news"; indeed, "gospel" derives from an old English word meaning "good news" or "glad tidings," in keeping with the Greek *euangelion*. Just as kerygma reflects this practice of *proclaiming* the good news, is there something that one can perhaps take from the name of the Islamic scripture in order to come up with a conceptual framework that is better suited to studying the Qur'an but at the same time is familiar to us here, given our location in a Western academic context? Whereas kerygma denotes "proclamation," "Qur'an" is generally translated as "recitation" since the act of reading in Muḥammad's day (and for many centuries afterward) was primarily an oral practice invariably accompanied by voice. People generally read texts out loud, even when they were sitting by themselves.[31] It follows that the practice of *recitation* is closer to the Qur'an's self-image than that of *proclamation*, thereby highlighting the performative, and even poetic, dimension of the scripture. It is my contention here that the question of conceptual language is best answered by exploring the *oral* dimension of the Qurʾan, using existing tropes that express how we imagine and study *oral* texts.

I base this approach on the observation that the Qurʾan has its primary function (and early *Sitz im Leben*, or "setting in life") in the liturgy, where it is recited during communal (and private) prayers.[32] To be sure, the scripture's early social context may have been quite different from the contemporary one. Nevertheless, there are hadith reports that depict the prophet's reciting Surat al-Baqara in its entirety during formal prayer (*ṣalāt*) – even though the tradition depicts him as illiterate and therefore unable to read.[33] For example, according to one of the major collections, the prophet's companion Hudhayfa (d. 11/633) narrates the following: "I happened to pray one night with the Prophet, peace and blessings be upon him. The Prophet started reciting al-Baqara and I thought he would stop and bow at 100 verses. But he continued, so I thought that he would recite it in one prayer cycle (*rakʿa*). But he continued and started reciting al-Nisāʾ."[34] Even today, al-Baqara – indeed, the entire Qurʾan – is recited during the nightly *tarāwīḥ* prayers in Ramadan, performed out loud in mosques all over the globe. It is also recited during formal visits of condolence and other occasions. Although to native English speakers it may be hard to imagine listening to 286 verses in one shot – a feat that can take an hour or more – in the Muslim world it would not surprise. Technological developments have made it even easier to listen to the Qurʾan for lengthy periods of time; in fact, because there are radio stations entirely devoted to recitation of the Qurʾan, people can listen to it at any point during the day. It is not unusual to hear it in taxis and shops, similar to background music in other geographical regions. Like pop stars, various reciters have made a name for themselves, their recitations sold in the form of CDs and other media all over the world and even made available on the Internet.[35] Moreover, there are women reciters, particularly in Indonesia, such as the famous Maria Ulfah.[36] Oral recitation serves a purpose, for the musicality of this practice can move the emotions and facilitate internalization.[37] Thus there can be no doubt of the Qur'an's vibrant oral dimension, even as it also functions as a written text.

Today, the debate over the nature of literature and the literary is experiencing a shift toward a focus on *method* rather than the object of study, allowing more room for notions of orality and the oral in literature.[38] In the realm of the Qur'an, the subject of orality has often appeared in connection with the text's origins to account for the divergence in its renderings of Biblical stories, which are sometimes studied from the perspective of folk literature, but it has also arisen more generally to argue for the Qur'an's dependency on the Bible.[39] In this avenue of scholarly reflection, the Qur'an becomes a garbled version of the Bible, the inexactness of oral transmission being the reason for the many "flaws" in the Qur'anic retellings of the "Biblical" stories. Some have even mustered modern-day technologies and computer programs in order to make this connection.[40] In contrast, some more recent scholars emphasize the uniqueness and originality of the Qur'an in search of more constructive approaches to Qur'anic narrative.[41] Either way, the Qur'an's Bible-related content is the focus of attention, few venturing further afield into the sphere of method. So to date, the orality of the Qur'an has been approached within scholarship through the lens of the Qur'an as an *object* of study that is distinctive and singular in its own way, but there has been little focus on *how* the Qur'an's oral dimension affects knowledge production and its communicated meanings.[42] Hence there is a growing need to understand how the oral dimension of this piece of "world literature" conveys meaning, structure, and aesthetics.

Nonetheless, the words "literature" and, by extension, "literary" have their drawbacks since they emphasize the written dimension of the Qur'an at the expense of the oral recitation. Today, we are used to absorbing most texts through our eyes, relying on visual techniques to organize text as a way to grasp the bigger picture. As a result, we use things like section headings, paragraph indentation, footnotes, and colour to divide, unify, and emphasize text. However, these graphic signals are not available to texts that are transmitted orally, as was generally the case with ancient literatures. Oral texts used a different set of structural markers, ones that a listener can discern without the help of visual aids. Therefore, to understand the organization of the Qur᾽an, one must develop new reading habits and pay attention to methods that function on the nonvisual, acoustic plane.

Most of the known oral organizational tools consist of special patterns of repetition, which are incidentally also known and studied in the more visual, written domain of literature. For example, Wadad Kadi (al-Qāḍī) and Mustansir Mir have pointed to some of these devices, including special repetitions such as the chiasmus.[43] Thus oral structuring tools can be referred to as "literary" devices to emphasize their literary qualities. They can also be termed "rhetorical" devices, thus highlighting their oral, rhetorical dimension.[44] Moreover, they can be called "poetic" devices since they occur in poetry and imbue compositions with artistic merit. These tools help to explain the poetics of Surat al-Baqara's structure and function as a kind of "oral typesetting" within the sura that sets up the text to be displayed in oral form. This unusual term is best known from the work of H. Van Dyke Parunak,[45] who addresses the differences between visual and oral organization techniques in the realm of the Bible. The term captures the technical, almost mechanical, aspect of this method of analysis, as well as its attention to minutiae that may be of little interest to the nonspecialist but are necessary for a proper grasp of the text's general layout. Describing these tools in detail and showing them at work in Surat al-Baqara provides the specialist with the "tools of the trade" for analyzing the poetics of Qur᾽anic narrative structure. They are inescapable if one wishes to provide a solid, scholarly foundation for delineating al-Baqara's compositional schema. Since most of these devices are not well studied in the Qur᾽an but are known from Biblical studies and other disciplines, one needs some interdisciplinary acumen in order to be able to spot enough of them to construct Surat al-Baqara's layout and unifying themes. Thus identifying these oral structuring devices and how they organize the text and pinpoint its structure is a first step in reading the sura holistically.

The Qurʾan and Literary Theory

Although identifying the oral devices at work in a sura can help to pinpoint its general structure, more is needed if one is to understand how the sura's contents revolve around its common theme. New reading methods from the field of literary theory can help to accomplish this goal. Foremost among these developments are the reader-oriented approaches, which emphasize that the reader has a role in the creation of meaning and is therefore an active participant in the process. In contrast, the older, more established author-oriented approaches are based on the assumption that meaning lies with the author and are concerned with uncovering the meaning that an author originally intended for his audience. This change from author- to reader-oriented is sometimes expressed by the catchy phrase "death of the author," which is the title of an article by the literary theorist and philosopher Roland Barthes.[46] In the realm of scripture, these developments have made inroads into the study of the Bible, where this shift is also reflected in the modern holistic approaches, which treat the Bible as a whole text, independent of origins. They are also termed "synchronic" approaches, being largely ahistorical, and are contrasted with the historical, diachronic approaches, which emphasize the Bible's collation from multiple sources and its development through time. In the realm of the Qurʾan, identifying the method used as synchronic and reader-oriented is another step in the process of reading a sura holistically. "Synchronic" suggests a concern with the text as it stands, independent of origins and development over time, whereas "reader-oriented" opens the door to specialized readings that help to adjust the focus on common themes that form the sura's backbone and hold its contents together.

The notion of using a reader-oriented approach has a history within Qurʾanic studies, even if the exact nature of such an approach may be up for debate. One of the earliest scholars to have recognized the potential of the literary developments is Andrew Rippin, who addressed reception theory as early as 1983.[47] Using the ideas of Hans Robert Jauss (d. 1997), Rippin advocates situating the Qurʾan within twentieth-century reader-response theory (or reception theory), which is preoccupied with the reader's response to a text not only in terms of negotiating the text's meaning but also in terms of the history of its reception. As with other reader-oriented approaches, the reader is thus not merely a passive listener but an active co-creator of the Qur'an's meaning. Although he acknowledges the value of studies that attempt to uncover the author's intention or how the Qur'an's earliest audience understood it, Rippin maintains that the focus should be on the present-day response.[48]

Although Rippin's contribution has value, what such an approach would look like and exactly what constitutes a reader-oriented approach are more difficult to fathom from his work alone. Rippin's only well-explained example of approaching the Qur'an as literature is the work of John Wansbrough (d. 2002), which is difficult to classify as "reader-oriented," just as it is difficult to similarly classify the parallel Biblical diachronic approaches. Both are preoccupied with sources, original authors or redactors, and the genesis of the texts and are thus more fittingly described as "author-oriented." In the Biblical diachronic approaches, there is no clear consensus on the division, dating, and authorship of the text's compositional subunits, just as Wansbrough, the only significant scholar to put forward a similarly "Biblical" diachronic theory for the Qur'an, does not present a concrete scheme identifying such details. In general, reader-oriented approaches, particularly if the reader is located in the twenty-first century, receive the text "as is" rather than delving into redaction criticism or other methods of how the text came to be put together. Even though Rippin's proposal of using reception theory is compelling and Wansbrough's theories are not without interest, the relationship between the two methodologies is not entirely clear. In the realm of reception theory, the most useful contribution of Wansbrough's work is probably as a contrast to help clarify the distinction between reader- and author-oriented methods, as well as between synchronic and diachronic analyses, and to show the breadth of literary approaches to the Qur'an.

Whereas Rippin highlights reader-response theory, Angelika Neuwirth uses the term "listener-response."[49] By replacing "reader" with "listener," she not only brings in nuances of orality and a conversational dimension but also ties the listening experience to that of the early communities of the Meccan and Medinan periods, as well as to the variety of religious identities that these communities entailed. Neuwirth's term "listener-response" is useful in highlighting the oral dimension of the Qur'anic text; however, I restrict myself here to "reader-response," which is more common in the field of literary theory. Of course, one should keep in mind that the "reader" can also be a "listener" and that the "reading" can also be a "listening," both of which involve a process of interpretation and are therefore a "reading" of sorts. So although I highlight the oral nature of the Qur'anic text, I bring it into the visual realm and use the "reading" phraseology.

Neuwirth also employs other terminology derived from literary theory, particularly the notion of "intertextuality." For Neuwirth, this notion takes on a special significance in relation to the Qur'anic texts, where thematically related passages are in a dialogic relationship with each other, functioning as a type of commentary or "exegetical" method. Her approach is diachronic in the sense that the chronologically later texts function as a kind of commentary on the earlier ones. Pictured on the visual plane, her method can be imagined as vertical, as moving up and down through time, and as representing different stages in the community's development. Although very different in scope, both Neuwirth and Wansbrough's approaches are diachronic.

Like Neuwirth's method, a synchronic reading also presupposes a high degree of intertextuality but in a horizontal sense. Rather than being concerned with which verse or passage historically came first, such a reading proceeds from the beginning of the book to the end in a seriatim manner, with texts located in a *sequentially* later position functioning as commentaries on former texts. In this approach, the known ordering of the Qur'anic verses and suras need not be changed since the Qur'an is in its universally recognized, acknowledged form – which it reached at the end of the composition process and which could even be considered an integral part of this process. Thus verses located sequentially later in the final composition expound, elaborate, and explain verses in an earlier position, whereas verses located sequentially earlier introduce later verses.

If a synchronic reading highlights the value of studying the text in its current arrangement, a reader-oriented approach allows for narrowing the lens to highlight special aspects of the composition. Today, literary theorists have come to recognize that it is possible to read the same text in multiple ways, exploring more specialized readings, such as feminist or Marxist readings, as well as a host of other possibilities. The question of how to read scripture is intricately tied to readers' expectations and to what they are looking for when they are reading. For example, the choice of a feminist reading may be prompted by a concern for gender equality, whereas a Marxist reading may have underlying notions of social justice. Although feminist and Marxist readings are worthy pursuits, some other expectations are posited here, highlighting certain characteristics of scripture that make it distinct from any other genre of writing. Yet what is it that readers look for and expect to find in scripture that makes it unlike, say, a novel, a journal article, or even a cookbook? As with any reading, there is a subjective factor in the choice of focus since different readers have different expectations. Here, the readings are based on the assumption that what makes scripture distinct from other genres is its portrayal of the divine and an accompanying pedagogical delineation of certain expectations for humanity. In fact, the underlying assumption is that these two features form the basic objectives of scripture that this genre aims to accomplish. As a result, the proposed readings are focused on these two features, using each as a lens through which to read the Qurʾan. Choosing these two foci is thereby another important step in the holistic reading process, one that gives it a certain individual, subjective flavour and rationale.

An added benefit in using a reader-oriented approach is the avoidance of absolutism and methodological rigidity – a fault for which Aysha Hidayatullah, among others, has criticized feminist interpretations of the sacred text.[50] Like male-centric, gendered, traditionalist Qurʾan interpretation, which tends to be prescriptive and exclusionary of new interpretations under the pretext of blameworthy personl judgment (*raʾy*), feminist exegetes have been accused of being just as unaccepting of alternate modes of reading. A reader-oriented approach acknowledges the existence and validity of different readings, including traditionalist, atomistic ones, and by highlighting the inherent assumptions behind each reading, it moves the conversation in the direction of method. Whether one perceives God or Muḥammad as the author of the text, we must ask whether one can ever truly uncover authorial intent? Thus a reader-oriented approach takes us from the unknown, or possibly unknowable, to the known, even as it obliges us to express and take responsibility for our interpretive choices.

Divine Self-Revelatory Reading

The first of the two proposed readings places God at the focal point, and the text is read to determine what it reveals about the deity. Since the text also portrays "God" as its author, I call this reading a "divine self-revelatory" reading, suggesting that the text describes this deity in the form of a narrative from the deity's perspective, which recalls, for example, a novel written in the first person. The concern, therefore, is not to investigate the claim of divine authorship but to take it as a literary depiction since the text revolves around God as a central protagonist. Given that the focus of the reading has been narrowed down to depictions of the deity, Surat al-Baqara's common theme in this reading is a dominant idea or attribute that describes "God" in some way or other.

The idea of divine self-revelation has received a fair amount of scholarly attention and is not without some kind of theoretical basis, even though it is not a well-established reading method. The scope of a divine self-revelatory reading is also substantially less than that of other readings since it is most fruitful when applied to texts that portray the divine as a tangible protagonist with a distinct voice, a feature that is relatively uncommon, except in texts of a scriptural nature. Theoretical precursors that serve to substantiate the reading stem from several fields, mainly Islamic and Biblical scholarship, in addition to literary theory.

In the area of Islam, the idea of divine self-revelation recalls the Qur'anic "beautiful names of God," which are central to the Muslim conception of the deity and have been a focal point of contemporary piety, as well as classical Muslim theology, philosophy, and mysticism.[51] These numerous and often repeated attributes systematically describe the Islamic deity and are therefore a major Qurʾanic form of divine self-revelation. They are often mentioned among the themes and topics of the Qurʾan. Daniel Madigan, for example, has organized the themes and topics around some of these central names, which include Creator, Merciful, and Guide. He explains, "God could be said to be the subject of the Qurʾan in a double sense: first in that God is the speaker – the Qurʾan's 'I' or 'We' – and second that in many respects God is the center of the text's attention. For this reason it would be inaccurate to speak of God as one theme among the many treated by the revelation; each of its themes revolves around the divine nature and the divine initiative."[52] However, not all scholars present God or the divine epithets in the same way. Some portray God and God's attributes as one theme among many, whereas others do not even present them among the major themes of the Qurʾan. For example, both Fazlur Rahman and Faruq Sherif list "God" as the first major theme, wheres Jaques Jomier and Muhammad Abdel Haleem do not include God or his attributes in their major subheadings.[53]

It should be noted that the term "self-revelation" is not commonly used in connection with the deity's attributes; "self-disclosure" is much more widespread, often being a translation for *mukāshafa* or even *tajallī*, although the latter is more usually translated as "manifestation." The term is quite central to the Sufi tradition, where it has mystical and experiential connotations since the focus is on the transformational aspect of these attributes within people's lives, not on the literary delineation of the Qurʾan's central protagonist. The divine self-revelatory reading described here is not intended as a spiritual exercise and should therefore not be classified as a transformational reading; rather, the aims are much less profound and are confined to the literary, descriptive sphere. Therefore, even though the term "self-disclosure" is well established and very close in meaning, I generally avoid it. Also, "self-revelation" is more suitable for a literary context since "revelation" incorporates nuances of "scripture" – the Qurʾan depicts itself as a "revelation" –

whereas "self-disclosure" is not book-oriented but carries nuances of direct communication between the deity and the mystical practitioner.

Within the Qur'an's broader intellectual context, divine self-revelation has been recognized as a major theme of the Bible, and the notion is well established in Biblical studies. However, there is a difference between Jewish and Christian discourses, each often associating divine self-revelation with a central figure within its tradition. In Christian discourses, divine self-revelation often takes the form of Jesus Christ and occasionally takes on a theological character; the Christian theologian Karl Barth (d. 1968), for example, has examined the idea of divine self-revelation in great depth.[54] In these discourses, this central event is sometimes foreshadowed by divine self-revelation through ancient Israelite history as portrayed in the Hebrew Scriptures.[55] This view has been criticized in Jewish discourses, which do not generally utilize the New Testament but draw on Midrashim and Rabbinic texts.[56] Events that have been connected to divine self-revelation often feature Moses, such as the burning bush theophany (Exodus 3:6–15) and Yahweh's self-revelation on Mount Sinai (Exodus 34:6–8).[57] Not only have these events engaged students of the Bible, but they also have some Qur'anic parallels.[58]

Although divine self-revelation through historical events is a noteworthy notion, other approaches are perhaps more relevant to the idea of a divine self-revelatory reading and the Qur'anic divine names. For example, Mary Mills investigates God's image in each of the books of the Bible, pointing out how each book presents a different aspect of this multifaceted deity.[59] They include descriptions such as "God of the fathers" (Genesis), "God of Law and Covenant" (Exodus), the "king" (Psalms), the "loving" and the "wrathful" (Deuteronomy), and the "first" and the "last" (Isaiah). Many of these names occur practically verbatim in the Qur'an, such as the "king," the "first," and the "last." The Qur'anic divine names are thereby not generally alien to Jewish and Christian conceptions of the deity but have many parallels. Many of these parallels have been recognized and systematically pointed out in Rev. David Bentley's *The 99 Beautiful Names for All the People of the Book*. Thus the theme of divine self-revelation is common to all three Abrahamic scriptures and has been explored in various ways, even in connection with divine names, titles, or attributes. The most relevant approaches to divine self-revelation within Biblical scholarship are those that explore how some of the books of the Bible emphasize certain aspects or attributes of God and revolve around this portrayal.

Pedagogical Reading

I call the second reading a "pedagogical" reading. It situates the general category of human being at the centre, focusing on the pedagogical content that people receive. Like its divine self-revelatory counterpart, the pedagogical reading narrows down Surat al-Baqara's common theme to a central idea that has pedagogical connotations. This method of reading the Qurʾan is also new and differs substantially from previous methods. Nevertheless, it has at least one forebear in the approach of Nimat Hafez Barazangi, who also uses the term "pedagogical reading." Like Wadud and Barlas, she too has contributed to a feminist reading of the Qurʾan, *Woman's Identity and the Qurʾan: A New Reading*, in which the expression occurs as the title of the first chapter.[60] Speaking as an educator (*murabbiyya*), Barazangi seeks to empower women to read the Qurʾan autonomously, as opposed to through the lens of tradition, and to attain "Islamic higher learning," by which she means the entire range of early Qurʾanic sciences. She links this autonomy to the basic monotheistic tenet that "there is no god but God" (*lā ilāha illā allāh*), arguing that to accept the authority of traditional interpreters as binding is to veer away from this tenet. As a result, for Barazangi, monotheism denotes not acknowledging the religious authority of anyone other than God, including that of the early exegetical authorities.

There are similarities and differences between Barazangi's approach and the pedagogical reading described here. The similarities are very general and include the focus on pedagogy and "autonomous" thinking, which is not bound by the often patriarchal exegesis by transmission (*tafsīr bi'l-maʾthūr*). The method serves as a foil for both readings; however, whereas Barazangi's main critique is of the patriarchal aspect of traditional interpretations, here it is of atomism. There is also a difference in scope: whereas Barazangi addresses dispersed verses with woman-relevant content that are scattered throughout the Qurʾan, the proposed reading is generally restricted to Surat al-Baqara (and Surat al-Fātiḥa) and does not directly address women's issues. Rather, the focus here is on the pedagogical function of repetitions and patterns, as well as how they shed light on the structure and organization of al-Baqara as a whole.

It is hard to find a reading of the Bible that identifies as a "pedagogical reading," although there are many studies that address the pedagogical value of the Bible. The most relevant "pedagogical" approach is probably that of Umberto Cassuto (d. 1951), who criticized Julius Wellhausen's (d. 1918) documentary hypothesis, refuting his views on repetitions and incidentally also addressing the pedagogical function of repetitions.[61] He also discussed the Torah's purpose, recalling the work of the Mālikite scholar Abū al-Faḍl Muḥammad ibn Muḥammad al-Maghribī al-Bijāʾī (d. 865/1459) and Burhān al-Dīn al-Biqāʿī (d. 885/1480), who describe a unifying agent for each Qurʾanic sura and term it *gharaḍ* or *maqṣūd*.[62] Both terms refer to the sura's purpose and are in circulation today. The two terms have slightly different nuances: whereas *gharaḍ* is more clearly "purpose" or "objective," *maqṣūd* can also refer to the "intended meaning."

Al-Bijāʾī's and al-Biqāʿī's explorations of the Qurʾan's purpose recall my assumptions for the proposed divine self-revelatory and pedagogical readings of the Qurʾan since both foci are assumed to be objectives that give scripture a distinctive character as a genre. To be sure, al-Bijāʾī and al-Biqāʿī were not concerned with the features of scripture as a literary genre but with the purpose of each of the Qurʾan's suras. As a result, they have also come up with a very different purpose for each sura. However, like al-Bijāʾī and al-Biqāʿī, I suggest that the purpose, or "aim," is a common feature running throughout the sura that connects its different parts. The pedagogical lens is therefore a means of narrowing down the reading to the pedagogical aspects alone in order to help clarify the text's organization.

In light of the above, the divine self-revelatory reading and the pedagogical reading narrow the focus to certain aspects of the text in order to facilitate identifying the central theme and how it links the sura together. Consequently, Surat al-Baqara's running theme is restricted twice, resulting in two running themes, one limited to a divine characteristic and the other to a pedagogical feature. It follows that any special rhetorical devices that unify the sura and hold it together as a unit must be read within these two reading frameworks in order to pinpoint the common theme and give meaning to the otherwise cold, mechanical devices. The device is part of the text, the substance that the reader uses to co-create the text's meaning, whereas the reading is the process of generating this meaning with the help of the special lens. The reading is thereby the method of crafting the common theme out of the bare bones of the device. This concern with a common theme imparts holistic qualities to these methods, distinguishing them from atomistic and linear-atomistic readings. For this reason, identifying the common theme within each of the two readings is yet another step in reading Surat al-Baqara holistically.

Nevertheless, there is more to a text than just its organizational tools, no matter how well one may read them in special ways. Indeed, the rhetorical devices are just a small part of Surat al-Baqara that happen to embellish it and highlight the shapes and patterns of its contents. As a result, the readings accomplish more than merely generating the common themes; they also shape the meaning of the rest of the sura's contents. Narrowing the focus to divine characteristics or the pedagogical dimension helps to show the relationship between each respective central theme and the sura's subject matter. The reading thereby helps to isolate a special aspect of the text in order to show the internal connections. Indeed, it provides a framework within which to demonstrate how the sura's contents connect to the central theme and revolve around it. The common theme thus acts as the spine around which the sura's contents flow, holding them together to form the whole sura. Since revealing the divine and conveying the accompanying pedagogy are posited as distinct objectives of scripture as a genre, the reading process illustrates how Surat al-Baqara is organized in ways that revolve around these two objectives. In other words, these readings suggest that the rationale for al-Baqara's unusual configuration is that it is organized in ways that best meet the objectives of scripture as a genre. They provide a vivid illustration of how the sura's odd arrangement has to do with its status as "scripture" and with the organization of the material to best meet its special aims.

It is noteworthy that in literary theory "readings" can sometimes become "critiques" when the text is subjected to preconceived principles or ideas. For example, in the case of a Marxist critique, the text may be scrutinized on the basis of a principle such as economic justice, which can act as a kind of measuring stick for the text. However, in the divine self-revelatory and pedagogical readings, there is no predetermined image of the deity or a certain pedagogy against which to compare and evaluate the results. Rather, the intent is to let the text speak for itself and to explore the resulting image and pedagogy, searching for patterns and central themes. This exercise can therefore be classified as a "reading," not a "critique," of scripture. A divine self-revelatory or pedagogical "critique" of scripture requires a preconceived notion of the deity or predetermined pedagogical ideas. Such endeavours may not be without interest for theologians and educators; however, they are not generally holistic since their main concerns are not coherence, central ideas, and the aesthetics of organization.

To sum up, reading Surat al-Baqara holistically entails placing the sura's contents, including its structuring devices, in a reading framework that enables one to identify the sura's common theme and understand how the contents revolve around it. The reading framework chosen here is based on the assumption that the genre "scripture" has two main features: a portrayal of the divine and the outlining of pedagogical expectations. As a result, the readings focus on each of these two features in turn and are termed "divine self-revelatory" and "pedagogical" respectively.

Enantiodromia: Bringing the Two Readings Together

Although the divine self-revelatory reading and the pedagogical reading can each stand on its own, they are far more interesting when viewed together so that one may see how they complement each other and form yet another "whole." This notion becomes clearer in conversation with another idea from literary theory, Bakhtinian dialogism – at least as this idea is applied in Biblical studies.[63] This conversation is not meant to exhaust the possible connections between Mikhail Bakhtin's work and the study of Surat al-Baqara. Rather, the purpose is to shed light on the divine self-revelatory and pedagogical modes of reading and on the dialogical relationship between them. Bakhtinian dialogism is formally defined as follows:

> Dialogism is the characteristic epistemological mode of a world dominated by heteroglossia [the presence of two or more "voices" or viewpoints within a text]. Everything means, is understood, as part of a greater whole – there is constant interaction between meanings, all of which have the potential of conditioning others. Which will affect the other, how it will do so and in what degree is what is actually settled at the moment of utterance. This dialogic imperative, mandated by the pre-existence of the language world relative to any of its current inhabitants, insures that there can be no actual monologue.[64]

Thus no text is created in a vacuum; its components are in a dialogic relationship with other discourses within their surroundings, conditioning the meaning of these discourses and being conditioned by them. The notion of dialogism is thus more broad-ranging than intertextuality, which is confined to the relationship between texts. It should be noted that dialogical interactions are not limited to the relations of the text to the outside world but apply to the characters within a text, the interplay between them shaping the meaning of their utterances. Thus dialogism can refer to the relationship between expressed viewpoints within the same text. Theorists describe dialogism as holistic since Bakhtin sought to attain a better understanding of the "whole" through the dialogue of the various parts. Bakhtin was keen on the life sciences of his day, which have been used to clarify this aspect of his thinking; for example, it has been shown that a living organism or even an ecosystem has "a high degree of complexity, a systematic, ramifying interconnectedness. The whole is in a most pragmatic way more than the sum of the parts."[65] Thus the "other" forms a part of the whole and is necessary for the survival and self-identification of the situated subject.

Dialogism is sometimes contrasted with dialectic. In a dialectical relationship, the "other" is often an opponent, whereas in dialogism, which is nonconfrontational, the "other" serves the important function of facilitating self-identification and is thus vital for the construction of our own consciousness.

Dialogism is also open-ended, for it does not come to an end with the discovery of a solution but is a continuous process of "experimentation on the part of the situated subject."[66] In contrast, with dialectic, there is an end in sight since one is arguing with one's opponent in order to reach some kind of solution to a distinct problem. Whereas dialectic has parallels with dialectical theology (*kalām*), a practice that flourished in the early centuries of Islam and one at which the Muʿtazilites particularly excelled, dialogism recalls Sufi ideas, such as the universalism of Muḥyī al-Dīn Ibn al-ʿArabī (d. 638/1240) and the modern scholar Seyyed Hossein Nasr. Both Sufi universalism and dialogism are nonconfrontational and look at the self and the "other" as part of a whole, as can be noted in the concept of "oneness of being" (*waḥdat al-wujūd*), associated with the school of Ibn al-ʿArabī.

In light of the ideas of Mikhail Bakhtin, understanding the dialogic relationship between the different viewpoints, or protagonists, within a text can help to clarify its meaning and can even contribute to the process of constructing each protagonist's separate identity, for which the "other" is essential. Although the legitimacy and value of directly appropriating this theorist's ideas is debatable, particularly when applying them to Surat al-Baqara, seeing them at work in the Hebrew Scriptures may prove helpful. In Biblical studies, Barbara Green is one of the foremost scholars to apply Bakhtin's theories to the study of the Hebrew Scriptures, most often in connection with the story of King Saul in 1 Samuel. She presents that book's various protagonists, portraying each voice as a separate strand. Accordingly, she describes the strands attributed to Elqanah (Samuel's father), Eli (the high priest), Peninnah (Elqanah's first wife), and Hannah (Samuel's mother), showing the interaction and disjunction between these characters.[67] However, the most important of these strands is that of Yahweh, omnipresent and prevalent, as can perhaps be noted in the way this strand has been isolated in a similar way elsewhere in the Bible.[68] Very broadly, the divine self-revelatory reading of Surat al-Baqara foregrounds in the Qur'anic text the voice of the Qur'anic Yahweh, which describes and defines this character.

In the Qur'an, God is the central protagonist, occasionally presented by speech in the first person but also addressed in the second person and even described in the third person. God's pervasiveness is underlined by the prolific doxologies – that is, refrain-like statements that often occur at the end of verses or passages, outlining some attributes of the deity. However, a genuine dialogic relationship requires two or more protagonists, each with a distinct voice, set of experiences, and placement in the world.[69] In the proposed reading framework, the dialogic counterpart is posited as the general category of "human being," which appears in various forms throughout the text, as well as in speech in the first, second, and third persons. Whereas God is the central protagonist in the divine self-revelatory reading, the human being takes centre stage in the pedagogical reading, forming another party in the dialogic relationship. To be sure, it is possible to isolate more than one "voice" or strand within this broad category when exploring the interaction between "human being" and "God" in Surat al-Baqara. For example, al-Baqara also contains a short passage that portrays other characters from the Saul story, primarily Samuel, Saul (Ṭālūt in the Qur'an), David, and Goliath. However, these characters are not a suitable dialogic counterpart for the permeating character of "God" since they appear only in a short passage and do not form strands that recur throughout the sura. The general category of human being is therefore a better fit for Surat al-Baqara as a whole. So in very general terms, the divine self-revelatory reading and the pedagogical reading each elucidate one aspect of the text, centred on one category of protagonist. Because both protagonists and associated readings are in a dialogue with one another, together they form a greater "whole." The Qur'an may not be the text for which Bakhtin developed his theories, and the way they have been applied is not in keeping with what he had in mind, but seeing dialogism at work in the Bible helps to elucidate the complex, interactive nature of the relationship between the two Qur'anic readings.

Just as the notion of dialogism highlights the relationship between readings, the twofold, binary character of the readings has support elsewhere in the Qur'an and related scholarship. It is noteworthy that in this scripture, certain opposites seem to be balanced, such as day and night, heaven and hell, and male and female. This feature was recognized quite early in Islamic history, along with how opposition forms connections between verses, passages, and even suras.[70] In contemporary scholarship, Todd Lawson has explored this phenomenon in great depth when exploring the question of the Qur'an's genre. He has identified many other types of duality and opposition, such as narrative and anti-narrative, and even a duality of dualities, where these dualities form a literary contrast to the one who is One.[71] In connection with this phenomenon, he has used the term "enantiodromia," which originated in the literary domain but was most recently made current by the psychiatrist Carl Jung (d. 1961).[72] In psychology, it is used to describe extreme feelings or attitudes turning to their opposites and thereby enabling the patient to achieve some kind of psychic balance. In the literary field, Lawson has shown that these dualities are distinct from dualism and are a striking feature of the Qur'an's general style that lends it a unified character.[73] The binary nature of the new readings is therefore in conversation with the work of Lawson since one can imagine God and human being as forming another such duality, perhaps even as opposites. The readings can therefore be qualified as "enantiodromatic," or oppositional, readings – not in the sense of "extreme" or "confrontational" but in the sense of forming contrasting or counterbalancing literary foci. Thus, if one thinks of the Qur'an as depicting a relationship between God and human being, the readings complement each other, together forming one greater, well-balanced whole.

The Feminist Dimension

The above exposition does not draw the outlines of a feminist reading of Surat al-Baqara in the sense that it is not concerned with women-related content. Therefore, the reading framework developed in this chapter is not that of a typical Islamic feminist reading. Nevertheless, it has feminist undertones since it is based on women's scholarship and is similarly concerned with developing new methods of reading the Qur'an that contest patriarchal, traditionalist interpretations. It ties into the work of Amina Wadud, who first used the word "holistic" when describing such an approach. Although Amina Wadud is the earliest well-known scholar to identify her reading as a distinctly woman's reading, the very first woman Qur'an scholar in over a thousand years is actually ʿĀʾisha ʿAbd al-Raḥmān, who stands out for inaugurating the literary approach, which gives more weight to literary context than to the atomistic interpretations that have traditionally been assigned to the text. Following ʿAbd al-Raḥmān, this monograph is similarly located in the literary domain, thereby reaching out across the boundaries of faith orientations and persuasions. Moreover, the work of Barlas also builds mutual understanding across the broad range of scholarship she consults, including Biblical studies, such as the work of Ricoeur. This hermeneutical framework continues in her footsteps, developing common terminology and highlighting the value of interdisciplinary insights from Biblical studies. Likewise, the stress on "coherence" reflects the work of El-Awa, the pedagogical reading recalls Barazangi, and the focus on divine epithets links to the work of Bakhtiar. The use of a reader-oriented approach takes into consideration Hidayatullah's critique. As one can see, the hermeneutical framework that I develop here has its feminist undertones, for it builds upon the work of women scholars before me who are similarly concerned with the question of how to read the Qur'an in today's world.

One should note that women's Qur'an hermeneutics is a relatively recent phenomenon since Qur'an exegesis, like that of other scriptures, has historically been dominated by men. Indeed, in the period between the two ʿĀ'ishas – the seventh-century ʿĀ'isha bint Abī Bakr, one of the prophet Muḥammad's wives, and the twentieth-century exegete ʿĀ'isha ʿAbd al-Raḥmān – I have been unable to find a single woman among the authors of the great classical Qur'an commentaries. There is a reason for this dearth in premodern women's interpretations. As Aisha Geissinger convincingly demonstrates in her analysis of gender and Muslim constructions of exegetical authority, early and classical exegetes presented socio-political and religious authority as emblematically masculine, constructed in contradistinction to femaleness, which they associated with intellectual, moral, spiritual, and physical deficiency. Within this worldview, not only were women denied the ability to interpret the Qur'an, but the legitimacy of their interpretations was also refuted. That some of these interpretations have survived is due in part to the historical predilection for transmitted traditions and the associated *ma'thūr* method of interpreting the Qur'an. There are comparatively few of them, mostly attributed to Muḥammad's wives ʿĀ'isha bint Abī Bakr and Umm Salama and to a few other of his women companions, thus conveying the notion that exegesis is a typically male occupation, with a few notable exceptions. Moreover, these women's interpretations remain limited in scope and subject to the authority of male exegetes who had access to higher learning.[74]

Can it be that women's readings can bring a new dimension to the interpretation of the sacred text, as Wadud has suggested?[75] For some, the answer is no, as women's efforts, even today, are not always well received. Commenting on this general neglect, Farid Esack observes, "Qur'anic scholarship is really the domain of men; the contribution of women, when it does occur, is usually ignored."[76] Reflecting this phenomenon, he too makes no mention of the work of Amina Wadud or Asma Barlas in a small publication entitled *The Qur'an: A User's Guide*. Thus the curious lack of recognition of women's exegetical authority in premodernity has its continuation even today. Accordingly, there is a need for a greater understanding of the historical and possible contributions of women to the study of the Qur'an.

The women scholars mentioned in this monograph are some of the leading names of the Western academy in the area of women's Qurʾan scholarship. But there are others whose names are not as well known, such as the Morrocan Nadia al-Sharqāwī, who speaks of "holistic interpretation" (*al-tafsīr al-shumūlī*) within a transnational Islamic feminist network (*shaqāʾiq*).[77] It is no accident that women scholars from across the globe are exploring the Qurʾan and have a decided interest in holistic approaches. They are part of a larger question that is of great concern to women today: how to read the Qurʾan in gender-egalitarian ways, or even how to read it in ways that allow women to reach their full potential. Within this emerging movement of women's Qurʾan scholarship, if holistic approaches are to become a viable alternative to the well-entrenched, patriarchal method of exegesis by transmission, they have to work – and do so consistently. In this field, sura-centric holistic approaches can be very challenging, most notably when applied to Surat al-Baqara. If one can answer the riddle of its structure, then one has drawn a step nearer to the goal. When one has identified al-Baqara's structure, one can delve deeper into the minutiae of the sura, examining discrete passages of women- and gender-related content and setting them within their immediate literary context – as delineated by the sura's compositional schema. Of course, there is no guarantee that such readings will prove to be more advantageous for women; however, it is a tantalizing possibility, particularly given the existing body of feminist interpretation that accomplishes this feat. For example, I have used a similar method of analysis in my approach to Surat al-Naml, showing how the sura's structure impacts women-related content.[78] So although the above hermeneutical framework is not strictly a feminist one per se, it arises directly out of feminist concerns and is in conversation with a budding Islamic feminist hermeneutic.

Nevertheless, the question of Surat al-Baqara's organization is of interest to more than just Islamic feminists,[79] for it reaches out to all those who are interested in a better understanding of the Qurʾan. Like the work of ʿAbd al-Raḥmān, El-Awa, and Ingrid Mattson before me,[80] this work addresses a broader constituency and moves women's scholarship beyond that which expressly addresses women's issues. Among other things, it functions as an invitation to take the work of women scholars more seriously and to see that they too can make valuable contributions to the study of the Qur'an.

Conclusion

In light of the above, there is no one way of reading the Qur'an; there are as many ways as there are readers. All readers bring ideas, assumptions, and a rationale to their interpretation of the text that give it its distinctive character. One of the basic assumptions here is that there is value to be gained from viewing a sura as a whole rather than as a conglomeration of isolated pericopes. It is this assumption that forms the basis for holistic readings. Within this holistic reading framework, I analyze al-Baqara's oral structuring devices, based on the assumption that the sura has an oral dimension and therefore needs such devices to organize it. To do so, I employ a synchronic reader-oriented approach since it allows for narrowing down the focus of the reading to help highlight the sura's central theme and how it connects the sura's contents. The reading foci I have chosen here are two: the portrayal of God and the text's pedagogical dimension – the first producing what I have dubbed a "divine self-revelatory" reading and the second a "pedagogical" reading. This choice reflects the assumption that what makes scripture distinctive as a literary genre is its portrayal of the divine and its pedagogical directions on how to live one's life. Placing these two aims at the focal point of the readings highlights the text's character as "scripture" and brings out the special qualities of the individual text. More importantly, these aims provide an explanation of why Surat al-Baqara is organized in the way that it is. In other words, they suggest that the sura is arranged in ways that are centred on its literary aims and that best convey these aims.

2

Beginning at the Beginning

Al-Fātiḥa as a Prelude to Surat al-Baqara

The Qur'an begins with Surat al-Fātiḥa, a short seven-verse prayer that introduces Surat al-Baqara,[1] as well as the entire Qur'an, and therefore sets the stage for the unfolding narrative.[2] The sura also presents the key players in this narrative – "God" and "humanity" – and the first speech act that connects them. In fact, al-Fātiḥa frames the longer sura as a divine answer to humanity's prayer, a form of introduction that contributes to the dialogic relationship between God and humanity within the text.[3] Therefore, the conversation between these two central protagonists extends to both suras, each sura forming a piece of the exchange. It follows that placing the two participants, one by one, at the focal point and reading al-Fātiḥa for related content can help to clarify the different strands of this conversation.

However, a conversation is composed of words, strung one after the other to form ideas, which are in turn assembled into larger edifices. What special devices can one see in the sura that bind its ideas together and turn it into a coherent composition? What shape do these structures give to the sura? And what about emphasis, a feature that highlights certain portions of the text and renders others in shadow, like vales and mountains on an otherwise flat, monotonous surface? These questions all have to do with the Qur'an's special compositional style, and they help to clarify the conversation's distinctive features. Moreover, they are incidentally also the first forays into exploring methods of organizing the text, beginning at the most basic structural level.

On Literary Devices, Poetics, and Poetry

The search for literary devices and organizational structures takes us into the realm of poetics, which has a long history in the study of the Qurʾan. It is important to note that a focus on "poetics" does not necessarily mean that the subject of study is poetry. Indeed, the term is also used in conjunction with prose texts since they too can have literary features with aesthetic qualities that are deemed "poetic." For this reason, the study of poetics within literary theory can apply to prose, poetry, and a variety of styles of writing.

Although the Qurʾan has certain rhythms and rhymes that sound like poetry to our modern ears, it is very clear in its denial of being poetry, or *shiʿr* (Q. 36:69; 69:41). Indeed, Arabic poetry is characterized by very specific structures to which the Qurʾan does not conform. That the Qurʾan is not the kind of poetry deemed *shiʿr* is very clear. However, there is another kind of poetry, called *sajʿ* in Arabic and "rhymed prose" in English, that has been the object of scholarly attention. Devin Stewart has made a convincing argument that the Qurʾan falls within this stylistic category, based on a very careful study of its prosody and structures.[4] Michael Zwettler has also made a major contribution along this line, showing that in ancient Arabia "rhymed prose" was the expected form of mantic (or prophetic, supernatural, divine-related) speech, on the one hand, and just how different in size, scope, provenance, and subject matter the Qurʾan is from this genre, on the other hand.[5] For example, the soothsayers of ancient Arabia, who used this mode of expression, generally made short cryptic answers to questions that had to do with things like the timeliness of a battle or the search for lost camels, whereas the Qurʾan deals with morality and a whole way of life, among other things. More recently, Michel Cuypers has approached the subject from a different angle – that of rhetoric – examining features such as parallelism, which is known from Biblical Hebrew poetry. He has shown that the Qurʾan does not follow the linear organization of Greek rhetoric but rather the symmetrical one of Semitic compositions.[6] Thus, to contemporary English-speaking listeners whose native poetry is not subject to the metric constraints of Arabic poetry and who are more attuned to English rhetoric, the Qurʾan does seem like poetry, just a unique kind of poetry.

On the subject of poetics and style, the works of two major classical scholars along this line are widely studied today: ʿAbd al-Qāhir al-Jurjānī (d. 471/1078) and the previously mentioned Jalāl al-Dīn al-Suyūṭī (d. 911/1505).[7] The latter is of particular interest for his focus on *badīʿ al-Qurʾan* (the poetics of the Qurʾan).[8] In this regard, he cites the monograph of Ibn Abī al-Iṣbaʿ al-Miṣrī (d. 654/1256), listing about a hundred different kinds of literary devices, including simile, metaphor, allegory, repetition, assonance, and antithesis, among others. Although al-Suyūṭī incorporates these figures into his own book, he does not restrict himself to them but expands his own section on *badīʿ* by adding other devices that he has found in the course of his own investigations. Among this lengthy repertoire, one device in particular stands out: *iqtiṣāṣ* (intertextual clipping). It is this device that is of special interest here for the way it binds parts of the text together and contributes to a very distinctive compositional style.

What Is *Iqtiṣāṣ* and How Does It Function?

Like other words that are borrowed from different languages and introduced into English, it is difficult to find an exact equivalent when attempting to translate *iqtiṣāṣ*, which is probably why it has gained currency among contemporary Qurʾan scholars in its transliterated form. For example, Abdel Haleem has introduced it to English speakers as referring to the expansion and clarification of a single word in another verse,[9] as a kind of intra-scriptural gloss. Nevertheless, the word's etymology and exact meaning are somewhat obscure and therefore need some clarification. The Arabic term *iqtiṣāṣ* derives from the root *q-ṣ-ṣ* and takes the *iftiʿāl* pattern, which has the meaning "following in someone's tracks," "to relate exactly," "to retaliate," and even "to take a clipping from something."[10] Among these meanings, "to relate exactly" and "to retaliate" do not pertain to *iqtiṣāṣ* since the first is associated with storytelling or narration and the second is a juridical meaning applied in criminal law and elsewhere. Accordingly, the etymology of *iqtiṣāṣ* is best explained as coming from the idea of cutting or taking a snippet from something. However, if the meaning of "cutting" alone were intended, it would have been possible to use the passive participle form *maqṣūṣ min* (Form I). Using instead the passive participle form *muqtaṣṣ min* (Form VIII) layers the idea of cutting with the idea of following a trail to its origins.

Iqtiṣāṣ is most commonly known through al-Suyūṭī's multivolume masterpiece *Al-Itqān fī ʿulūm al-Qurʾan* (Mastering the Qurʾanic Sciences), in which he defines it as follows: "It is that the speech is taken (*muqtaṣṣ*) from speech in another sura or in the same sura."[11] He provides four examples, in which he uses *muqtaṣṣ* and *maʾkhūdh* (taken) interchangeably. In his first example, he describes Qurʾan 29:27 as taken (*muqtaṣṣ*) from Qurʾan 20:75.[12] The relationship between the two verses seems to be an explanatory one, since Qurʾan 20:75 explains the concept of the ones in accord with morality (*ṣāliḥīn*) in Qurʾan 29:27. However, semantically the words *muqtaṣṣ* and *maʾkhūdh* imply that an expression or concept in the first verse is "taken" from the second verse, implying that the latter is the "origin" of the former and is in a "donor" relationship to it. Al-Suyūṭī's other examples also show an explanatory relationship between the verses.[13] In every case, there is a word from a certain verse or verses that is "taken" from and used in another verse, bringing certain nuances and layers of meaning from its "original" context to the new one. In fact, it is not only the word that is "cut" from a certain context and brought over to the new verse but also its associated meanings. These meanings explain the otherwise ambiguous word. There does not seem to be any organizational or chronological order behind which verses are described as *muqtaṣṣ* or *maʾkhūdh* and which ones are described as the "donor" verses. For example, both a verse from Qurʾan 50 and a verse from Qurʾan 4 are used to explain Qurʾan 40, even though one precedes it and the other follows upon it. Thus, the term *iqtiṣāṣ* seems to have a truly synchronic, intertextual character, disregarding chronological origins and organizational placement.

It is noteworthy that although al-Suyūṭī's examples more often than not contain verbal repetitions, he uses two synonyms in his last example, *yafirru* and the geminate *tanādd*,[14] both of which indicate "fleeing." In this way, *iqtiṣāṣ* can also involve synonyms and the repetition of concepts, as opposed to only verbatim repetitions. Therefore, *iqtiṣāṣ* entails taking a word, expression, or idea from a certain context and repeating it in a different one, thereby carrying nuances and layers of meaning over to the new context.

The above analysis is mostly concerned with meaning; however, there is another side to *iqtiṣāṣ* that touches the aesthetic imagination and makes this device worthy of being included among all the poetic figures al-Suyūṭī lists in his section on *badīʿ*: the way it contributes emphasis. Repetition is one of the most established ways of adding emphasis in oral texts, and since *iqtiṣāṣ* invariably consists of repetition, it also contributes emphasis, thereby inserting high points into the compositional landscape. Like stepping stones within a lake of meaning, it is possible for a reader to follow these repetitions and thereby envision how the text moves from one idea to the next.

Concatenation: A Special Kind of *Iqtiṣāṣ*

Unlike *iqtiṣāṣ*, concatenation is more commonly known from the study of the Bible, even though it has also been identified in the Qurʾan. David Heinrich Müller (d. 1912), who discovered it, also pinpointed other important rhetorical devices, describing their occurrence in both the Qurʾan and the Bible, among other Semitic texts.[15] Concatenation denotes the recurrence of a keyword at the end of a strophe or other structural unit and the beginning of the next, and it has the effect of transition and unification.[16] It can be considered a special case of *iqtiṣāṣ*, or more precisely, it is the occurrence of *iqtiṣāṣ* in a transitional context, linking two structural units. In the Qurʾan, these kinds of keywords generally move beyond transitions, as can be noted in the analysis of Surat al-Fātiḥa below, so the more broad-ranging term *iqtiṣāṣ* is better suited to describing the phenomenon. However, "concatenation" is a useful term when explaining transitional contexts.

The *Iqtiṣāṣ* Pattern in al-Fātiḥa

But why is *iqtiṣāṣ* so important for understanding the Qur᾿an's style, its coherence, and particularly the connection between al-Fātiḥa and al-Baqara? This device highlights the way text is constructed in the Qur᾿an and how disparate elements are linked together to make one coherent whole. It is this device that permits the knitting together of variegated clusters of new ideas in a style that is characterized by a high density of content but that flows smoothly for the listener. From a structural perspective, it also allows for linking various compositional units and is therefore what binds together the various elements of the design and makes cohesion in structural poetics possible. A good way to understand how it works is to begin at the beginning by analyzing al-Fātiḥa and then to explore the sura's connection to al-Baqara.

Al-Fātiḥa begins with "In the name of God, the Compassionate, the Merciful," a verse often referred to as the *basmala.* Since it is repeated at the start of every sura (other than sura 9), classical commentators were divided on whether it should be considered part of every sura or an independent verse acting as a divider. Thus the structural function and independent character of this particular repetition were recognized quite early in the history of Qur᾿anic commentary. It is this feature that also indicates the beginning of al-Baqara and marks it as a separate unit, distinct from a-Fātiḥa. Although today there are other, visual methods of designating the beginning of suras in printed editions, in a primarily oral environment or in a liturgical setting, the *basmala* functions as a signal for the commencement of a new sura. In al-Fātiḥa the *basmala* functions as its first distinct compositional subunit (see table 2.1).

Al-Fātiḥa's second subunit begins with verse 2. It consists of a short statement of praise to God, who is further identified as the educator of everyone in the world.[17] The repetition of "God" serves as a verbal and ideational link between the two verses with which the central activity of praise is introduced. It indicates a special technique of composition, in which the repeated word forms a nucleus around which the new material is constructed. The repeated word is "taken" from the preceding verse and placed in the new one, making it the first occurrence of *iqtiṣāṣ* in the Qurʾan. *Iqtiṣāṣ* is therefore a method of achieving lexical cohesion, since it ties verse 2's new content of praise to verse 1. It is also possible to use John Wansbrough's (d. 2002) term "organic" in connection with this form of textual growth since it mimics growth in nature.[18] However, whereas he applied it to the historical compilation of the text, here it is used in a literary, compositional sense.

The second repetition, "the Compassionate, the Merciful" (v. 3) is composed of two words and has subsequently not gone unnoticed among scholars. For example, in keeping with conventional wisdom, Abū Ḥayyān al-Andalusī (d. 754/1353) and Abū ʿAlī al-Ṭabarsī (or al-Ṭabrīsī) (d. 548/1153) associate it with emphasis,[19] whereas Muḥammad Sayyid Ṭanṭāwī (d. 2010) suggests that it mitigates any harshness accompanying "educator" in the previous verse since presumably teachers are known to be harsh to their students in some educational settings.[20] The so-called mitigation effect establishes a connection between "educator" (v. 2) and "the Compassionate, the Merciful" (v. 3), but it also links verse 3 with the following "master of the Day of Judgment" (v. 4) since this day can evoke images of hell and a vindictive God. When one looks at verse 4 in conjunction with verses 2–3, a string of divine attributes becomes evident, all of which are grammatically in apposition: God, educator of everyone in the world (v. 2), the Compassionate, the Merciful (v. 3), and master of the Day of Judgment (v. 4). Thus the three attributes forming the latter part of verse 1 are expanded by two additional ones: "God" is expanded by "educator of everyone in the world" (v. 2), and "the Compassionate, the Merciful" is expanded by "master of the Day of Judgment" (vv. 3–4). From a structural perspective, these three verses form a transition between the *basmala* and the subsequent three verses and are therefore the first occurrence of concatenation in the Qurʾan. The repetitions link the first part of al-Fātiḥa (v. 1) to the second part (vv. 2–4) and unify the text.

Verse 5 contains the repetition of "it is You," which also happens to be the first occurrence of *iltifāt*, a poetic device composed of a change of person when referring to the same entity.[21] In this case, the entity is God, who is now directly addressed, as opposed to spoken about in the third person. The repetition emphasizes the *iltifāt*, which in this instant also functions as a structural demarcation between the first parts of the sura, in which God is spoken about in the third person, and the second part, in which God is directly addressed and supplicated. In the English language, this shift in pronoun is usually considered an error; however, not in the Arabic language and also not in the Hebrew Bible, where it functions as a poetic device. For example, there is a similar shift from the third person to the first person in the first verse of the Song of Songs, which Marvin Pope terms a "heterosis of person."[22]

The repetition of "it is You" also comes with an expansion: the first time it occurs, it is joined to "we worship," and the second time, it is repeated with and elaborated by "we ask for help." The "way" of verse 6 is also repeated and expanded in verse 7, identifying it as "the way of those whom God has blessed, not those who are the objects of anger, nor those who go astray." As we can thus see, in the third part of al-Fātiḥa, the two repetitions follow successively one upon the other, each separated by a single Arabic word.[23] Repetitions now follow closer to one another, so the tempo is increased. This change in pattern, together with the *iltifāt*, sets off these verses, signalling a subunit of text. Moreover, this subunit is also highlighted by a changing intensity since an increase in the speed of repetition is accompanied by a change in the intensity of the emphasis that repetitions generally add. This subunit is the third and last part of al-Fātiḥa (see table 2.1).

Al-Fātiḥa has a tripartite structure that contains four instances of *iqtiṣāṣ*: the repetition and expansion of "God," "the Compassionate, the Merciful," "it is You," and "way" (see table 2.1). These words are central within their repeated context, so removing them and their immediate

TABLE 2.1
The structure and repeated words of Surat al-Fātiḥa

Subunit	Text	Verse
Part 1	In the name of **God, the Compassionate, the Merciful.**	1
Part 2	Praise belongs to **God**, educator of everyone in the world,	2
	the Compassionate, the Merciful,	3
	master of the Day of Judgment.	4
Part 3	**It is You** we worship; **it is You** we ask for help	5
	Guide us to the right **way**,	6
	the **way** of those, whom you have blessed, not those who are the objects of anger, nor those who go astray.	7

attachments would reduce the text to little more than the initial *basmala*. These repetitions are therefore strongly fixed to their surroundings and have a special cohesive function that ties the verses of the sura together. Consequently, from the beginning of the Qurʾan, *iqtiṣāṣ* functions as a stylistic feature that permits knitting diverse ideas together into a coherent composition.

The Emphasis Pattern in al-Fātiḥa's Structure

But what about the emphatic dimension of *iqtiṣāṣ*? How does it tease the imagination and enliven an otherwise flat, monotonous text? In the realm of the emotive experience, emphasis translates into variations of intensity, like the ups and downs of musical compositions. If one imagines al-Fātiḥa's changing intensities in the acoustic space, the move from the simple one-word repetition (*Allāh*) to the more intense two-word repetition (*al-raḥmān al-raḥīm*) resembles an increase in volume. This rise in the "volume" of the emphasis is then followed by an increase in tempo formed by repeating each of the two words, *iyyāka* and *sirāṭ*, in quick succession, one after the other like a verbal staccato (vv. 5–7). Al-Fātiḥa therefore has a tripartite structure that displays subtle changes in intensity, moving from a simple augmentation to an increase in tempo. Indeed, when the sura is recited and this distinctive pattern enters into the acoustic space, its mounting intensities resemble a tripartite, accelerating crescendo, but instead of decibels, this figure is expressed through the medium of words. Al-Fātiḥa thereby introduces a tripartite figure with a distinctive crescendo-like dynamic that is subsequently reflected in al-Baqara's structure.

Does "Style" Convey Meaning? *Iqtiṣāṣ* and the High Density of Content in al-Fātiḥa

Although they number only seven, al-Fātiḥa's verses cover a variety of fundamental Qur'anic concepts, thereby contributing to a high density of ideas. The *basmala* designates who this text is from and the spirit of loving-kindness. In verse 2, the reader praises God and learns that he is the *rabb* (lord, master, educator) of everyone in the world.[24] Within the Jewish and Jewish-Christian milieu of the revelation,[25] the term *rabb* was used to denote rabbis or similar persons, an elite often highly educated in religious law. Before the Qur'an, it was uncommon to use this term to refer to the deity. Here, in this verse, God takes over the function of the rabbi, which may include educational, legislative, and authoritative aspects. This appropriation suggests a more direct relationship with the deity, a kind of monotheism in which religious authorities and similar figures recede in importance.[26]

Next, God reasserts his loving-kindness, and we learn that God is master of the Day of Judgment. No details are as yet provided; there is no mention of an afterlife, hell and the Garden only appearing in al-Baqara 2:24–5. This phrasing reaches a wider audience since the idea of a Day of Judgment appears in the Hebrew Bible, especially in the prophetic books, beginning with Amos (5:18 ff), but its accompanying afterlife in heaven or hell is not present, even if the concept survived in Christianity and Rabbinic Judaism and formed part of the cultural milieu of Islam. Its importance lies in epitomizing life's inescapable goal, for which individuals need to be prepared if they are to avoid failure and know ultimate success.

The third and final subunit of al-Fātiḥa contains the crux of the sura (vv. 5–7), for which the prior verses prepare. As humanity turns to God directly, readers affirm the sura's monotheistic message by stating that God is the only one to worship or to ask for help. It is this portion of the sura that contains the supplication for guidance to which al-Baqara responds.

Thus al-Fātiḥa focuses on God's loving-kindness to humanity, on praising God, and on the judgment to come, and it directs individuals onto the right path – all of which comprise the basic information readers need to receive in their religious education. In fact, the sura condenses the most rudimentary fundamentals of established faith traditions – at least from an Islamic perspective. If this were everything one managed to read or hear, and one were suddenly to pass away, the contents of al-Fātiḥa would provide the rubrics for entry into the hereafter. This style of organizing text has its pedagogic dimension and caters to the requirements of the learner – as there is less immediate need for a specialist to lay down a curriculum. For example, if one compares this style with the linear progression of Genesis, the first book of the Bible, pages and pages of details of the creation process provide little information for the uninitiated person wanting to learn the faith, necessitating the help of a teacher to pick the most relevant passages from each of the well-ordered books of the Bible. For the expert, the Bible can serve as an excellent reference source, the linear organization making its contents easily accessible. In contrast, in the Qurʾan readers/listeners have direct access to the most important information they need to know, relying more on the text than on the specialist for this information. Therefore, the idea of the deity taking over the role of educator, or "rabbi," shows itself in the very organization of the sura and is consistent with the Qurʾan's literary style. Within this compact style, *iqtiṣāṣ* is the smoothing agent and the tool that knits together this cluster of variegated ideas.

To sum up, *iqtiṣāṣ* is a rhetorical device that makes for a smooth, compact style by linking together diverse ideas. Within this particular sura, this style allows for conveying the rubrics of faith as briefly as possible in a coherent way. The method in which these rubrics are expressed is not devoid of meaning since it suggests a directness of communication between individual and deity that leaves the intermediary out. This special style goes hand in hand with the distinctive monotheism of "it is You we worship; it is You we ask for help" (v. 5) and also with the use of *rabb* to describe the deity (v. 2), a word that historically is more commonly applied to religious and other leadership. Contemporary readers wishing to access the text directly without restricting themselves to interpretations that the classical exegetical tradition has assigned to the text may find some support for their intellectual enterprise. As one can thus see, the Qur'an's compositional style, as it appears in al-Fatiḥa, carries hints of the sacred text's monotheistic message and is of interest for feminists, reformists, and others from among the intellectually curious.

The Concatenation Pattern in the Beginning of al-Baqara

Al-Baqara, indeed the entire Qur'an, comes in the form of a response to the request for guidance in the latter section of al-Fātiḥa (v. 6), as can be noted in the first two verses of al-Baqara, which designate this book (the Qur'an) as a doubt-free source of guidance (vv. 1–2). This connection has been previously identified – for example, by the medieval scholars al-Suyūṭī and Burhān al-Dīn al-Biqāʿī (d. 885/1480), in addition to the modern scholar Ṭanṭāwī.[27] The supplication in al-Fātiḥa ends with the designation of three different paths, which in turn provide the nucleus around which the first twenty verses of al-Baqara are constructed. Accordingly, the ones whom God has blessed (Q. 1:7) are elaborated as the mindful of God, who believe, establish prayer, and spend in charity (Q. 2:1–5), whereas the ones who are the objects of anger (Q. 1:7) are explained in al-Baqara 6–7 as the ones who are ungrateful and whose hearts are sealed off. The last group mentioned in al-Fātiḥa (v. 7) are the ones who go astray, which is again described in thirteen verses in al-Baqara (Q. 2:8–20). As one can thus see, the first twenty verses of al-Baqara expand the ideas of al-Fātiḥa's last verse, thereby establishing the connection between the two suras and indicating another instant of "organic" progression, or *iqtiṣāṣ*. The strong link between the end of al-Fātiḥa and the beginning of al-Baqara, in addition to the progression and elaboration of ideas, indicates that this is a special case of *iqtiṣāṣ*: a transition that is yet an integral part of the sura, similar to the concatenation in the beginning of al-Fātiḥa.

Many medieval and modern exegetes do not connect al-Fātiḥa's three paths to the three groups in the beginning of al-Baqara but instead identify the last group as the "hypocrites," a group so named in subsequent suras of the Qur'an. For example, Fakhr al-Dīn al-Rāzī (d. 607/1210), Muḥammad Ḥusayn al-Ṭabāṭabā'ī (d. 1981), Abū Ja'far al-Ṭūsī (d. 460/1067), and Shihāb al-Dīn al-Alūsī (d. 1270/1854) identified this group as insincere Medinan Muslims at the time of the prophet.[28] Some modern commentators, such as Muḥammad 'Abduh (d. 1901) and Sayyid Quṭb (d. 1966), have expanded this group to include modern-day insincere Muslims.[29]

However, the connection between al-Fātiḥa's *ḍāllīn*, or "the ones who go astray" (v. 7), and al-Baqara's last group is clearly established by a reiterated term: verse 16 describes them as "the ones who purchased *ḍalāla* (going astray) at the price of guidance," thereby repeating the same root in a different grammatical form. This repetition indicates that it is indeed the same group. As expounded later in the Qur'an, the *ḍāllīn* seem to be a large umbrella group, which includes the Muslim hypocrites and some members of the "people of the book," as well as others (Q. 4:44, 88; 7:179).

Al-Biqā'ī and al-Suyūṭī are among only a few who have commented significantly on the link between al-Fātiḥa and al-Baqara, tying al-Baqara's third group to the *ḍāllīn*. Al-Biqā'ī writes, "The classification of people at the end of al-Fātiḥa into three categories – guided, rebellious, and those gone astray – is like their classification at the beginning of al-Baqara: God-conscious, manifest ungrateful ones (these are the rebellious) and those gone astray (these are the hypocrites). Their concision in al-Fātiḥa and their elaboration here [in al-Baqara] is of a marvelous style; it is the pattern of the great Qurʾan: concision and then elaboration."[30] Al-Biqāʿī's words recall *iqtiṣāṣ*, which is similarly used when a concise word, expression, or idea is elaborated elsewhere. Al-Suyūṭī does not use the term *iqtiṣāṣ* in this context, even though he was instrumental in disseminating it. Rather, he uses words designating concision (*ijmāl*, *iyjāz*) and elaboration (*tafṣīl*), tying al-Fātiḥa in its entirety to verses in al-Baqara. Although al-Suyūṭī's exposition recalls al-Biqāʿī's, he does not mention him by name, even though he does quote and name another lesser known scholar.[31] That al-Suyūṭī was well aware of al-Biqāʿī's work is clear since he refers to it in his magnum opus *Al-Itqān fī ʿulūm al-Qurʾan* and summarizes aspects of it in a shorter work, even using a very similar title, *Tanāsuq al-durar fi tanāsub al-suwar* (Correlation of Pearls: On the Correlation of Suras). Thus al-Suyūṭī does not seem to have been ashamed of associating his work with that of al-Biqāʿī but in fact underlined the connection. That he saw no need to mention al-Biqāʿī's name hints at how well entrenched in the tradition al-Biqāʿī's work was for this particular genre of literature. This deep entrenchment can also be inferred in the contribution to al-Suyūṭī's manuscript by its editor, who saw fit to supply al-Biqāʿī's name in a footnote.[32] Al-Suyūṭī's curious omission of the term *iqtiṣāṣ* can be explained by the fact that it was unknown to al-Biqāʿī; the latter did not use it, and his work seems to have been influential in determining the associated terminology, as scholars read his work and reformulated it in their own words. Furthermore, the ideas of concision and elaboration imply a kind of linear progression, a nuance that is not necessarily present in *iqtiṣāṣ*.

In light of the above, there is a strong connection between al-Fātiḥa and al-Baqara since the three groups mentioned at the end of al-Fātiḥa are elaborated in the first twenty verses of al-Baqara. Those whom God has blessed, the ones who are the objects of anger, and the ones who are astray in al-Fātiḥa (v. 7) are elaborated as the mindful of God, the ungrateful, and the ones who have purchased error at the price of guidance in al-Baqara (vv. 1–20). There is some disagreement among commentators on whether the third of these groups, the ones who are led astray

(Q. 1:7; 2:8–20), is actually the same group in both suras; however, lexically, the connection is made by the use of a different form of the same root in both texts (*al-ḍāllīn* in Q. 1:7; *al-ḍalāla* in Q. 2:16). So there is a strong ideational link between the last verse of al-Fātiḥa and the beginning of al-Baqara, one that is bolstered by the lexical connection. Furthermore, there is an additional lexical connection between the two suras in the form of the word "guidance" and its derivatives since verse 6 of al-Fātiḥa is a supplication for guidance using a verbal form (*ihdinā*), whereas the noun (*hudā*) occurs in the beginning of al-Baqara (v. 2). The lexical link is an instance of concatenation, which affects smooth transitions between the two suras. This method of transitioning is also present in the beginning of al-Fātiḥa since concatenation ties the *basmala* to the rest of the sura. As one can thus see, concatenation seems to be a feature of the Qur'an's compositional style, one that has been used consistently so far.

The verbal link between al-Fātiḥa and al-Baqara also highlights a second aspect of the connection between the two suras. Repeating the word "guidance," even if it is in a different grammatical form, emphasizes it, thereby underlining the framing of al-Baqara as a response to the request for guidance in al-Fātiḥa. Those who form the collective supplicating God for guidance in al-Fātiḥa receive their answer in al-Baqara, thereby setting up both God and humanity as central protagonists within the text. The prominence of both these major players within the beginning of the text further supports the rationale for conducting divine self-revelatory and pedagogical readings, placing each of them in turn as the focus of a reading. It further reinforces the suitability of choosing "humanity" as the focus of the second reading, as opposed to say Muḥammad, the Muslim community, or some other group of persons. Since the Qur'an is not introduced as a relationship between God and specific persons or groups but rather as a relationship between God and humanity as a whole, it makes sense to centre the second reading on humanity as a whole. By emphasizing "guidance," concatenation inherently highlights the associated relationship between God and humanity and therefore the rationale for the divine self-revelatory and pedagogical readings.

Opening Up the Communication Channel: A Divine Self-Revelatory Reading of al-Fātiḥa

When al-Fātiḥa is read in the divine self-revelatory mode, God surfaces as the central subject of the prayer, which is indicated in the repetitions of "God" and "the Compassionate, the Merciful." The transition from third person to directly addressing God establishes the connection between the person and God, underlined by the repetition of "it is You." God does not yet emerge as the supreme guide since the intricacies of the right way are not yet outlined. Rather, the deity teaches humankind to reach an awareness of God's existence, to depend on God, and to turn to God for guidance on the right way. The sura thereby establishes a relationship and opens up a communication channel between humanity and the deity. Thus God emerges as being there for humanity.

Assembly of Humankind: A Pedagogical Reading of al-Fātiḥa

In a pedagogical reading, al-Fātiḥa is shown to prepare human beings to receive guidance. Repetitions functioning as didactic tools stress the need to depend on the loving and kind God, and on God alone, so that the individual may find the right track. In addition, repetitions have a special, cohesive function, knitting together a text that is characterized by a concentrated assortment of fundamental ideas. This stylistic feature reflects a distinctive monotheism in which the deity takes over the educational role of human religious authorities. The pedagogical content of the sura, when viewed as a whole, consists of the basic rubrics of faith in general, presented to the reader/listener in a succinct, easily accessible form. In addition, the brevity of al-Fātiḥa helps individuals to achieve focus and underlines the prayer's role in preparing one to receive instruction on the different ways.

On the collective level, the opening prayer affirms concepts common to all three Abrahamic faiths. Taking the repetitions as keywords, the common concepts include monotheism, loving-kindness as the relationship between God and humankind, dependence on the deity, and the need to be on the right track. Al-Fātiḥa does not contain any ideas that may be unacceptable to most Jews or Christians but assembles members of the cultural milieu of Islam around the most fundamental of shared principles. The Qur'an thereby begins by affirming simple foundations that were established in other traditions, for it is upon these foundations that its distinctly Islamic elements are based, similar to the way that a teacher in a classroom may begin a new course by reviewing basic information that students learned in previous courses. The sura is thereby concerned with assembling humanity on shared principles and establishing common grounds.

Style and the Question of Genre

The subject of the Qur'an's style and format as a prayer and response may raise the question of where this composition fits in the plethora of discourses that form the Bible – that is, if it fits in at all. One may expect such a connection since the Qur'an did not emerge in the absence of similar scriptures of a like nature but materialized amid a rich and well-established world tradition. Thus, for the sake of completeness, a brief glimpse at Biblical discourses is in order. It may even contribute insights into the ongoing conversation on the Qur'an's genre, which so far has remained unresolved within contemporary scholarship.

If one attempted to locate the Qur'an within the Biblical literary tradition, where would one start? It is noteworthy that narrative is not the only type of discourse in the Bible; the twentieth-century interest in the Bible's literary aspects has led to the development of a typology of canonical discourse. Paul Ricoeur (d. 2005), in particular, stands out in this respect, having pointed to five different types in the Hebrew Scriptures alone: prophetic, narrative, prescriptive, wisdom, and hymnic. He has also added three more in the New Testament: biographical-historiography, epistle, and apocalyptic.[33] Vernon K. Robbins and Gordon D. Newby have provided a brief synopsis of this classification, indicating that the Qur'an represents a substantive reconfiguration of these types of discourse.[34] In addition, they have pointed to the contributions of social rhetorics to the classification of New Testament discourse, noting that a further six modes are interwoven into the discursive landscape: wisdom, miracle, prophetic, suffering-death, apocalyptic, and precreation.[35] It is these categories that they think have substantive parallels in the Qur᾽an.[36]

In the Hebrew Scriptures, hymnic discourse or even prophetic discourse may pose interesting parallels. For example, the *basmala* is similar to the formulaic "thus said the Lord" (*koh amar adonai*), which introduces prophetic speech in the Bible, where the prophet is speaking in the name of Yahweh.[37] Then again, what follows the *basmala* is not in the form of direct speech from the deity but is closer to hymnic discourse, where people praise God and direct their supplications for guidance toward God. It has been suggested that some of the early Meccan suras have a hymnic character, particularly those dealing with creation.[38] In addition, the Qur᾽an's rhymed prose is closer to the poetry of Psalms than it is to the nonrhymed prose of Genesis.[39] Thus, although there are no exact counterparts in the different discourses of the Hebrew Bible, there are some intriguing meeting points.

Probably the most fascinating parallels come from the New Testament apocalyptic discourses. The word "apocalypse" comes from the Greek ἀποκάλυψις, or *apocálypsis*, and means "revelation." It is also the name of the concluding book of the New Testament and the last to be canonized. With regard to the Qur᾽an, Robbins and Newby have shown interesting parallels with apocalyptic literature, as has Todd Lawson, who has studied specific features in depth, such as typological figuration, duality, and opposition, arguing that they form an apocalyptic substrate. Within this analysis, he has even pointed to the contrast between the Qur᾽an's narrative passages and those passages that defy the classification of "narrative," terming them "anti-narrative."[40] It is tempting to take this argument to its conclusion and suggest that the Qur᾽an falls into the apocalyptic genre – that this third major installment of the Abrahamic scriptures is in the same vein as the last book of the New Testament, as a kind of "Islamic apocalypse." However, this determination is not so easy to make because of the major differences in scope and contents, as well as the Qurʾan's focus on the present, among other things. Indeed, the differences between apocalyptic literature and the Qurʾan are probably as great as those between pre-Islamic Arabic rhymed prose and the Qurʾan's distinctive *saj*ʿ-like style of writing. Thus, although Biblical (and non-Biblical) apocalyptic discourse poses a tantalizing avenue of inquiry, the search for the Qurʾan's literary genre continues.

Conclusion

The supplication for guidance in al-Fātiḥa and al-Baqara's answer designating the "book" as that guidance frame al-Baqara as a divine response to humanity's prayer. This arrangement highlights the dialogic nature of the God-human relationship as it is expressed in the sura and, by extension, the associated divine self-revelatory and pedagogical readings of the text. "God" and "humanity" become the main actors in this unfolding narrative and form the focal points of the two readings. Whereas God is one, humanity is a broad collective that is not limited to special groups or specific persons, which validates the choice of "humanity" as the focal point of the pedagogical reading.

Like well-placed stepping stones, *iqtiṣāṣ* and concatenation emphasize certain words that draw attention to the relationship between the two suras and thereby also inadvertently highlight the rationale for the two readings. The emphasis that these repetitions provide varies in intensity as it moves throughout the text, giving interest to an otherwise flat compositional landscape. The pattern that these repetitions take resembles an accelerating verbal crescendo that permeates the sura's tripartite structure. In addition, these devices have a cohesive function, knitting the basic rubrics of faith into a smooth, coherent composition. This style of writing reflects the educational role of the deity and suggests a distinctive monotheism of looking directly to the deity for guidance.

Reading al-Fātiḥa in the divine self-revelatory and pedagogical modes also highlights the sura's introductory role in the Qur'an and how it prepares the reader for al-Baqara. On the one hand, the divine self-revelatory reading of al-Fātiḥa indicates its theme and function of opening up the communication channel between God and humanity and establishing the deity as being there for humankind. On the other hand, the pedagogical reading illustrates how the sura's instructional content consists of the fundamental basics of faith in general, assembling humanity on shared principles. The prayer thereby prepares readers for what is to come, leaving them with a sense of impending expectations.

3

Symmetry and a Mounting Dynamic
Al-Baqara's Skeletal Outline

When confronted with the vast material of Surat al-Baqara, I recall Rumi's story of the elephant and the blind men, who each focused on a small portion of the beast's anatomy and described it as if it were the animal in its entirety. How does one begin to see the sura as a whole and not get lost examining its smaller portions? A good starting point is to organize its massive contents into smaller, more manageable units so that one can start exploring how they fit together and give shape to the sura's structure. Most scholars who have attempted to do so have used a thematic approach, dividing the sura into segments with common themes. Each time they saw the sura's theme change, it would mark the beginning of a new thematic unit in their analysis. Although this approach has merit, I have decided to start with a different set of tools, looking at rhetorical devices to signal the beginning or end of a subunit. In the history of similar texts that have an oral dimension, such devices are known for their organizational function and cue their listeners to a change in the compositional schema of the text they are hearing. They also take the delineation of section borders from the purely heuristic domain and move it to more tangible methods of organization. As it turns out, scholars who have used a thematic approach have come up with divisions similar to the ones marked by the oral indicators. Is it purely by chance that the devices I have chosen just happen to coincide with the borders of thematic units, or do they really mark the sura's thematic layout in a more concrete way? It is my contention here that the consistent location of the *rhetorical* devices at the borders of *thematic* units indicates that these figures are not haphazard but worthy of close attention.

Before I begin to explore the various organizational devices, a brief glimpse into al-Baqara's historical setting and a preview of its main themes and flow of ideas are in order so that readers may gain their bearing in the considerable expanses of Surat al-Baqara and its initial context. The sura is termed a "Medinan" sura because of the circumstances of its revelation during the prophet's sojourn in the city of Medina, to which he had fled after heavy persecution in his birth city, Mecca. One of his first initiatives in Medina was to negotiate a peace accord between the various warring Arab tribes and their Jewish allies, a feat contemporary historians refer to as the Consitution of Medina. As Saïd Amir Arjomand has pointed out, it gave all the inhabitants of the city equal protection in this God-secured pact, irrespective of religious or ethnic idenitity, since "the protection of God [*dhimma*] is one and undivisable."[1] Although not necessarily related, this event has parallels in al-Baqara and its theme of "covenant," as can be noted in the use of similar words to depict the different events in al-Baqara and in the historical constitution, such as *ʿahdī* (my covenant) (Q. 2:124) and *ʿāhadahum* (he made a covenant with them).[2] Moreover, it is also reflected in the sura's inclusion and favourable depiction of the Jewish community as having been privileged by God (vv. 40–123). These are two examples that pinpoint possible relationships between al-Baqara and its immediate context. The sura's various other themes may also reflect nation building and related concerns in this ancient backdrop; however, enumerating these historical relationships is outside the bounds of this monograph. Moreover, the Islamic exegetical tradition has developed a genre of literature that is specifically devoted to recounting circumstances that surround the revelation, known as *asbāb al-nuzūl* (occasions of revelation, reasons for revelation, contexts of revelation). Although these anecdotes historicize the Qurʾan or specific portions of it, the historicity of some or all of these reports is disputed. Nevertheless, this variegated material suggests possible avenues of historical-critical scholarly pursuit.

As noted earlier, Surat al-Baqara consists of 286 verses and follows immediately after Surat al-Fātiḥa, the Qurʾan's short, opening sura.

Al-Baqara begins with a response to the supplication for guidance at the end of al-Fātiḥa, delineating the Qur᾽an as a doubt-free source of guidance. It is followed by a general instruction to human beings to worship their lord and by a depiction of their primeval origins, along with their election in the form of the story of Adam and Eve. This theme is followed by a narrative that has the Children of Israel at the centre, beginning with a set of divine commands, followed by a recounting of their ancient roots, and ending with a give-and-take with the Muslm community. At the centre of the sura lies the founding story of Mecca and the Ishmaelite covenant, incidentally the primeval origins of the Muslim community. It is followed by a voluminous set of instructions, which include almost every topic related to Islamic beliefs and practices, ranging from rituals to legal regulations. The sura ends in a prayer.

What Is an Inclusio and How Does It Function?

There are many rhetorical devices that have an organizational dimension and can help to provide structure for this massive sura. Some of these devices are composed of verbatim repetitions, whereas others are thematic ones, consisting of changing topics set in special patterns. The most important of the verbatim devices is the inclusio. This tool divides Surat al-Baqara into sections, outlining all the sura's main compositional subunits and thereby almost singlehandedly delineating Surat al-Baqara's skeletal structure.

To understand what this device is and how it accomplishes this feat, a close look at its function and history is in order. An inclusio is a rhetorical device that consists of a repeated word or phrase located close to the beginning and end of a text, forming a frame for the enclosed unit, the "includitur." It is similar to a known classical device, the epanadiplosis, more commonly known as "epanalepsis" in English.[3] However, the latter usually denotes a more immediate repetition – one word or more occurring at both the beginning and the end of a sentence or phrase – whereas inclusios frame longer passages. They are better known from the study of Biblical Hebrew texts, the burgeoning interest in the study of the Bible's literary aspects providing an impetus for their discovery. Richard G. Moulton, who drew attention to them as early as 1895, called them "envelope" figures;[4] however, they should not be confused with contemporary "envelopes."[5] Whereas inclusios are simple repetitions, the latter are twofold inverted structures (chiastic), which generally take the form (AB/B'A'), A and B signifying repetitions of similar words or phrases. Thus today's envelopes have an added, inverted repetition within the outer, framing one, whereas the inclusio is a simpler figure.

Although Moulton used the term "envelopes," his continental contemporary, David Heinrich Müller (d. 1912), used "inclusio" to describe the same device.[6] It is this term that has survived. It is noteworthy that Müller did not restrict himself to identifying inclusios in the Bible alone but attempted to establish commonalities with other Semitic literatures, such as the Babylonian cuneiform inscriptions and the Qur᾽an. He identified several inclusios in some of the Meccan suras and also noted their function in framing sections, for which he has used the term "strophes." He pointed out that inclusios form the borders between sections, close them off, and highlight their individual character.

Although inclusios are best known from the study of the Bible and have been identified in a broad range of Semitic texts, including the Qur᾽an, they occur in other literatures as well. They are characterized by their long and effective history, ranging from as early as Middle Egyptian compositions up to present-day bestsellers. For example, Gary A. Rendsburg, also a Biblical scholar, identified an inclusio in *The Shipwrecked Sailor*, a well-known ancient Egyptian text that dates to the Middle Kingdom, roughly 2040–1640 BCE.[7] Rendsburg has explained how this inclusio serves to "heighten the sense of cyclic completion."[8]

As with many rhetorical and poetic devices, the art precedes the theory, and one need not be a scholar to fully appreciate their aesthetic and rhetorical effect. It is likely that many contemporary readers have come upon inclusios in their everyday reading but have not realized what they were, even as the beauty of this device contributed to the artistic merits of the writing. For example, in J.K. Rowling's bestselling Harry Potter novels, the central prophecy includes one such inclusio, which frames it and signals its closure.[9] As one can thus see, inclusios permeate our literature from the early compositions of ancient Egypt and Babylon all the way to the present time; they have their aesthetic and rhetorical effects, which may be appreciated by those unfamiliar with the terminology that today's literary analysts use to describe them.

In addition to this sense of completion, inclusios can affect the text in other ways. H. Van Dyke Parunak has discussed some of their functions in "Oral Typesetting: Some Uses of Biblical Structure," showing how ancient composers used them to organize and unify their material. He defines an inclusio as a "three-membered (A B A) chiasm whose outer members are short, compared with the center member."[10] He has confirmed the device's segmenting function – previously identified by Müller and other Biblical scholars. Then again, segmentation is not its only function; it also has unifying and emphasizing effects. It is the "emphasizing" function and its rising and falling undercurrents that contribute to Surat al-Baqara's unique dynamics. This function is a feature of repetitions in general, one that classical Muslim scholars have noted in their discussions of repetition (*tikrār*). For example, Aḥmad ibn Muḥammad al-Thaʿlabī (d. 427/1035) has offered a catalogue of such occurrences in the Qurʾan and has explained their linguistic function as follows: "A majority of the people of rhetoric (*ahl al-maʿānī*) are of the opinion that the Qurʾan was revealed in the language of the Arabs and according to their linguistic habits of discourse (*khiṭāb*). One of their habits is repetition of words in order to emphasize and elucidate – just as brevity is one of their habits for a more streamlined prose."[11]

However, other than general discussions of repetitions, these scholars did not recognize inclusios as independent rhetorical devices, nor assign them a distinctive name. Thus inclusios as distinctive rhetorical figures are best known from the study of Biblical Hebrew texts. Although these texts were not originally composed in Arabic, they too arose within the general cultural milieu of the region and have an oral dimension.

Inclusios can exhibit variations in form. Whereas some are verbatim repetitions, others vary the repeated components for artistic purposes, such as guarding against monotony and introducing an element of surprise. Martin Kessler notes, "The ancient Hebrew writers used literary conventions creatively; though they seem always to have been aware of them, they felt quite free to modify, to transform, or even to turn them upside down.[12] The Biblical student must therefore allow the literature to speak for itself; each literary piece must be permitted to set forth its own characteristic features."[13]

Accordingly, although the general framing characteristic of inclusios is used as a starting point in this study, the literature – in this case al-Baqara – should be allowed to speak for itself. As I show below, the sura is characterized by multiple consecutive inclusios that divide it first into three successive panels, which are major sura subdivisions that contain distinct subject matter, and then into sections and subsections. Their form is very distinctive since they are heavily weighted toward the end of the enclosed unit and display incrementation by increasing the repeated element. It should be noted that the notion of incrementation and the term "incremental" in connection with inclusios are not widely known. Then again, they do appear in connection with repetitions: those that are similarly augmented are termed "incremental repetitions," particularly in connection with oral poetry.[14] Therefore, in order to bring out the distinctive, intricate quality of these inclusios and distinguish them from simpler devices, I describe inclusios that are augmented in this fashion as "incremental inclusios." This special term underlines their distinctiveness and paves the way for understanding how they contribute to the sura's changing intensities.

Before I begin analyzing the inclusios that organize al-Baqara into panels, sections, and subsections, I should explain my somewhat unusual choice of the word "panel" to signal a major subdivision in the sura – unusual, that is, in the realm of Qur'anic studies. This word suggests a discrete compositional unit within a larger entity, like a well-defined panel within a multi-unit painting or decorative wall element. It therefore has compositional and artistic nuances that are well suited to explorations of the Qur'an's poetic and aesthetic dimension. Moreover, this term is used in similar ways in the analysis of the Bible, which provides analytical homogeneity.

The Inclusio Framing Panel 2 (vv. 40–123)

Only one of al-Baqara's inclusios has been recognized and described as such. It frames the sura's second panel, which has the Children of Israel as its topic. The inclusio is incidentally composed of the longest repetition, comprising two full verses at the end. Muḥammad Ḥusayn al-Ṭabāṭabāʾī (d. 1981) notes in his commentary on the latter verses, "The two verses return the conclusion of this speech to its starting point, and its end to its beginning. A section of the discourses of the Children of Israel is thereby concluded."[15] Al-Ṭabāṭabāʾī's description recalls the words of his contemporary, Mitchell Dahood (d. 1982), one of the first Biblical scholars to work on the inclusio; he defined it as that "rhetorical device also called 'cyclic composition,' in which the author returns to the point where he began."[16] Thus al-Ṭabāṭabāʾī recognized the function of these repetitions and considered the panel a distinct unit, even if he did not identify the repetitions as a separate rhetorical figure.

Two other medieval scholars also recognized that verses encompassed by these repetitions form a unit. Burhān al-Dīn al-Biqāʿī (d. 885/1480) quotes Abū al-Ḥasan al-Ḥarāllī (d. 637/1239) as follows:

> Because of the distance between the beginning of this speech and its end, may He be Exalted [God] has repeated it, thereby joining the end of this speech to its beginning, so that this articulation and teaching may have a foundation from the rest of the Qurʾan to which it can be brought back; it is as if the speech, when it concludes to a final objective, the heart must observe the starting point of this objective, so it recites it, so that in its recitation both ends of the structure are joined, and in its comprehension, the meanings located at both ends of the meaning are joined.[17]

Hence al-Ṭabāṭabāʾī and others recognized the function of this particular inclusio, even if they did not classify it as a separate device. However, there is one scholar who has made this valuable observation, Matthias Zahniser, who refers to it by its technical name, "inclusio."[18]

Zahniser relies largely on thematic analysis when subdividing the sura into clearly demarcated sections, although he also considers rhetorical features, such as the above-mentioned inclusio. He is not the first to use such methods but was preceded by other scholars, the most relevant being Neal Robinson and Amīn Aḥsan Iṣlāḥī, the latter of whom writes in Urdu but whose section demarcations are known to Western scholarship through the work of Mustansir Mir.[19] Robinson and Mir do not use the term "inclusio." Thus the only al-Baqara inclusio to have been identified so far is the one framing Surat al-Baqara's second panel. It divides the sura into three panels in a quasi-chronological fashion. The first panel deals with humanity at large, the second panel addresses the Children of Israel, and the third panel has the emerging Muslim nation as its topic (see table 3.1).

TABLE 3.1
The panels of Surat al-Baqara

Panel	Theme	Verses
1	Humanity at large	1–39
2	The Children of Israel	40–123
3	The emerging Muslim nation	124–286

Zahniser, al-Ṭabāṭabāʾī, al-Biqāʿī, and al-Ḥarāllī recognized this particular device because it is so striking. It begins in verse 40 with the sentence "O Children of Israel remember the blessings with which I have blessed you," which is repeated in verses 47–8 and 122–3. However, in the latter two occurrences, the repeated element is extended, covering two entire verses: "O Children of Israel remember the blessings with which I have blessed you and that I have privileged you over all the peoples of the world. And be mindful of the day when no person shall avail another, nor interception be accepted, nor compensation be taken, nor shall they be aided" (vv. 47–8). In the last occurrence, these words are repeated verbatim, except for the switching of the two final verbs: "nor interception be taken, nor compensation be accepted" (vv. 122–3). In light of the great length of this repetition, one would not want it to be monotonous after all. The repetition of an entire sentence from verse 40 in these subsequent verses is unmistakable.

The incremental character of this inclusio also stands out. Rather than following a simple ABA arrangement, they display a pattern of ABAA'CAA', with A and A' representing short repeated units of text and B and C representing the long, enclosed includitur. Augmenting the repetition in the last part of the figure is a particular feature of all the al-Baqara inclusios. Here the initial sentence, "O Children of Israel remember the blessings with which I have blessed you" (v. 40), is expanded by two whole sentences: "and that I have privileged you over all the peoples of the world. And be mindful of the day when no person shall avail another, nor interception be accepted nor compensation be taken nor shall they be aided." The bracketing effect is thereby increased in the latter part of the inclusio, as is the emphatic intensity – for increasing the repeated element also increases the emphasis. Thus panel 2 is framed by a three-pronged (or three-repetition) inclusio that relays emphasis to the end. This buildup heightens the sense of anticipation and closure.

Yet what exactly is being emphasized here? The word "remember" (*udhkurū*) comes in the form of a plural verb and is addressed to the "Children of Israel." It refers to events that feature Moses and the ancient Israelites in the wilderness, which a large portion of the panel portrays in detail. These are all events that individual Jews living in Muḥammad's time could not possibly have recalled since they had happened eons before their time. Then again, these events form an important founding narrative of the Jewish community of Muḥammad's day and age. The word therefore carries nuances of a collective history, a social memory that speaks to Jewish group identity and is in conversation with it. Hence the inclusio emphasizes this collective memory, warning of a day to come when people are assessed individually, not according to the group to which they belong. After all, none from that group may avail, help, compensate, or intercede for another in any way. Like the Children of Israel, God is also emphasized: not only is God the implied interlocutor who is speaking in the first person, but God is also the provenance of the Children of Israel's blessings and privilege. This distinctive rhetorical figure thus emphasizes the relationship between God and the Children of Israel, evoking the past to segue into the present and future as it exhorts the Children of Israel to remembrance and mindfulness.

The Inclusio Framing Panel 1 (vv. 1–39)

In case the listener has not noticed that panels 1 and 2 deal with entirely different topics, their respective inclusios frame them and set them off rhetorically as distinct units. Indeed, panel 1 also has its own bracketing device, even if it is not as strongly pronounced as that of panel 2. Nevertheless, although the inclusio framing panel 2 has been recognized within scholarship, the inclusio framing panel 1 has not. Perhaps the reason for this curious discrepancy is that inclusio 1 is very short, being formed by a single word, and therefore easy to overlook. This unexpected variance in length suggests that even though the two devices share important features, they are also very different and make their own distinct, aesthetic contribution to the sura.

When one is on the lookout for it, inclusio 1 is hard to miss. It has some of the same features as inclusio 2, including the three repetitions with an incrementation of the repeated element – a highly unusual feature in the history of inclusios. The first appearance of the repeated word "guidance" (*hudā*) occurs in the first line of Surat al-Baqara: "Alif Lām Mīm. This is the book in which there is no doubt, a guidance for the mindful" (vv. 1–2). It appears in verse 2 rather than verse 1 because the latter is composed of only three letters and can be disregarded. "Guidance" also appears at the end of the panel in verse 38: "whenever guidance comes to you from Me, whoever heeds My guidance need have no fear nor sadness." It occurs in verse 38 rather than verse 39, which rounds off the panel, because these last two verses form a single unit. Verse 39 is the antithesis of verse 38, so they form a contrasting pair, similar to a merismus, a figure formed of two contrasting words denoting an entirety. Whereas verse 38 outlines the fate of those who follow God's guidance, verse 39 contrasts it with the fate of those who reject it, both verses together giving a sense of completeness by delineating the fate of humanity as a whole. Antithesis is a well-known figure from various types of literature, including Biblical Hebrew poetry, where antithetical parallelism is quite common. Such figures occur quite frequently in the Qurʾan, often concluding compositional subunits. Thus panel 1 is framed by the repetition of "guidance," located near the beginning and end of the panel.

It is undeniable that compared to the very striking inclusio 2, inclusio 1 is very short, so small, in fact, that if one were not conversant with the versatility of inclusios, one would miss it. Nevertheless, what inclusio 1 lacks in size, it makes up for in quantity. "Guidance" occurs profusely within the sura and in very distinct patterns. Although it appears only once in the first bracket of the inclusio, it is doubled in verses 16 and 38, the second and third brackets of this tripartite device. In each of these verses, the word occurs twice. Here, too, the special, incremental character of the al-Baqara inclusios is evident, even when the repeated element is a single word.

Although inclusio 2 stands out for the length of the repeated element, inclusio 1 is also singular in its own way: it is formed by the *Leitwort*, a special keyword that occurs throughout the sura, as shall be demonstrated below. The inclusio's unusual character is indicated by the occurrence of "guidance" two more times throughout the section (vv. 5, 26), for a total of seven times, signalling its special status as a running keyword. Indeed, as is well established in other literary works, this special kind of keyword is known to occur in different grammatical forms. That is why in verse 16 – the inclusio's middle bracket – it occurs once as the substantive "guidance" (*hudā*) and once as the participle "guided" (*muhtadīn*). Is this grammatical variation also an alleviation of monotony or maybe a display of artistic skill? Either way, in light of the profusion of this repeated element, and despite its small size or perhaps because of it, "guidance" sets the tone for the whole sura and is highly significant.

As al-Thaʿlabī has so eloquently pointed out, repetition denotes emphasis. So what exactly is the inclusio emphasizing? Or in other words, what is so special about this word "guidance" that makes it worthy of being emphasized? Is it only because it happens to be the sura's *Leitwort*, or is there more? Emphasizing this word also highlights its function within the sura. It is pivotal in its location, not only tying al-Baqara together as a unit but also tying al-Baqara to the preceding sura, al-Fātiḥa. The listener's ears are already attuned to hearing the word from listening to al-Fātiḥa, which ends in a prayer for guidance. The listener therefore expects to hear it and is on the lookout for it. As an implied supplicant among the collective praying to God in al-Fātiḥa, the listener has asked for guidance and desperately wants it. The use of "guidance" in the inclusio therefore underlines the character of al-Baqara as the answer to that prayer and thereby the sura's connection to al-Fātiḥa. As the emphasized word in this particular inclusio, "guidance" is therefore immanently suited to the figure's location at the beginning of the sura. Not only does it highlight the sura's central idea, but it also ties it to al-Fātiḥa.

One should perhaps note that inclusios can have an inner and an outer bracketing function since the middle bracket can serve to delimit an internal subdivision, as is evident in this panel. In fact, two of the verses in which "guidance" occurs round off internal thematic units. In verse 5 the phrase "these are the ones who are on *guidance* from their lord and they are the successful ones" wraps up a thematic subunit dealing with those mindful of God, whereas in verse 16 the phrase "these are the ones who have purchased going astray at the price of *guidance* so that their trade does not profit nor were they *guided*" wraps up the description of those gone astray, prior to a lengthy parable-like comparison. Thus inclusios serve to signal major divisions within the sura, but they can also organize content internally within each panel.

The Three Inclusios of Section 3.1 (vv. 124–51)

So far, analyzing Surat al-Baqara's inclusios has yielded inclusio 1 and inclusio 2, which consecutively and methodically frame panels 1 and 2.

Each panel has a different topic, the first one addressing humanity as a whole and the second one focusing on the Children of Israel. The rest of Surat al-Baqara comprises panel 3 and has the emerging Muslim nation as its theme. This panel is much longer than the other two panels, covering 164 verses. This broad expanse of verse is also in need of organization, as it seems to be a hodge-podge of stories, injunctions, and prayers. How then is it organized? Not unexpectedly, one finds the selfsame device bracketing its subunits: this panel contains no fewer than five inclusios. Three occurrences of this device divide it into three consecutive sections. I number the three sections 3.1 (vv. 123–51), 3.2 (vv. 152–242), and 3.3 (243–86) (see table 3.2). I have chosen to call these units "sections" rather than "panels" because this term is a better fit: it signals a smaller subdivision within the larger "panel" grouping of verses, depending on the length of the respective repetition. The different terminology reflects the special character of inclusios 3–7, which are not as pronounced as inclusio 2, even though they too are clear and unmistakable. Whereas inclusio 2 makes a bold statement, inclusios 3–7 echo it while tuning down the intensity. Accordingly, from a *rhetorical* perspective, the changing intensities of al-Baqara's rhetorical figures suggest three overall panels, with smaller subdivisions in the last one. Moreover, the tripartite configuration is borne out by a *thematic* perspective since panel 1 clearly revolves around humanity in general, panel 2 undoubtedly addresses the Children of Israel, and panel 3 is focused on the Muslim community. The following analysis addresses each of the last three sections in turn.

Section 3.1 speaks of the Abrahamic origins of the emerging Muslim nation and contains one overarching inclusio (inclusio 3), which envelopes the entire section (vv. 124–51). It consists of Abraham and Ishmael's prayer for God to send a prophet to their offspring, one who will teach them scripture, wisdom, and purification (v. 129). Its final bracket is the realization of this prayer in the form of the prophet Muḥammad, who traced his genealogy to these ancient patriarchs, as did all the Arabian tribes of his day (vv. 151); non-Ishmaelite Arabian tribes, known as the *ʿĀriba* Arabs, had died out by then. The two patriarchs are portrayed

TABLE 3.2
Skeletal outline of Surat al-Baqara

Panel	Themes of inclusio-bracketed units
1	§1 Humanity (bracketed by inclusio 1)
2	§2 The Children of Israel (bracketed by inclusio 2)
3	§3 The Muslim nation
	§3.1 Founding narrative (bracketed by inclusio 3)
	§3.1.1 The Abrahamic covenant (bracketed by inclusio 4)
	§3.1.2 Becoming a middle nation (bracketed by inclusio 5)
	§3.2 Legislation (bracketed by inclusio 6)
	§3.3 Testing of faith (bracketed by inclusio 7)

making the prayer while building the ancient sanctuary in Mecca, the birth place of Muḥammad. Indeed, this pre-Islamic pilgrimage site is depicted as the first house of worship established for humankind (v. 125).[20] This section thereby showcases the founding narrative of the Islamic faith tradition, Mecca's origins, and incidentally its long-lived, popular pilgrimage.

Whereas the first two inclusios have three brackets, inclusio 3 has only two – one not quite at the beginning of the section and one at the very end (vv. 129, 151). To be sure, it is a rather long one: "send unto them a prophet from among themselves, who will recite to them your verses, teach them the book and wisdom and purify them" (v. 129). Although it is not as long as inclusio 2, it is similar in the way it also displays variation by inverting the last elements when repeated: "we have sent unto you a prophet from among yourselves, who recites to you our verses, purifies you, and teaches you the book and wisdom" (v. 151). But the first bracket is missing. It is not where one expects it to be: as close as possible to the beginning of the panel. It would seem that in multiple consecutive inclusios, it is not as important to define the first element since the end of one panel automatically signals the beginning of the next. Accordingly, inclusio 2's extensive repetition signals not only the end of panel 2 but also, by extension, the beginning of both panel 3 and section 3.1. Thus there is no need for inclusio 3 to define the exact beginning of section 3.1. However, it does define the end of the section since it has a "middle" bracket and a final one to signal closure. The inclusio's bracketing function is thereby upheld, as is the distinctive construction of the al-Baqara inclusios, which relays emphasis to the end.

Like inclusio 2, inclusio 3 has a transcendental quality, connecting past and present. Just as inclusio 2 evokes the Children of Israel's primeval past as a segue into the present moment, so too does inclusio 3 highlight the Muslim community's Abrahamic past, connecting it to the advent of Muḥammad in the here and now. Indeed, the connection to God is also emphasized since the inclusio stresses the deity's benevolence in gifting the Muslim community with Muḥammad, just as inclusio 2 highlights God's privilege to the Children of Israel. In both cases, inclusios underline the "God" component in the respective people's founding narratives, evoking a sense of responsibility as the communities look to the future.

Yet inclusio 3 is not the only inclusio evident in this section. Two smaller inclusios split section 3.1 into two compositional subunits, each with its own distinct idea. It would seem that the founding narrative of the Muslim community is too important to make do with only one inclusio but is in need of two extra devices to add more emphasis. The first of the highlighted subunits is section 3.1.1 (vv. 124–41), which speaks of the Abrahamic covenant and its three different heirs: Jews, Christians, and Muslims. The subunit's respective inclusio (inclusio 4) contains a whole repeated verse: "This is a nation that has passed away; they have their deeds and you have yours, and you will not have to account for what they did." The sentence occurs in the middle of the unit (v. 134) and at the end (v. 141), repeated word for word. Like inclusio 3, this internal inclusio has only two brackets since the initial element is missing. Here, not surprisingly, emphasis is again relayed to the end of the section.

Like all the previous inclusios, inclusio 4 also underlines the crux of the enclosed section and distills its contents. This inclusio's respective subsection (§ 3.1.1) is composed of two halves, split into two by the inclusio's middle bracket. Whereas the first half maintains that Abraham and his immediate descendants were Muslim (vv. 124–33), the second half argues against the claim that they were either Jewish or Christian (vv. 135–40). Accordingly, this idea is further underlined by the repetition of "This is a nation that has passed away; they have their deeds and you have yours, and you will not have to account for what they did" (vv. 134, 141), which detaches the patriarchs from the activities of their later offspring, whether Israelite or Ishmaelite, making each generation responsible for its own deeds. As in inclusios 2 and 3, the distant past is evoked and linked to the present, thereby highlighting the sense of responsibility. Although Abraham and his immediate offspring have passed away, the implication is that he has left behind a faith tradition and a tangible sanctuary for performing his religion's rituals for which his descendants are responsible.

It is noteworthy that in this subsection, Abraham's faith tradition is described as Islam; in fact, the patriarch is portrayed as the first Muslim, exhorting his children to hold fast to this religion (vv. 131–2). Even his son, Jacob, also known as "Israel," is depicted preaching this religion to his children on his deathbed (v. 133). To be sure, "Muslim" and "Islam" here have broad connotations and do not necessarily refer to followers of Muḥammad. Rather, this word has a different etymology and means "wholeness makers, peacemakers, well-being makers and safety makers."[21] Putting this word into the mouths of Abraham and Jacob and having them use this name to describe followers of the Abrahamic faith further underlines the primeval origins of Islam, connecting past to present and using social memory to evoke a sense of responsibility.

After portraying the origins of the Meccan sanctuary in the first half of section 3.1, the second half of the section establishes it as the new prayer orientation, to which Muslims are required to turn (vv. 142–51) (see table 3.2). Within the early history of Islam, this move separated followers of Muḥammad from Medinan Jews who did not convert to the new religion, whereas both groups were known to have prayed together before this change. It is this step that set apart Muslims as a distinct people. The historic weight of this event is mimicked within the sura, since its numeric centre occurs here (v. 143), thereby making it a high point in the text. The verse reflects this event, establishing Muslims as a middle nation with its epicentre in Mecca. It is framed by another striking inclusio (inclusio 5), one that is almost as pronounced as the illustrious inclusio 2. As has been the established pattern so far, the device is incremental, defining the end border of the section much more strongly than its beginning. The first bracket contains a single repeated word, *wallāhum*, from the root *wly*, meaning "to turn" (v. 142). The middle bracket features a much longer repeated element (v. 144), which is duplicated twice at the end of the section (vv. 149–50), providing a robust, accentuating frame for the sura's numeric centre (see table 3.3). The repetition consists of the injunction to turn toward the Meccan sanctuary, making it into the new prayer orientation, or *qibla*. Past and present fuse together as Muslims turn their faces in the direction of the primeval sanctuary. The numerous reiterations of the words highlight their textual significance, thereby inadvertently matching their historic impact.

TABLE 3.3
Inclusio 5 (bracketing section 3.1.2)

Brackets	Text	Verse
1	… *turn* …	142
	[Numeric centre]	143
2	… *turn* …, so *turn* your face [O Muḥammad] toward the sacred sanctuary; and wherever you may be [O Muslims], *turn* your faces toward it …	144
3	From wherever you come forth [O Muḥammad], *turn* your face toward the sacred sanctuary …	149
	From wherever you come forth [O Muḥammad], *turn* your face toward the sacred sanctuary; and wherever you may be [O Muslims] *turn* your faces toward it …	150

The inclusio 5 repetitions are so striking that they caught the eye of commentators of old, who nonetheless did not recognize the recurrent pattern of incremental inclusios and sought other means to account for them. For example, al-Biqāʿī explained the first as the good news (v. 144), the second as the realization (v. 149), and the third as the proliferation of Muḥammad's nation (v. 150).[22] For his part, the modern scholar al-Ṭabāṭabāʾī speculated that the repetition of the injunction to turn to Mecca during ritual prayer may indicate its legal application under any circumstances.[23] The repetitions do have legal and other meanings, but for the purposes of this chapter, their main function is to frame the numeric centre and signal thematic closure. From a rhetorical perspective, they also relay emphasis to the end of the subsection, thereby contributing to the sura's underlying dynamics.

To sum up, just as the inclusios framing panels 1 and 2 each have their own distinctive characteristics, the framing devices of section 3.1 are singular in their own way. This section is the only part of the sura that actually has two layers of inclusios, one superimposed upon the other for extra emphasis. Accordingly, it has one overarching inclusio (inclusio 3) and two internal inclusios (inclusios 4 and 5), which split the section into two parts. All the inclusios highlight ideas that have to do with the Muslim community's founding narrative and making them distinct from the Jewish and Christian faith communities. The layering of the devices in this section heighten the intensity and imbue the section with extra emphasis, like the heightening of the tempo in a musical composition. Whereas inclusio 2 is bold and strong, inclusios 3–5 pick up the pace.

The Inclusio Framing Section 3.2 (vv. 152–242)

Section 3.2 contains special legislation for the emerging Muslim nation. It begins with "so remember me, that I may remember you" and is followed by a command to seek help in patience and prayer (vv. 152–3). The two components, "remember" and "prayer," are repeated near the end of the section (vv. 238–9), forming part of a complex, interwoven

TABLE 3.4
Repeated elements of inclusio 6

	Repetitions	Verses
Initial elements	"remember," "prayer"	152–3
	"signs," "have sense"	164
	"divorced women"	228
	"and those of you who die and leave widows"	234
	"monetary endowment"	236
Concluding elements	"remember," "prayer"	238–9
	"and those of you who die and leave widows"	240
	"divorced women," "monetary endowment"	241
	"signs," "have sense"	242

inclusio, which reflects something of the breadth of legislation introduced in this section (see table 3.4).

Verses 238–9, which contain the two words, stand out in particular due to their placement between seemingly unrelated material pertaining to widows and divorcees. This placement has long puzzled commentators such as Abū Ḥayyān al-Andalusī (d. 754/1353), Shihāb al-Dīn al-Alūsī (d. 1270/1854), Sayyid Quṭb (d. 1966), and Muḥammad Sayyid Ṭanṭāwī (d. 2010),[24] who have sometimes suggested linking them through the positive effect of prayers in divorce situations or by elevating alimony and the other instructions to the level of worship. However, from a structural perspective, the odd placement of these verses is rhetorical and serves to signal the end of the section.

The inclusio's bracketing effect is heightened with the repetition of content about widows and divorcees in the subsequent two verses (vv. 240–1). In the case of widows, a whole phrase is repeated: "Those of you who die and leave widows" (vv. 234, 240). And in the case of divorcees, the repeated words are "divorced women" and "monetary endowment" (*matāʿ*) (vv. 228, 236, 241). The oddly placed verses on prayer and remembrance are thereby sandwiched between the repeated material on widows and divorcees, heightening the bracketing effect. One more repetition closes off the inclusio, the repetition of "signs" (*āyāt*) and the idea of "having sense" (*ya'qilūn/ta'qilūn*) (vv. 164, 242). As a result, inclusio 6 differs somewhat from the above figures in the way it is formed by seven elements, chosen from throughout the section and woven together in its final bracket (see table 3.4). They include belief-related elements ("signs" and "have sense"), tangible ritual-like activities ("remembrance" and "prayer"), and legal regulations dealing with vulnerable women ("those of you who die and leave widows," "divorced women," and "monetary endowment"). This inclusio therefore contains only two brackets. In keeping with inclusios 3 and 4, which also consist of only two brackets, inclusio 6 follows upon a very strongly defined bracketing device (inclusio 5). It would seem that every time there is a very strong bracketing device (inclusios 2 and 5), subsequent devices are missing their initial bracket. After all, it is not as important in these cases to mark the exact beginning of the section. Like Surat al-Baqara's other figures, each of which has its own distinguishing characteristics, the interwoven quality of inclusio 6 transforms it into a unique device.

Finally, the odd placement of verses 238 and 239, which sandwich the content about remembrance and prayer in the midst of material pertaining to women, is not without purpose after all. These verses grab one's attention. If not for them, an avid listener may never notice this last inclusio. The profusion of alternating material could shift attention away from it. Because these verses draw in the listener, the special quality of this section's last five verses, notably the way they interweave material from within the entire section, becomes more evident (see table 3.4).

The Inclusio Framing Section 3.3 (vv. 243–86)

The "interwoven" quality of inclusio 6 prefigures Surat al-Baqara's final inclusio (inclusio 7). However, there is one major difference between the two devices. Whereas inclusio 6 weaves together elements from within one section, inclusio 7 reiterates elements from the sura in its entirety. The special eclectic character of inclusio 6 thereby provides a buildup for inclusio 7, which is broader in scope and draws upon the entire text, tying it together. It is a fitting closure for the sura.

Surat al-Baqara's last section also has its own distinct theme, portraying tests of faith for the emerging Muslim nation, which consist of spending in charity and fighting in the cause of God. A verbatim repetition ends this section, initially part of an Israelite prayer (v. 250), which is taught to Muslims at the conclusion of the sura (v. 286). The prayer consists of "Grant us victory over the ungrateful people" and is reiterated verbatim without any changes. Once more, the prayer does not occur at the beginning of the section but provides closure only for the end, forming the sura's last words. Like some of Surat al-Baqara's other inclusios, inclusio 7 has only two brackets. However, as with all the al-Baqara inclusios, the delayed emphasis is still in evidence, the final repetition closing both the panel and the sura.

There is more. Neal Robinson has convincingly shown that Surat al-Baqara's last three verses carry multiple echoes from within the entire sura, terming them the "epilogue."[25] Although there is only one strongly defined verbatim repetition, "grant us victory over the ungrateful ones" (vv. 250, 286), the multiple echoes function in much the same way as an inclusio in emphasizing and providing closure for the unit. That the sura's last verses close off not only the last section but also the whole sura is a rhetorical signal that the entire sura should be considered a single unit, not three independent panels.

Rhetorical and Thematic Convergence in Section Demarcation

Like the various parts of the above-mentioned elephant in Rumi's story, the different sections of Surat al-Baqara join together seamlessly, making it difficult to pinpoint the exact dividing line between them. The above border definition relies primarily on the analysis of inclusios and therefore on specific rhetorical figures. Only a few scholars have noted one or more of these bracketing devices since most of those who partitioned the sura into sections relied on thematic analysis, grouping together pericopes with similar themes. But what of their findings? Must one be familiar with the theory of inclusios to understand al-Baqara's layout, or is it possible to come to the same conclusion purely by following the change in themes? Three established scholars have conducted a mostly thematic analysis of the sura: Robinson, Zahniser, and Mir – the latter relying on Iṣlāḥī's work. It is noteworthy that their findings parallel the divisions outlined rhetorically by the inclusios, confirming the function of inclusios as frames for thematic subunits. Although there are minor variations in the subdivisions of the various scholars, they consist of only three disputed borders. As I show below, the borders outlined *rhetorically* are also a better fit *thematically*, confirming that these verbatim frames also signal thematic changes. This feature suggests that understanding the function of inclusios and the way they demarcate thematic borders can help to clarify the sura's thematic flow, moving it out of the heuristic realm and onto methodologically more tangible ground.

Although there is no dispute over the delineation of panel 1, there is a two-verse difference in the border of panel 2. Whereas I count verses 122 and 123 as part of panel 2, others count them as part of panel 3 (see table 3.5).[26] However, these verses address the Children of Israel and are therefore a better thematic fit with panel 2, which has the Children of Israel as its subject, compared to panel 3, which deals with Abraham and his Ishmaelite offspring. Consequently, from a thematic perspective, verses 122 and 123 should be considered part of section 2. Here, too, the *rhetorical* demarcation signalled by the inclusio is also a better *thematic* fit. However, the connection between the Children of Israel and Abraham indicates the general connectedness of the discourse.

Similar to the border disputes between panels 2 and 3, there is some disagreement over the demarcating line between sections 3.1 and 3.2. Zahniser and Robinson end section 3.1 with verse 152, whereas Iṣlāḥī suggests verse 162 (see table 3.5). Thus there is a difference of one verse between Robinson's thematic analysis and my inclusio-dependent one. He ends it with verse 152 instead of verse 151, as I do.[27] Here, too, there is thematic evidence in favour of considering verse 151 to be the suggested end border: verse 152 is better connected to the subsequent section (§3.2) since the verse sums up and introduces section 3.2. The verse

TABLE 3.5

Disputed borders in section demarcation

Verses	Iṣlāḥī	Robinson	Zahniser	Reda	Comments
122–3	§3	§3	§3	§2	Verses are a closer thematic fit with §2, which deals with the Children of Israel, than with §3, which deals with Abraham.
152	§3	§3	§3	§3.2	Verse is a closer thematic fit with §3.2 (equivalent of §4 in Iṣlāḥī's, Robinson's, and Zahniser's numbering systems) since it sums up and introduces §3.2.
153–62	§3	§4	§4	§3.2	Verses fit thematically with §3.2, which elaborates v. 152, and are joined to §3.2 through v. 152.
284–6	§6	§6	§6	§3.3	Verses are a close thematic fit with §3.3 since they round off §3.3 and the entire sura.

states, "So remember me, that I may remember you, and thank me and do not be ungrateful towards me." Section 3.2 outlines in detail how the emerging Muslim community is to accomplish this task, delineating basic beliefs and practices such as praying, fasting, and pilgrimage. It therefore introduces these disparate elements and ties them together, making it a better thematic fit to section 3.2, as I have suggested. Not surprisingly, there are also the inclusios: inclusio 5, which ends with verse 151, and inclusio 6, which begins with verse 152. Thus there seems to be an almost symbiotic relationship between rhetorical and thematic demarcations – that is, between inclusios and thematic borders.

The last of the disputed borders are the sura's final three verses, their special character leading Robinson to allot them a section of their own, termed the epilogue, as do Mir and Zahniser. I have incorporated these verses into section 3.3. Thus there is a three-verse difference between the end demarcation of my analysis and that of previous scholars, my analysis combining the last two sections into one (see table 3.5). The diminutive size of the epilogue is one indication that it does not stand alone. Moreover, from a thematic perspective, it rounds off the entire sura, in addition to concluding section 3.3, and is therefore better grouped within it.

In light of the above, section borders delineated by the inclusios are largely congruent with those identified by means of thematic analysis, except for three disputed borders. Differences are minor, ranging from one to three verses in Zahniser's and Robinson's demarcations and numbering eleven verses for the border between sections 3.1 and 3.2 in Iṣlāḥī's analysis. In each of these cases, I have shown that the disputed territory is *thematically* better suited to the sections delineated by the inclusios than to the ones proposed by Zahniser, Robinson, and Iṣlāḥī. It follows that the borders marked by the inclusios are actually the boundaries of thematic units, with the inclusios helping to identify and bracket these thematic units. The existence of these devices moves the thematic partitioning process out of the purely heuristic, subjective domain and onto more tangible, rhetorical ground.

The congruence between the inclusios and thematic borders is not the only indication that the device outlines the sura's structure, for the neat, consecutive pattern of the inclusios also strengthens the case for an organizational purpose. Furthermore, this immediate quality is highlighted by some of the beginning repetitions, which dovetail nicely with the concluding repetitions of their respective, preceding inclusios. This pattern is evident since the beginning of inclusio 2 follows immediately upon the end of inclusio 1 and the beginning of inclusio 6 follows immediately upon the end of inclusio 3 (see table 3.6). These borders are thereby doubly defined – first by a long final repetition of the former unit and then by a small repetition of the latter unit. The sura's two internal inclusios (inclusios 4 and 5), which subdivide the middle section into two parts, also feature this immediate quality: the beginning of inclusio 5 follows immediately upon the end of inclusio 4. Inclusio 3's concluding repetition (v. 151) also follows immediately upon inclusio 5's concluding repetitions (vv. 149–50), fitting neatly into the pattern. The inclusios thereby clearly cover the entire sura and define its internal thematic borders. They form the structural skeleton upon which the thematic units are mounted.

Symmetry

Surat al-Baqara contains seven inclusios that demarcate thematic borders. Yet what of the final shape they give to the sura? If one sketched a plan of its layout, what would it look like? Each of these inclusios frames a unit of text that forms a building block of the sura's skeletal structure. A bird's-eye view of these segments yields five consecutive parts, following one after the other in a linear fashion. The first, third, and last of the units are of similar length and relatively short, whereas the second and fourth are also of similar length but much longer. Hence the al-Baqara compositional units are laid out in a distinct pattern, alternating between short and long segments. The remaining two inclusios split the midmost section of the sura into two more or less equal halves, thereby accentuating this particular unit. Thus the inclusios give balance to the

TABLE 3.6
Surat al-Baqara's symmetrical outline

Panel 1 (framed by inclusio 1)	
Panel 2 (framed by inclusio 2)	
Section 3.1.1 (framed by inclusio 4)	Section 3.1 (framed by inclusio 3)
Section 3.1.2 (framed by inclusio 5)	
Section 3.2 (framed by inclusio 6)	
Section 3.3 (framed by inclusio 7)	

sura's basic outline, with a strong focus on the middle of the sura. In other words, the sura's seven verbatim figures are laid out in a more or less symmetrical fashion, with the axis of symmetry roughly in the middle of the sura (see table 3.6).

The Mounting Dynamics of the al-Baqara Inclusios

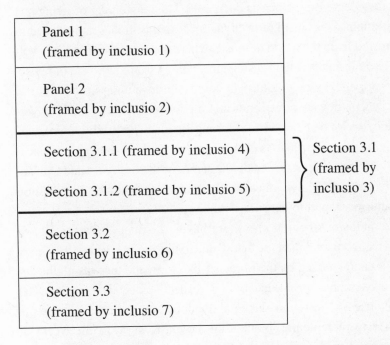

Inclusios delineate the bare bones of Surat al-Baqara's structure, organizing its contents into a pleasing symmetrical shape. Since they are poetic figures, they also enhance the sura's beauty and rhetorical qualities. Yet are organizational value and artistic merit the only contributions that this device brings to the sura? Or is there something else? As al-Thaʿlabī and others have pointed out, repetition adds emphasis. All of these inclusios are composed of repetitions, so they all add emphasis to varying degrees. When repetitions increase, emphasis also increases, and when they decrease, emphasis decreases. This movement of rising and falling emphasis is what I term "dynamics" in this monograph. The term is borrowed from the world of music, where it refers to variations in volume. There is a rationale for using terminology from the world of music. Both Surat al-Baqara and musical compositions belong in the acoustic realm, where they are active and can function to their full potential. Volume, too, is a kind of emphasis – a change in intensity that highlights certain pieces of music. Just as changing dynamics can enliven a musical piece, changing emphasis can do the same for the orally recited Qur᾽an. Therefore, changing dynamics are also part of the aesthetic contribution that inclusios impart to the sura.

The inclusios of Surat al-Baqara have a distinct character. I have termed them "incremental inclusios" due to the general pattern they take, which is characterized by their bracket-like form and the way all the devices relay emphasis to the end of their respective unit. They are unusual not only because of the incremental dynamic but also because they are consistently incremental, blanketing the entire sura. In the world of music, mounting dynamics that relay emphasis to the end are referred to by the term "crescendo." This figure consists of a steadily rising volume that abruptly falls, signalling closure of the figure and leaving the listener with a sense of heightened expectation. Each of the al-Baqara inclusios is like a minute crescendo, which keeps listeners on their toes in the expectation of more to come. Collectively, they layer the sura with a sense of anticipation.

The dynamics inherent in Surat al-Baqara's inclusios also have structural implications, for each inclusio reflects its location and interacts with it. Indeed, each of these seven inclusios has its own unique features that set it apart as an art form. Variation is built into the inclusios to avoid the ennui of too much repetition. In a display of literary artistry, each one is different, yet they work together to form a single figure, rendering the entire sura a rhetorical masterpiece. As in a symphony, they fit seamlessly together and have their own internal logic.

Accordingly, inclusio 1 consists of a single word, "guidance," to which the listener's ears are already attuned from hearing it in al-Fātiḥa, which ends in an elaborate supplication for guidance. This running keyword underlines the connection to al-Fātiḥa and is judiciously placed in the beginning of al-Baqara. Incidentally, it also highlights a common thread that binds al-Baqara together as a unit – perhaps not surprisingly since the sura comes in the form of a response to that supplication. If one imagines this running keyword in the musical realm, it is like the *Leitmotif*, or theme, of a musical composition, which is highlighted in the overture and echoed in the rest of the composition. Inclusio 1 is thus well suited to its placement within the sura as the first of these special figures, underlining the sura's common idea, or "spine," and tying it to al-Fātiḥa.

In contrast, inclusio 2 has the longest, most pronounced repetition, which divides the sura into three panels. Its increase in intensity is similar to a burst of volume. As with its precursor, inclusio 2's special character is well suited to its function and location within the sura. Not only does it draw attention to the sura's tripartite construction, but it also makes a bold statement – asserting the incremental inclusio to be a figure of interest and drawing the reader's attention to the distinctive pattern early on in the sura. It is here that an attentive reader will notice the figure for the first time and either understand the sura's special organizational technique or explore further, depending on how familiar the reader is with oral structuring methods.

With inclusio 3, things increase in complexity. This device defines the midmost section and features two additional smaller inclusios, which add depth to the sura's dynamics. Thus, if one imagines inclusio 2 as amplifying the volume, the added complexity increases the tempo. However, this added layer is not the only way that one can discern a general rise in the complexity of the structuring devices of this section. The two internal inclusios also display a steady rise in complexity: inclusio 4 consists of a simple, verbatim repetition of a verse, and inclusio 5 is the most pronounced inclusio after inclusio 2, emphasizing the numeric centre of the sura. The simplicity of inclusio 4 builds up to the complexity of inclusio 5, the delayed emphasis continuing to imbue this section with a sense of anticipation. As one can see, like the previous inclusios, the three that occur in section 3.1 also interact well with their location within the sura, highlighting the sura's epicentre and adding complexity. Moreover, since this special, layered emphasis coincides with the sura's midmost section, it also adds to the sense of balance and symmetry.

Singular in its own way, inclusio 6 interweaves seven elements from within its respective section, knitting them together while also providing closure for the unit they frame. This interwoven quality is less intense than in the three superimposed inclusios of the preceding section, winding down the intensity and forming a prelude to closure. This inclusio thereby paves the way for inclusio 7, with its distinctive finale (vv. 284–6), which echoes elements from throughout the sura and provides closure for it as a whole. Thus, although each of these inclusios follows an incremental pattern, they are also unique and interact judiciously with their location within the sura, moving from the simple figures to the more complex interwoven ones.

Although each of the al-Baqara inclusios is different in its own way, together they cover the entire sura, following one after the other in a well-proportioned, symmetrical manner. The development of emphasis throughout the sura can be described in musical terms. Inclusio 1 (panel 1) emphasizes the gentle pitter-patter of the theme, which is then followed by a burst of volume in inclusio 2 (panel 2). Inclusios 3–5 (panel 3) then display an increase in tempo, followed by a decrease in intensity in inclusio 6 and then by closure in inclusio 7. But is this variation purely an expression of literary craftsmanship and rhetorical mastery, or is there more to it? The way the inclusios interact with each other and with their respective placement within the sura reflects a deep connection. Indeed, this congruence suggests that they are not independent entities at all. Rather than seven distinct and completely separate inclusios, they should be considered a single figure that is tailor-made to fit the sura's contents. Although it is useful to analyze each inclusio on its own, like the blind men surrounding Rumi's elephant, one must move beyond these minutiae if one wants to gain an understanding of the picture the inclusios form in their entirety. This picture is that of *one* symmetrical figure that has a distinct incremental dynamic built into it. This dynamic relays emphasis to the end, even as it embellishes and highlights each of the sura's subdivisions.

Affirming al-Baqara's Skeletal Outline: Parallels with al-Fātiḥa

There is both symmetry and a mounting dynamic in al-Baqara's skeletal structure – symmetry due to the location of its inclusios and a mounting dynamic due to the delayed emphasis. In the above, I have considered all the sections framed by inclusios 3–7 as part of panel 3, not independent panels of their own, despite the fact that panel 3 does not have a separate inclusio framing it (see table 3.2). There are good reasons for this organization. Inclusios 3–7 are all composed of a single verse or less that is repeated verbatim, and they therefore pale beside inclusio 2, which repeats two entire verses. As a result, inclusio 2 has a much more pronounced bracketing effect. It organizes the sura into three major divisions, or "panels," and renders the less pronounced subdivisions "sections." This classification is also borne out by the sura's thematic configuration since each panel deals with a different theme: "humanity as a whole" (panel 1), "the Children of Israel" (panel 2), and "the Muslim community" (panel 3). Thus there are good reasons for considering sections 3.1, 3.2, and 3.3 "sections," not "panels," even though they do not seem to have an inclusio framing them as a whole.

However, there is more. There are structural parallels between al-Baqara and al-Fātiḥa that support a tripartite configuration for al-Baqara, assuming one can consider al-Fātiḥa a prelude to al-Baqara. After all, it does immediately precede it. Al-Fātiḥa also has a tripartite structure, a template that features three parts of increasing length, the last of which again has three components. The first part consists of the opening formula, the *basmala*. The second part is verses 2–4. The third part is verses 5–7 and consists of a supplication for guidance to the right way. The threefold split at the end of the unit can be noted in the three different ways that are outlined in the supplication – "the way of those whom God has blessed, not those who are the objects of anger, nor those who go astray." Like panel 3 of Surat al-Baqara, the last portion of al-Fātiḥa is emphasized. It acts as a kind of finale, the previous portions functioning as a prelude to it, just as panels 1 and 2 do the same for al-Baqara. As one can thus see, both al-Baqara and al-Fātiḥa have a tripartite construction that delays emphasis to the end, the last portion of each sura again having a threefold character. Therefore, al-Fātiḥa's structure seems to prefigure that of al-Baqara in a very general, succinct way, which further affirms al-Baqara's configuration into three panels, the last of which has a threefold composition.

Conclusion

Inclusios are poetic figures that frame units of text and thereby set them apart as distinct segments. They can be discerned by both readers and listeners since they can be seen visually in the written word and heard aurally when the text is recited. Thus they are an ideal device for outlining al-Baqara's basic structure. There are seven of these figures in Surat al-Baqara, which systematically delineate the sura's panels and sections in a palpable way, the boundaries they set incidentally coinciding with the sura's thematic subunits. They resemble a composite frame that demarcates and embellishes a picture and inadvertently underlines its internal subdivisions. The picture that these figures sketch is one with an escalating tripartite structure but also an underlying symmetry.

Although inclusios are rampant in literature, from the early writings of ancient Egypt to modern bestsellers, the al-Baqara inclusios are unusually sophisticated for a number of reasons. First, they are consecutive and systematically cover the entire sura in a symmetrical fashion, emphasizing its midmost section and numeric centre. Second, they are all incremental, each building up to and accentuating its end border. Third, each inclusio has its own character, similar to the way a piece of art displays its genius in the way each of its repeated elements are themselves unique masterpieces. Each figure is constructed so as to best suit its placement within the sura's flow of dynamics, building up to the finale, which echoes ideas from within the entire sura and effectively functions as closure for it. This composite feature suggests that together these seven inclusios are the building blocks of one complex, multilayered inclusio that blankets the entire sura.

The recurrent pattern of amplification and climax, buildup and release, as expressed in the special character of the al-Baqara inclusios, layers the sura with a sense of mounting expectation. When the text is orally performed and infused with the melodies of chanting, it enters the acoustic space, where these changing intensities recall the internal dynamics of musical compositions. Within this world, crescendos contribute similar effects through the medium of sound – the rise in volume and its abrupt fall also adding to a sense of fervid anticipation. But rather than decibels, the al-Baqara crescendo touches the aesthetic imagination through the medium of emphasis, even though a gifted reciter may also use volume to communicate rising intensities. As in a concerto, these sophisticated figures work harmoniously together, organizing the text and imbuing it with a mounting dynamic.

4

Thematic Affirmation

Al-Baqara's Chiastic Structure

So much hinges on al-Baqara's inclusios. In fact, Surat al-Baqara's entire structure depends on them. But if they were removed from the equation, would one still be able to base the sura's layout on a firm scholarly foundation? And would the in-built, crescendo-like dynamic be as evident, or would it be lost to posterity? To be sure, I am not suggesting changes to Surat al-Baqara; the intent of this mental exercise is merely to ascertain al-Baqara's structure using a different set of rhetorical tools in order to affirm previous results. Inclusios address only the borders of thematic units, and if one uses the analogy of a composite frame, they do not necessarily convey much about the content they enclose. However, this material, too, is worthy of close attention.

Alternations, Their Types, and Their Function

Whereas inclusios are verbatim repetitions, a second type of the same apparatus also organizes text and has been extensively studied in the Bible: thematic repetition. This particular device organizes the material *within* the frames, and just as one would likely be able to identify the beginning and end of a picture by looking at it without its external trimmings, so too do these tools convey compositional boundaries without a reader necessarily having to resort to the inclusio. These tools involve alternating topics, either in the same order or in an inverted order. When topics alternate in the same order, the device is called "alternation." Alternations add variation and aesthetic appeal to a text and come in different forms. In their simplest forms, they can take the pattern AB/A'B' or ABC/A'B'C'.

Like inclusios, alternations also segment and unify text, the changes in patterns providing emphasis.

When themes alternate in an inverted order, the figure is called a "chiasm," also known as a "chiasmus."[1] In its simplest form, a chiasm follows the pattern AB/B'A'. It can often be quite elaborate, as when it follows the pattern ABC/C'B'A' or even ABCDED'C'B'A', which is suggested for Ezekiel 26:15–18. These long, elaborate chiasms are termed "chiastic structures" when used to describe the structure of a text. Units containing the repeated elements are termed "panels." Thus the chiasm ABC/C'B'A' consists of two panels, of which ABC is the first panel and C'B'A' is the second panel. Like inclusios, chiastic structures are well known in ancient literatures, particularly of the oral variety, since they facilitate memorization, among other things. It is not unusual at all to find such structures within scripture.

Not only do chiasms provide structure for a text or a segment thereof, but they also divide texts by offsetting their compositional elements and unify texts through the imposition of a pattern. Chiasms can also emphasize certain elements within a text. For example, the central unrepeated element D in a chiasm with the pattern ABCDA'B'C' is in a unique position, highlighted by the surrounding repetitions. The chiasm thereby emphasizes this element. A broken pattern, where certain repetitions deviate from the expected, can also provide emphasis, as when the figure is expanded by additional elements at the end. A chiasm that displays an uneven pattern is called a "broken chiasm." For example, a broken pattern of ABCDE/E'D'C'A'B' draws attention to the final irregularity. A pattern of ABCD/D'C'B'A'B"A" relays emphasis to the end of the figure. Broken chiasms can therefore contribute to the movement of emphasis within a text.

Generally, chiasms have two panels, some spreading out from an additional middle element, as in the case of ring composition. But what does one call a sophisticated three-panel figure that similarly displays inversion, as in a pattern of ABC/B'C'A'/C"B"A"? This figure is highly relevant for Surat al-Baqara, as I show below. Does one call it a "broken chiasm" or a "chiastic structure"? Since alternations can have more than three panels and since chiasms and chiastic structures are alternations in an inverted order, I extend the terms "chiasm" and "chiastic structure" to include three-panel compositions – which can always be qualified with the term "tripartite" if one chooses to be more specific. After all, as I have pointed out in conjunction with Martin Kessler, one must allow creative literature to speak for itself, using the available vocabulary to describe it, limited as it may be.[2] Al-Baqara displays a high level of sophistication in its structural figures; however, they all have simpler counterparts in the language of literary devices, which can be used to describe them. The sura's thematic figures are no less ingenious than its inclusios and are in need of resourceful depiction.

Symmetry: The Overarching Ring Construction

Only one of Surat al-Baqara's chiasms has been identified in recent years: its ring construction. This figure is a special kind of chiasm that consists of a centre point with themes fanning out from it in both directions, similar to ripples within a lake. The advantage of using the term "ring" construction, instead of "chiasm," is in the way it conveys the symmetrical quality of the device. The "rings" are the sura's thematic components, laid out in concentric circles around a central theme located in the numeric centre of the sura or thereabouts. As Raymond Farrin has convincingly shown, the sura incorporates such a device, whose circles fan out from its numeric centre at verse 143 and display corresponding themes as they spread.[3] In a very simplified form, they roughly conform to a pattern of ABCDED'C'B'A', where A represents the theme of belief, B the theme of creation, C the theme of law, D the theme of test, and E the theme of election.[4] The ring construction layers the sura with a sense of balance, which recalls the symmetrical layout of al-Baqara's inclusios. Thus both the sura's verbatim and thematic repetitions display symmetry and balance.

Mounting Intensity: Al-Baqara's Incremental Chiastic Structure

Like the sura's inclusios, al-Baqara's thematic repetitions also display a mounting emphasis. But rather than lengthening the verbatim repetition, thematic emphasis is the result of increasing the space devoted to each individual theme. Accordingly, the Muslim community (panel 3, vv. 124–286) is emphasized in comparison both to humanity as a whole (panel 1, vv. 1–39) and to the Children of Israel (panel 2, vv. 40–123), as there are more verses devoted to panel 3. Indeed, panels 1 and 2 combined have only 123 verses, whereas panel 3 contains 163 verses. Panel 3 is therefore emphasized. Moreover, panel 1 has only 39 verses, whereas panel 2 has 84 verses and thus more than twice the number. As one can see, there is a rising emphasis in the sura, where panels are progressively emphasized by allocating them more space. The sura's structure thereby displays gradation leading to a finale, recalling al-Baqara's inclusios and their distinctive crescendo-like dynamic.

But is there more to al-Baqara's thematic repetitions? Can one identify another overarching figure that displays mounting emphasis, a device that is more reflective of al-Baqara's tripartite thematic structure than the ring construction described above? Thematic devices are formed by changing themes, so to locate such a device, one needs to pay attention to changes in themes. Such an analysis has its heuristic aspects; however, what takes it out of the purely experimental domain are the special patterns that one searches for in the text, namely alternations and chiasms. The chiastic structure in particular is so well established in ancient literature that it would not be at all surprising to find one overlaying al-Baqara's ring construction. How does one go about searching for this device? As already indicated by inclusios, panel 3 has a tripartite composition, each section incidentally also displaying a distinct theme. Can a close analysis of panels 1 and 2 yield similar thematic sections? To begin this line of investigation, I start with a closer look at panel 3 to determine these themes and their sequence, which I then follow with an examination of panels 1 and 2.

TABLE 4.1
Thematic structure of panel 3 (vv. 124–286)

Section	Verses	Theme	Character
3.1	124–51	Abrahamic origins	Story
3.2	152–242	Legislation for the new nation	Instruction
3.3	243–86	Testing of faith	Test

Panel 3 begins with the founding narrative of the city of Mecca and the emerging Islamic faith tradition, telling the story of how Abraham and Ishmael built the ancient sanctuary (vv. 124–51). Section 3.1 therefore has the character of a story of primeval origins that is set in the distant past. It is enveloped by a divine promise and its realization in the prophet Muḥammad, who is sent to Abraham's and Ishmael's offspring. It is therefore inherently a story of election, telling of this great privilege that was bestowed upon the emerging Muslim community in the form of an ancient covenant (*ʿahd*). The section is followed by section 3.2, containing legislation for the new nation (vv. 152–242), and ends with the testing of faith in section 3.3 (vv. 243–86), both of which are set in the present. Panel 3 thereby has the sequence of story, instruction, and test (see table 4.1).

Thematic divisions within panels 1 and 2 are highlighted rhetorically, in part by changes in addressees. Accordingly, just like panel 3 above, panel 1 has three sections, the transitions between them highlighted by a change in person. Its first section (1.1) speaks about humanity in the third person (vv. 1–20), its second section (1.2) addresses humanity directly in the second person plural (vv. 21–9), and its third section (1.3) speaks to a masculine singular entity, namely the prophet Muḥammad, directly in the second person (vv. 30–9) (see table 4.2).

Nevertheless, for these panels to form one of the known thematic figures, they need to have similar themes and follow a certain sequence. The sequence makes a big difference since it decides whether one calls

TABLE 4.2
Thematic structure of panel 1 (vv. 1–39)

Section	Verses	Theme	Character
1.1	1–20	Classification of humanity into three groups	Test
1.2	21–9	Direct address to humankind	Instruction
1.3	30–9	Story of Adam and Eve	Story

the figure a "chiasm" or an "alternation." In section 1.1, divine guidance in the form of "this book" functions as a test, by which humanity is classified into three categories, depending on how they perform. Therefore, panel 1 begins with a "test" section. Section 1.2 contains a direct address of the deity to human beings, who are instructed to worship their lord, identified as their creator. This section is therefore an "instruction" section that directs humankind to worship their lord. Section 1.3 is a story about Adam and Eve. It not only portrays the primordial origins of the human species but also delivers a divine promise of future guidance. It, too, is an ancient story of election, telling of human beings' special status as vicegerents on earth. Therefore, panel 1 follows the sequence of test, instruction, and story, the exact opposite of panel 3 (see table 4.2). The inverted sequence suggests that al-Baqara's structure may be chiastic.

But what would al-Baqara's midmost panel have to look like in order to confirm a chiastic structure? It would need to have the same three elements but in a different sequence and would also need to display inversion. Panel 2 is enveloped by the most clearly defined, three-pronged inclusio. The long, noticeable middle repetition (vv. 47–8) borders the first of this panel's thematic subunits, and a change in addressee from the Children of Israel to Muslims indicates the border of the third section (see table 4.3). Therefore, from a rhetorical perspective, this panel also has a tripartite structure, similar to panels 1 and 3 above.

TABLE 4.3
Thematic structure of panel 2 (vv. 40–123)

Section	Verses	Theme	Character
2.1	40–8	Present instructions for the Children of Israel	Instruction
2.2	49–74	Past interactions between them and the deity	Story
2.3	75–123	Present interaction with the Muslim community	Test

With regard to themes, section 2.1 begins with instructions to the Children of Israel in the present moment, followed by a recounting of their primordial history in the distant past (§2.2), and ends with a return to the present and an evaluation of their performance in several kinds of test situations (§2.3). The sequence here differs from section 1 and follows the sequence of instruction, story, and test (see table 4.3). Here, too, the story is one of election, and the term "covenant" (*ʿahd*) is again used to describe this special privilege.

Thus each of the sura's panels is composed of three sections, which in their entirety form the structure ABC/B'C'A'/C"B"A", where A is a test section, B is an instruction section, and C is a story. No two sections of the same type border one another. Accordingly, A does not border A', B does not border B', C does not border C', and so on. Otherwise, it would have been difficult to observe the change in topics, and the figure would not have come to fruition. In addition, the ABC sequence is upheld by the beginning element of each panel (i.e., A, B', C"). This sequence points to a general chiastic structure for the sura. Thus, although there are broad parallels in the composition of each panel and in the general character of the three sections, there is also a large external chiasm holding them together as a unit (see table 4.4).

Is there meaning embedded within this chiasm? Does this repeated grouping together of the elements of story, instruction, and test commu-

TABLE 4.4
The chiasms of Surat al-Baqara

	Section 1			Section 2			Section 3		
Large External chaism	A	B	C	B'	C'	A'	C''	B''	A''
Small internal chiasm			cba		mix of all three		abc		

nicate some kind of moral, idea, or piece of worldly wisdom? In each case described above, the story is one of primeval election set in the distant past, an election that then justifies ensuing instructions and testing in the present moment. Just as human beings as a whole were elected when their forefather became vicegerent on earth (§1.1), so too does this election come accompanied with the instruction to worship God and God alone (§1.2). Human beings are then subjected to a performance review when they are tested with a book coming directly from this deity (§1.3). Likewise, the Children of Israel are elected by means of the Mosaic covenant in the distant past (§2.2), which is then grounds for the deity instructing them (§2.1) and subjecting them to performance reviews in the present (§2.3). Only one word describes this relationship between being elected and the ensuing expectations and reviews: "responsibility." It is responsibility that also binds the primeval election of the Muslim community (§3.1) to the incumbent commandments (§3.2) and challenges (§3.3).[5] As the theme of responsibility moves from panel to panel, the repetitive cylindrical motion emphasizes the notion, amplifying it as it enters the context of the Muslim community through the increased space that it is allotted. The swelling narrative layers the sura and its theme of responsibility with a mounting dynamic.

Further Embellishment: An Internal Chiasm within the Story Sections?

Just in case the reader (or listener) has failed to grasp the significance of the elements of election, instruction, and test, they are repeated once more in each of the story sections, like a melody within a melody. Just as al-Baqara is organized by the external chiasm ABC/B'C'A'/C"B"A", the motifs of a, b, and c are played again within each of the C sections of the sura (see table 4.4). Accordingly, while illustrating the story of the first two human beings, section 1.3 presents Adam's election as a kind of vicegerent (*khalīfa*) on earth, followed by the instruction to eat from everything but the forbidden tree, and ends with the test. In this story, the elements of election, instruction, and test are clearly visible.[6] In terms of sequence, they follow the opposite order of the entire panel, like a chiasm within a chiasm or a sophisticated melody with different layers.

Likewise, in panel 3, Abraham is tested (*ibtalā*) by instructions (*kalimāt*) from God, and upon completing them, he gets elected as an imam for humankind (v. 124). In this story, the elements follow an inverted order, again adding a second layer to the larger figure (see table 4.4).

As one can see, the chiasm enveloping al-Baqara is unusually sophisticated. Not surprisingly, the three elements again combine in the story of Moses and the ancient Israelites, where they are elected and repeatedly instructed and tested (§2.2). Seven consecutive stories in this narrative display this combination: the departure from Egypt (vv. 49–50), the story of the calf (vv. 51–4), the request to behold God (vv. 55–6), entry into the city (vv. 58–9), food and drink in the wilderness (vv. 57, 60–1), the covenant and the violation of the Sabbath (vv. 63–6), and the story of the heifer (vv. 67–73). Here, the three elements are all jumbled up, in the sense that there are several occurrences of special instructions and testing that fill the narrative and do not necessarily display a specific order.

In light of the above, all the story sections of the sura display the three elements of election, instruction, and test, being designed in such a way as to form a second layer that embellishes the sura's main chiasm. The grouping together of these three ideas in these repetitive patterns sends the message that privilege invariably goes hand in hand with special expectations and performance reviews. In other words, the sura's mounting chiastic structure revolves around the idea of responsibility and lays it out in an aesthetically appealing form.

Raising the Tempo: The Belief-Practice Alternation of Sections 3.2 and 3.3

The most visible instance of alternation in Surat al-Baqara is an interlacing of "practice" (A) and "belief" (B) throughout sections 3.2 and 3.3, for a total of fifteen alternations between the two (see tables 4.5 and 4.6). It is somewhat different from a simple AB/A'B' or ABC/A'B'C' sequence since it follows a pattern of AB/A'B'/A"B"/A'"B'"/$A^{iv}B^{iv}$/$A^{v}B^{v}$/$A^{vi}B^{vi}$/A^{vii}. This interweaving recalls a similar combination in the beginning of al-Baqara, which describes the first of the three groups into which humanity is classified: the believers (vv. 3–4). Here, too, the verses begin by listing belief, followed by the more concrete activities of prayer and spending (v. 3). The next verse mentions scripture and the notion of a hereafter (v. 4), following the pattern BAB'. As we can see, the alternation in sections 3.2 and 3.3 repeats this initial pattern and extends it, making it visibly clearer. But what of the figure's contribution to the sura's dynamics? How is alternating fifteen times between belief and practice different from lumping all the practice-related material together in one section and the belief-related material in another? Increasing the number of alternations suggests a quickening of the pace. Thus, as practice and belief alternate in sections 3.2 and 3.3, they also increase the internal tempo of the piece, making their own contribution to the sense of urgency and anticipation.

However, there is another feature that adds to this sense of heightened expectation: the incremental character of the alternation. In both sections 3.2 and 3.3, the alternation begins with short segments of text and moves on to longer ones. Since lengthening the space devoted to each topic results in an increased emphasis, the al-Baqara alternations also have a mounting dynamic. The sura's crescendo-like dynamic is also in evidence here.

Adding Distinction: The Broken Chiasm of Section 3.2 and the Layered Alternations of Section 3.3

Although there is a clear alternation blanketing sections 3.2 and 3.3, it is overlaid with additional figures that give each section its distinct character. In section 3.2 this figure is a chiasm, whereas in section 3.3 extra alternations are layered onto the first one. These additional figures set the sections apart from each other and from the rest of the sura, while also highlighting certain meanings and passages.

To be sure, the material in each passage of section 3.2 is not repeated, even though the general topic is. For example, the idea of food occurs in verses 168–9 and in verses 172–3. However, whereas verses 168–9 are general, inviting humanity to eat from the good things available on earth and not to follow in the footsteps of Satan, verses 172–3 more specifically outline certain dietary restrictions. As they form the chiasm, the various topics fan out, with verses 170–1 as their centre point, changing themes in an inverted order that follows the pattern ABCD-C'B'A'B"A" (see table 4.5). Other than the two passages on dietary matters that flank verses 170–1, the rest of the "practice" elements all contain similar ideas, such as prayer, dealing with death or fighting, and pilgrimage, keeping in mind that there is a general trend of augmentation toward the end since the passages tend to increase in size (see table 4.5). The "belief" elements also display a similar pattern, spreading out from verses 170–1 and repeating similar themes on both sides of their centre point, while swelling in size toward the end of the section (see table 4.5). Both this feature and the recurrence of the A" and B" expansions render the figure a broken chiasm, with the chiastic emphasis toward the end. However, the centring of the chiasm around verses 170–1 balances out this emphasis, meaning that there is now a double emphasis: one in the beginning on verses 170–1 and another toward the end. The broken, uneven pattern layers section 3.2 with an internal dynamic and a delayed emphasis.

In section 3.3 belief and practice take on a markedly different character: no longer is scripture routinely mentioned in every passage on belief, but belief becomes geared toward God's mastery over life and death. The section contains three passages dealing with belief: verses 243, 246–53, and 255–60 (see table 4.6). The "practice" sections also change, exclusively centring on topics related to fighting and spending, with the exception of the epilogue, which closes off the sura (vv. 284–6). Accordingly, verses 244–5 enjoin fighting and spending, and verses 254 and 261–83 also deal with spending. Thus, although the alternation between belief and practice continues from the previous section, it takes on very different undertones, focusing on the portrayal of God as ultimately controlling life and death, as well as on spending one's money in charity and risking one's life for a noble cause as the ultimate tests of faith. Here, the general concern of the section is not ordinances for the newly minted Muslim nation but how its faith is going to be tested.

The different character that becomes apparent in section 3.3 can be summed up as a second alternation layered onto the first one. This time the alternation is between life and wealth, suggesting putting one's life and wealth in God's hands. These two motifs alternate a total of six times throughout the section, following a pattern of EF/E'F'/E''F'', where E represents a life-related topic and F a wealth-related topic (see table 4.6). They thus overlay the previous alternation of belief and practice from section 3.2 (see table 4.5) with another alternation distinctive to section 3.3 (see table 4.6).

However, there is more. The third alternation in this section, which intertwines with the other two, is an alternation of stories with other material. Again the number of alternating passages is six: three stories and three injunction passages (see table 4.6). The section begins with a story illustrating God's mastery over life and death (v. 243), followed by injunctions to fight and spend. The story of Ṭālūt (vv. 246–53), the

TABLE 4.5
Chiasms and alternations of section 3.2 (vv. 152–242)

	vv. 151–8	vv. 159–67	vv. 168–9	vv. 170–1
Alternation between belief (B) and practice (A)	A	B	A'	B'
Broad topical chiasm	A	B	C	D
Topics	Prayer; death or fighting; pilgrimage	Withholding scripture; those gone astray (group 3)	Food	Following scripture or ancestors; the ungrateful (group 2)

first Israelite prophet-king, who is often identified as the Biblical King Saul, is followed by the command to spend and by the passage containing the throne verse (vv. 254–7). The last of these story passages consists of three short stories (vv. 258–60) and is followed by a lengthy passage on money-related topics (261–83). Thus there is a third alternation overlaying the other two, this time between story and injunction passages, rhetorically highlighting the demarcation of this section as a distinct unit. The stories function as examples, reinforcing the commandments and the deity's mastery over life and death.

The three short story excerpts that form this alternation have a rather unusual poetic dimension. They briefly recall the three longer election stories of the sura: the story of Adam of panel 1 (§1.3), the story of the

vv. 172–4	vv. 174–6	vv. 177–203	vv. 204–14	vv. 215–42
A''	B''	A'''	B'''	A^{iv}
C'	B'	A'	B''	A''
Food	Withholding scripture; differing over scripture; components of belief; those gone astray (group 3)	Prayer; death or fighting; capital punishment; testamentary inheritance; pilgrimage; spending; fasting	Those gone astray (group 3); components of belief; differing over scripture	Spending; fighting; alcohol and gambling prohibition; prayer; women

ancient Israelites of panel 2 (§2.2), and the story of Abraham and Ishmael of panel 3 (§3.1). The first short story of the alternation (v. 243) has thousands of unidentified human beings as the protagonists, similar to the story of Adam in section 1.3, where the central protagonist is shared between all of humanity and is not exclusively affiliated with any one group. The second short story of the alternation, the story of Ṭālūt, the first king of Israel (vv. 246–3), has ancient Israelites as the protagonists, just like section 2.2, which features Moses and the ancient Israelites in the wilderness. The third short story excerpt of the alternation (vv. 258–60) is composed of three short stories in which the main protagonist is Abraham, who is also a central figure in section 3.1. Thus

TABLE 4.6
Alternations of section 3.3 (vv. 243–86)

		v. 243	vv. 244–5	vv. 246–53
1	Alternation between belief (B) and practice (A) continues from §3.2	B^{iv}	A^{v}	B^{v}

		vv. 243–4	v. 245	vv. 246–53
2	Alternation between topics of life (E) and wealth (F)	E	F	E'
	Topics related to putting one's wealth and life on the line for God	God as master over life and death; fighting (putting) one's life on the line for God)	Spending in charity	God as master over life and death; fighting (long)

		v. 243	vv. 244–5	vv. 246–53
3	Alternation between story (H) and injunction (I)	H	I	H'
	Story and injunctions alternate	Story	Injunction to fight and spend	Story

v. 254	vv. 255–60	vv. 261–83	vv. 284–6
A^{vi}	B^{vi}	A^{vii}	G

v. 254	vv. 255–60	vv. 261–83	vv. 284–6
F'	E''	F''	G
Spending in charity	God as master over life and death; (long)	Spending in charity; usury; loans (long)	Epilogue

vv. 254–7	vv. 258–60	vv. 261–83	vv. 284–6
I'	H''	I''	G
Injunction to spend; exaltation of God (throne verse)	Three short stories	Injunctions to spend; loans; usury prohibition	Epilogue

the same pattern reappears here, reinforcing the sense of progression from humanity in general to the ancient Israelites and then to Abraham and the emerging Muslim nation. This progression confirms God's mastery over life and death in all contexts, supporting the commands to spend and fight.

Furthermore, the last short story excerpt (vv. 258–60) consists of a story centred on Abraham, a story about an unidentified individual, and a story featuring Abraham again. Sandwiching the unidentified individual between two mentions of Abraham hints at the importance of the relationship of Abraham to humanity as a whole. Deviating from the previous pattern of one short story and instead presenting three seems to add to a sense of urgency. Moreover, the "thousands of human beings" story (v. 243) in the beginning of this alternation is noticeably shorter that the second segment, the Ṭālūt story (vv. 246–53), the increase in length contributing a rising emphasis. Indeed, the two single short story excerpts serve as a buildup to the finale with the three short stories, forming another crescendo-like dynamic. Therefore, the short stories of section 3.3 also display gradation, leading to a threefold climax that this time is composed of three consecutive anecdotes. Like the general structures of al-Baqara and al-Fātiḥa, the short stories of section 3.3 display a rise in emphasis as length increases from the first to the second segment, as well as a rise in tempo since there is a quickening of the pace of storytelling as the Abraham stories flow in quick succession one after the other. The short story excerpts of section 3.3 thereby carry echoes of Surat al-Baqara and Surat al-Fātiḥa in the way they are constructed.

It is no accident that of all the sura's sections, section 3.3 is the one to display three alternations layered onto the sura's general chiastic structure. After all, this section is the last one and therefore functions as the finale. In a way, it recalls the epilogue (vv. 284–6), which weaves together echoes from the entire sura, since the three alternations also weave together elements from throughout the sura. In fact, they blend together the three elements of its overarching chiasm – story, instruction, and test – even mimicking the sura's structure. Moreover, the one-layer, internal chiasm of section 3.2 functions as a buildup to the multilayer alternations of section 3.3, thereby paralleling the two interwoven inclusios of the same sections. Like the epilogue, these alternations also contribute closure but this time for the sura's thematic figure.

Alternations and Meaning

Surat al-Baqara's chiastic structure conveys the idea of responsibility since it invariably establishes a link between election to a privileged position and both added responsibility and performance reviews. But do the smaller structures that organize sections 3.2 and 3.3 also convey meaning, or are these ones purely aesthetic? What does an alternation between topics related to belief and practice convey? Alternations contribute meaning by highlighting a link between the alternating themes. Therefore, the belief-practice alternation highlights the notion that belief is invariably accompanied by practice, that the two go together. The structure thereby mimics the words of the verses that describe believers as "those who believe and do good deeds" (vv. 25, 82, 277), similarly combining the two ideas and placing them repeatedly in conjunction with one another. Additionally, in every occurrence of belief, scripture is mentioned (see table 4.5). The connection between belief and scripture is thereby strongly emphasized, confirming and elaborating on the message of verses 3–4, namely that true belief is invariably linked to scripture.

The broad chiasm covering section 3.2 helps to shape this meaning, as it highlights its midmost component (see table 4.5). The middle element in the chiasm (vv. 170–1) is given emphasis due to its location, similar to the ring construction discussed above (see table 4.5). These verses state, "When it is said to them: 'Follow what God has sent down,' they say: 'No, but we follow the ways of our fathers' – even though their fathers did not think and were not guided? The parable[7] of those who are ungrateful is like a shepherd calling out to what does not hear except for beckoning and shouting – deaf, mute and blind, they do not think."

Thus the idea of following scripture as opposed to ancestral traditions stands out in these verses, as does the negative portrayal of those who blindly follow their ancestors. They are pictured as animals who cannot properly hear, except for unintelligible sounds; they are "deaf, mute and blind." The word *yanʿiq* in verse 171 is a hapax legomenon and is usually used in the Arabic language to refer to a shepherd calling his flock. The parable is thus that of a shepherd calling out words that his followers cannot hear, absorb, and understand. The underlying metaphor suggests that those who fail to follow divine scripture when it is brought to their attention are like sheep, who can comprehend only meaningless sounds. Ancestral traditions are therefore likened to noise devoid of meaning, with the ones who prefer it over scripture being portrayed as "deaf, mute and blind." The chiasm thereby contributes to the "scripture" component of the meanings underlined by the alternation. The authority of scripture becomes superior to ancestral authority.

But what do the story-injunction and life-wealth alternations convey? Do they also link certain ideas? The stories serve as real life examples that illustrate and reinforce the injunctions, thereby highlighting the connection between ordinance and action. They suggest that theory and action go hand in hand, which in a way is well suited to this section with its character as a "test" of sorts. The life-wealth alternation also highlights this character, encouraging the emerging Muslim community to realize that God is master over life and wealth and to place themselves in the deity's hands. The interweaving of ideas related to fighting and spending in a threefold alternating manner implies a close connection between the concepts: after the previous sections have laid the groundwork for establishing the Muslim community and instructing its members in the new covenant, their ultimate test is to trust God with their lives and wealth. The community's performance will be evaluated with regard to these two aspects. The epilogue at the end of the sura underlines the hope that the deity will extend support to them in these endeavours.

Verbal and Thematic Convergence

It is noteworthy that the thematic segmentation of al-Baqara's chiastic structure coincides with its inclusios, just as a composite frame may highlight the borders of the pictures it encloses, even though it is possible to tell where these pictures begin and end from their contents alone. This correspondence therefore affirms that these figures are not haphazardly placed but are compositional devices that organize the text and provide structure. Moreover, the thematic figures work harmoniously with the sura's inclusios, adding complexity and embellishing sections 1, 2, 3.2, and 3.3 in turn, similar to the way an artist may use texture in a painting. In fact, all the sura's subunits, except the middle one, receive some kind of rhetorical embellishment of the thematic kind – perhaps not surprisingly since the middle unit is already adorned by the layering of additional inclusios (§3.1). Accordingly, sections 1 and 2 are garnished with the election, instruction, and test motifs. Furthermore, sections 3.2 and 3.3 are decked with a broad, extended alternation between the themes of belief and practice (see tables 4.5 and 4.6), which underlines the connection between what is in the heart and what becomes manifest in deeds. Moreover, these two sections are again adorned with additional thematic figures that are layered onto the alternation: the broken chiasm of section 3.2 and the three alternations of section 3.3. These additional figures further set off these sections as distinct units, contributing poetically to the threefold division of the sura's last panel and also to the rising complexity.

As a result, none of the sura's five main narrative segments is left without embellishment: sections 1, 2, 3.1, 3.2, and 3.3 are each adorned with an intricate design, whether it be the unfolding pattern of election, instruction, and test (§1, §2), the adding of internal frames (§3.1), or the additional layering of chiasms and alternations (§3.2, §3.3). Each of these embellishments is well suited to the section it adorns, moving from simple structures to more complex ones. Thus Surat al-Baqara's thematic figures also display variation and a steady rise in complexity that is well suited to its schematic layout.

So both the verbatim repetitions and the thematic ones converge, for while the verbatim figures enrich the sura's midmost section (§3.2), its thematic figures decorate the rest. As a result, they work harmoniously together and contribute to the sura's mounting dynamics. If one imagines these changing dynamics in the world of music, the increasing size of the panels resembles a steady climb in volume, and the growing complexity resembles a quickening of the pace. The internal dynamics of these poetic figures thereby contribute to a growing intensity and a sense of heightened anticipation.

Conclusion

Al-Baqara's alternations and chiasms corroborate the skeletal structure outlined by the sura's inclusios, independently conveying symmetry and a crescendo-like, mounting dynamic. The sura's *thematic* repetitions thereby affirm the results uncovered by analyzing its *verbatim* repetitions. Symmetry is conveyed by the ring construction centred on the sura's numeric midpoint, from which its themes fan out like ripples within a lake. Mounting intensity is displayed in its tripartite, chiastic structure, which is expressed through two methods: space allocation and frequency of alternations. As more space is allocated to a theme, it is also emphasized, and as the frequency increases, the intensity also increases. These two methods embed a clever, crescendo-like dynamic in the sura's structure. A bird's-eye view of the sura shows that it consists of three panels of increasing length, which display the same three overarching themes organized in an inverted order and augmented by fine-tunings, like a melody within a melody. In this bird's-eye view, the last two sections are revealed to possess other layers of complexity, which add to the sense of anticipation and produce closure. The sura thereby exhibits a sophisticated thematic organization, which takes the form of a chiasm that is embellished by an intricate, crescendo-like dynamic.

The sura's aesthetically pleasing organization does not serve artistic purposes alone but also has meaning. This additional dimension is contributed by the way certain components are highlighted and others are linked together. The highlighted components are first the election of the Muslim community (v. 143) and second the superiority of divine scripture to ancestral traditions (vv. 170–1), both emphasized through their location at the centre of a ring construction or a broken chiasm. These ideas therefore become significant in the sura. The linked components are belief and practice, theory and action, and life and wealth, the connection between them highlighted by the sura's alternations. However, the meaning that lies at the centre of al-Baqara's structure is the notion of responsibility, for as the sura repeatedly links the themes of election, instruction, and test, it suggests that privilege invariably comes accompanied by responsibility.

5

"God as Guide"

Surat al-Baqara's Running Theme in the Divine Self-Revelatory Reading

How does one begin to establish Surat al-Baqara's running themes? Does one follow a thematic method of analysis or a rhetorical one? Scholars who have followed a purely thematic method have had to face the challenge of synthesizing diverse topics, which can be as divergent as the subject matter of panels 2 and 3. As a result, they have tried to find something that addresses them both, coming up with very complex central themes. Sayyid Quṭb, for instance, suggests a central double axis: on the one hand, the sura deals with "the position of the Children of Israel regarding the Islamic missionary activity in Medina, their reception of it and their opposition to its messenger and the nascent Muslim community"; on the other hand, it discusses "the position of the nascent Muslim community, preparing to bear the responsibility of missionary activity and vicegerency on earth."[1] Others have looked to the numeric centre of the sura, with its reference to Muslims as a "middle nation," considering it to be a guide to al-Baqara's contents.[2] This latter approach can also be accompanied by rhetorical analysis since this numeric centre is located at the heart of the ring construction that covers the sura. As a result, the identification of this central theme is not based entirely on thematic experimentation on the part of the investigator but also has some rhetorical support.

Is it possible that the answer to the puzzle of al-Baqara's central theme is as simple as that – the numeric centre? Or would one expect something a little more sophisticated in a composition that displays the rhetorical complexity and aesthetic creativity of al-Baqara's structuring devices. To be sure, there is some merit in the notion of "middle nation" as a central theme. In a way, all the themes of panels 1 and 2 can be considered a buildup to this high point, namely the election and accompanying responsibilities of humankind and of the Children of Israel, as well as the primeval story of Abraham, Ishmael, and the founding of the sanctuary in Mecca. All these themes pave the way for the election of the Muslim community as a "middle nation." Furthermore, descending from this zenith, all subsequent themes somehow delineate the Muslim community's ensuing responsibilities and expectations. This high point is also underlined by the sura's lexical organizational figures, the inclusios. They do so not only in the form of the additional layer of inclusios that is added onto section 3.1 through inclusios 4 and 5 (see table 3.6) but also in the form of the extensive repetitions that are allotted to framing section 3.1.2 and that enclose the numeric centre (see table 3.3). In fact, these verbatim repetitions are so pronounced as to be unmistakable and highlight the numeric centre *rhetorically*. As a result, there can be no doubt as to the centrality of the theme indicated by the sura's midpoint: the election of the Muslim community as a middle nation and, by extension, the introduction of the Islamic covenant. It follows that scholars who have suggested this approach have made a valuable contribution by identifying a numerically centred peak that imbues the sura's meanings with an underlying symmetry.

However, here I opt for a different approach, something a little more in tune with the sophisticated verbatim and thematic structures that lend the sura its mounting, crescendo-like dynamic. In fact, I search for the spine that lies at the heart of these escalating structures and infuses them with meaning. Although there are two ways that rhetorical structures organize the sura – verbatim and thematic – in this chapter I address only verbatim repetition. I examine the rhetorical device of the *Leitwort*, or keyword, and follow its verbal cues to identify the first of the sura's running themes.

Nevertheless, there is one more thing to consider: the reading method, that playground in which the reader's subjectivity meets the impersonal text and brings it to life. For the divine-human relationship portrayed in the text is meaningless unless the text is similarly placed in a relationship with the reader. The question becomes how to read the verbal cues and then how to use that lens to explore the way that the sura's contents swirl and dance around its spine. In the pages of this chapter, I begin this endeavour with the first of the two protagonist-focused readings: the divine self-revelatory reading, which places God at the focal point and examines the text for how it depicts the deity.

The *Leitwort*

Similar to the inclusio, the *Leitwort* is also known from the study of the Bible, but its identification is more recent and is not as widespread in the literature. Martin Buber (d. 1965) discussed it in connection with the Pentateuch.[3] The term was subsequently picked up by Robert Alter, and it gained a wider audience.[4]

A *Leitwort* is a leading keyword that occurs throughout a text and imbues it with a unifying character or even – in the case of al-Baqara – with a central theme. It often appears in various grammatical forms since allowances can be made for case endings, gender, number, and other grammatical differences. It is similar to a *Leitmotif*; however, whereas *Leitwort* refers to a repeated word, *Leitmotif* refers to a repeated theme in a leading or central position.

In al-Baqara the profusion and relatively even distribution of the word "guidance," in addition to its tone-setting position in the sura's first inclusio, make it a good candidate for a *Leitwort*. Moreover, the inclusio's special construction and the way it builds the incremental effect reinforces this suggestion – for out of all the sura's inclusios, this one alone repeats the same word rather than expanding the repetition with different words. Furthermore, in addition to the expected threefold occurrence of "guidance" in the beginning, middle, and end of the panel (vv. 2, 16, 38), the word appears two more times in between (vv. 5, 26). As a result, "guidance" appears a total of seven times in the panel: four times as a nonsuffixed noun (vv. 2, 5, 16, 38), once as a suffixed noun (v. 38), and twice in alternate grammatical forms (vv. 16, 26). This device thus veers away from the usual pattern in al-Baqara, even as it maintains the basic shape of the inclusio. Therefore, the location and unusual profusion of the word within the sura's first inclusio signals its distinctive character as a keyword.

Furthermore, "guidance" occurs twenty-seven more times throughout the rest of the sura (vv. 53, 70, 97, 120, 135, 137, 142, 143, 150, 157, 159, 170, 175, 185, 196, 198, 213, 258, 264, 272). Thus the word occurs a total of thirty-four times in Surat al-Baqara, occasionally more than once in the same verse. This number is the largest among all the suras; for example, among the rest of the seven large suras, it appears ten times in Āl ʿImrān (sura 3), nine times in al-Nisāʾ (sura 4), ten times in al-Māʾida (sura 5), twenty-six times in al-Anʿām (sura 6), eighteen times in al-Aʿrāf (sura 7), and not at all in al-Anfāl (sura 8). It appears 316 times throughout the entire Qurʾan. As one can see, the concentration of this word in Surat al-Baqara is noticeably higher than the average concentration in the Qurʾan, further affirming "guidance" as the sura's *Leitwort*.

Whereas the inclusio divides al-Baqara into subdivisions, the *Leitwort* ties the text together and linguistically serves to provide cohesion. It should be noted that linguists agree that there is a difference between cohesion and coherence, even though they are not always in accord on what this difference actually is. In general, however, cohesion refers to the grammatical and lexical elements connecting a text, whereas coherence has the reader at its focal point and is the outcome of a connection between the reader and the text. Thus, when the reader is taken out of the picture and the focus is only on the lexical repetitions connecting a text, the investigation concerns cohesion. Although cohesion is an important function of the *Leitwort*, that is not its only function. Similar to the inclusio and any other form of repetition, it also has an emphasizing function, as identified by the medieval commentators mentioned in chapter 3. This verbal emphasis suggests that guidance is a common thread or running theme within the sura, like stepping stones for readers to follow and take note of every time they encounter one along the path of reading.

It is noteworthy that the most prominent of the early exegetical works to suggest a central theme for Surat al-Baqara, the medieval commentary of Burhān al-Dīn al-Biqāʿī (d. 885/1480), also uses the word "guidance" in its formulation. Al-Biqāʿī's method is to look to the sura names as a means to identify each sura's purpose. Accordingly, he describes al-Baqara's intent in a twofold manner: first, by means of its eponymic heifer; and second, through another of Surat al-Baqara's names: al-Zahrāʾ, "the radiant." When relating the sura's intent to the story of the heifer, he writes, "Its intent is to establish proof that the book constitutes *guidance* to be followed in everything it says. The greatest of what it *guides* [one] to is belief in the Unseen, and its sum is belief in the hereafter: it deals with belief in resurrection, articulated by the story of the heifer, which deals with belief in the Unseen. This is why the sura was called after it."[5] When relating al-Zahrāʾ to the sura's intent, he states, "It was called 'the radiant,' because it lights up the path of *guidance* and sufficiency in this world and the next and because it confirms the lighting up of faces on the day of accounting."[6] Thus, although the central theme identified by al-Biqāʿī is elaborately expressed, it is centred on the notion of guidance and therefore carries echoes of the *Leitwort*. Al-Biqāʿī's thematic analysis therefore displays some congruence with the results of the rhetorical one above.

Identifying the Divine Self-revelatory Central Theme

The central theme of the divine self-revelatory mode is relatively easy to identify since it is indicated by the numerous occurrences of the *Leitwort.* In every instance, "God" is either directly or indirectly depicted as the supplier of the guidance. Examples of direct guidance include verse 38, in which the deity speaks in the first person, identifying the guidance as "from me" and referring to "my" guidance. Verse 120 describes it in a similar fashion: "it is God's guidance which is guidance." Examples of the term coming through a vehicle of sorts include verse 2, in which the book is described as "guidance for the mindful." Verse 5 describes the same group as being "on guidance from their Lord," implying that the book constitutes God's guidance. The "book" is again portrayed as a means of guidance in verses 159 and 175 in connection with the ones who suppress this gift.

Whereas in the last two verses, the "book" may be a reference to other scriptures, such as the Torah, in verse 2 it points to the Qur'an specifically since it specifies "this book." In verse 185 the Qur'an is mentioned explicitly, with the instruction to glorify God for this guidance. Other vehicles of God's guidance include Moses (v. 53), who conveys guidance to the Israelites, and Gabriel (v. 97), who conveys guidance to Muḥammad. The deity is also portrayed withholding guidance from certain groups, such as the unjust ones and the ungrateful ones (vv. 258, 264).

All the instances of the *Leitwort* in this sura occur in connection with God, who is thus the ultimate guide, whether portrayed directly as such or shown to function through an intermediary like the prophets, angels, or scriptures. As a result, when placing God at the focal point and reading the text in the divine self-revelatory mode, the *Leitwort* becomes "God as Guide," forming a *Leitmotif* that runs throughout the text. How does the theme of God as Guide play out in the sura and hold its contents together? How does it develop, panel by panel? I explore these questions below, beginning with the first panel.

Panel 1: Humankind (vv. 1–39)

Since section 1 is framed by the *Leitwort* "guidance," the theme of God as Guide is particularly noticeable here. It is established in the beginning of the panel, where this book (the Qur'an) is identified as a doubt-free source of guidance (v. 2). God is portrayed not only as the book's sender but also as the transcendent guide, who has provided past and present guidance (v. 4). Having the ability to place a seal over the minds, eyes, and ears of individuals, he can prevent them from perceiving it, thereby emerging as the ultimate controller of guidance (vv. 6–7). In addition, he can remove the guiding light from those who rely on others to guide them (v. 17). He thereby becomes the guide par excellence: no others may fulfil this role.

The deity's active guiding role in the present moment is outlined in his direct address to humankind (vv. 21–5). He is referred to as *rab-bakum*, recalling his description in al-Fātiḥa (v. 2), and is identified as the creator of humankind, the heavens, and the earth. His creations are another aspect of his guiding function since even a mosquito can serve as a parable, having the purpose of either guiding to success or leading astray (v. 26). In the distant past, God became the primordial guide, providing guidance for angels and the first human couple, while promising to send future guidance (vv. 30–9).

Panel 2: The Children of Israel (vv. 40–123)

In panel 2 God blesses the Children of Israel with guidance in the form of the covenant (v. 40), which is a central idea here. The concept occurs in several verses dispersed throughout the panel, and multiple terms are used to refer to it. In verse 40 it appears as *ʿahd*, as is highlighted by the word *awfū*' (be loyal). In the Hebrew Scriptures, the notion of covenant is an important theme. Loyalty (Hebrew: *ḥesed*) is the convenant's foundation, for it is what binds both parties together. *ʿAhd* can also be translated as "testament"; the Hebrew Scriptures, also known as the Old Testament, are called *al-ʿahd al-qadīm* in Arabic, and the New Testament is known as *al-ʿahd al-jadīd.* Both "covenant" and "testament" have similar meanings, but whereas "covenant" highlights the contractual nuances of the historical event, "testament" underlines its enduring, textual attestation. *Mīthāq* is another term for the covenant and occurs several times in this panel (vv. 63, 83–4, 93), and the two terms even occur together (v. 27). Yet another reference to the covenant occurs in verse 51, which discusses "appointing Moses forty nights."[7]

Related to this ancient covenant is the expectation to fulfil a specified set of instructions, which include believing in the new prophet, practising charity, and performing communal prayers with the followers of the new faith (vv. 41–7). The deity thereby provides the Children of Israel with substantive guidance for the present moment. In the distant past, he provided Moses with guidance in the form of the book (v. 53) after saving the Israelites from Pharaoh's abuses (vv. 49–50) and splitting the sea (v. 50), and he supplied them with food and water in the wilderness (vv. 57–60). The section also shows how the deity dealt with their repeated transgressions, punishing the wrongdoers and providing restitution (vv. 51–74). God thereby fulfils his part of the covenant, guiding Israel in the present as he did in the past.

Whereas in section 2.2 the actions of the Children of Israel have a general, idyllic quality, in section 2.3 the tone changes, the location of the keywords underlining this change. Thus in section 2.2 they occur in verse 53 in connection with God giving Moses the book and in verse 70 in connection with the Israelites' ultimate wish to be guided and their eventual success in spite of their stumbles. In contrast, in section 2.3 the keywords occur in connection with God sending Gabriel to Muḥammad (v. 97), thereby moving the prophetic privilege from the Israelites to their Ishmaelite cousins. This notion is reinforced by the subsequent location of the keyword, where it occurs in connection with the Israelite's failure to realize that guidance is God's and that they have no monopoly over it (v. 120). Thus the location of the keywords underlines both the change in Israel's fortunes and God's ultimate control over who receives his gifts.

In section 2.3 the deity criticizes some of the Children of Israel's contemporaneous activities, providing the nascent Muslim community with guidance on these issues (vv. 75–123). He directs his reprimands toward the falsification of scripture (vv. 75–9), the attack, capture, and ransom of fellow Jews (vv. 84–6), and the refusal to follow the new scripture and prophet (vv. 87–91, 99–101). In addition, he spells out serious consequences for those who commit these offences, which include humiliation in this world, torment in the next, and being cursed (vv. 80–1, 85–6, 88–90). The deity also instructs the prophet Muḥammad how to respond verbally (vv. 80–2, 91–8) and directs the Muslim community not to copy some of the Jews' past and present actions (vv. 104, 108), to pardon and forgive them (v. 109), and to establish regular prayer and charity (v. 110).

This panel thereby brings the Muslim community into the conversation about Israel's past and present, in preparation for the upcoming panel, and incidentally also brings the Children of Israel back into the present and their current situation. The panel thereby establishes the continuity of God's guiding actions by portraying his role in the past and in the present: God is affirmed as the transcendent guide.

Panel 3: The Emerging Muslim Nation (vv. 124–286)

Panel 3 begins with Abraham fulfilling God's appointment of him as a religious leader for humankind, indicating the universality of his role (v. 124). The words of this appointment constitute guidance from the deity and recall Adam receiving similar words (v. 37). Central are Abraham's and Ishmael's prayers for a prophet to recite God's verses to their progeny, to purify them, and to teach them the book and its wisdom (v. 129). These prayers underline the deity's responsiveness to requests for guidance (v. 151) since God becomes the active sender of prophets with scriptures, who are the vehicles of his guidance, rendering him the universal guide.

In this section the deity also responds to Muḥammad's wish to change the prayer orientation (vv. 144, 148–9), an action that sets his followers apart from the Children of Israel and establishes them as a distinct nation (vv. 143). Incumbent upon this status are certain prescriptions and prohibitions (§3.2), with the relationship between the election section (§3.1) and the instruction section (§3.2) thus paralleling the relationship between verse 40 and verses 41–7 in panel 2. Whereas the covenant established the Children of Israel as a distinct nation (v. 40), the new prophet and the distinct prayer orientation accomplish the same for Muslims (§3.1), and since the Children of Israel had certain obligations associated with their status (vv. 41–7), Muslims are also given injunctions here (§3.2). As one can see, sections 3.1 and 3.2 reiterate and expand upon ideas similar to those that occur in panel 2.

However, there is more to this systematic repetition of ideas. Noteworthy is the set of instructions given to the Israelites in panel 2, many of which are repeated and elaborated in section 3, such as belief, prayer, and the giving of alms (e.g., vv. 40–8, 136, 150–3, 261–74). Neal Robinson has also noted parallels between the sequence of events connected with the Children of Israel and some of the legislation contained in panel 3:

> In vv. 178 ff., legislation is laid down for dealing with cases of manslaughter. This seems out of connection with the previous material until one recognizes that the sequence of topics in the address to the believers bears some relation to the sequence in the address to the Children of Israel. The Children of Israel were commanded to revere the One God (cf. v. 40), but they fell into idolatry and worshipped the calf (cf. vv. 51–54). Their idolatry led them in turn to be discontent with the food with which God provided them (cf. v. 61) and to commit manslaughter (cf. v. 72).[8]

The command to revere the one God is paralleled in verses 163–7, whereas the food theme occurs in verses 168–72. The legislation for dealing with cases of manslaughter (vv. 178–9) is followed by legislation dealing with the occurrence of death in general, namely with reference to the will of the deceased (vv. 180–2). We can thereby observe a similar pattern between the panel addressing the Children of Israel (vv. 40–73) and verses 124–82 of the current panel. The deity thereby seems to have systematically given a similar set of instructions to both Israelites and Muslims. Therefore, God emerges as a consistent, systematic, and methodical guide.

Again, the location of the *Leitwort* underlines the move away from the Children of Israel and the establishment of the nascent Muslim community as a distinct nation. It appears in verse 137, which designates the guided ones as those who believe as Muslims believe and identifies those who turn away as being in dispute. It then appears three times in the verses that relate to the change in prayer orientation (vv. 142–3, 150), of which verse 143 occurs at the sura's numeric centre, designating Muslims as a middle nation (*umma wasaṭ*). The status of "being guided" thereby moves along with the addressees, passing from the Children of Israel to the Muslim community.

In sections 3.2 and 3.3, the *Leitwort* occurs in a variety of locations and is associated with seemingly disparate topics, such as catastrophe and death (v. 157), suppressing scripture (v. 159), true belief (vv. 170, 175), fasting (v. 185), pilgrimage (v. 198), nations and the book (v. 213), Abraham (v. 258), and charity (vv. 264, 272). The topics covered in the two sections are also very broad and include practical topics, such as fasting, war regulations, pilgrimage, women, charity, trade, and usury, alternating with the ideas of monotheism, scripture, and belief. Many of these topics appear twice in what has previously been identified as a roughly alternating, broken chiasm, topics such as pilgrimage (vv. 158, 196–203), food laws (vv. 168, 172–3), and withholding truth (vv. 159–62, 174–6). Since there do not seem to be any precisely repeated phrases, other than in the inclusios, this doubling does not suggest any further major structural demarcation but rather a plurality of individual, intertwining themes that are equally emphasized. These disparate and intertwining elements underline the broad, interrelated, and substantive nature of the deity's guidance. Accordingly, God counsels remembrance and patience in moments of distress (vv. 152–7), the disclosure of scripture (vv. 160–3, 174–6), and monotheism (vv. 164–71). He prescribes dietary restrictions (vv. 172–3), regulations related to death and dying (vv. 178–82), and how and when to fast (vv. 183–7). In addition, he outlines rules for war (vv. 190–5, 216–18), for pilgrimage rituals, and for marriage, divorce, and menstruation (vv. 158, 196–203, 221–42), and he warns against insincerity, the consumption of alcohol, and gambling (vv. 204–14, 219). The deity is thereby concerned not only with the broad outlines of guidance but also with some of its minute details. God is thereby portrayed as a thorough, meticulous, and careful guide.

In the last subsection, God appears as the provider of concrete guidance in the form of the monetary and fighting injunctions. Not only can he ordain death, but he can also revive the dead (vv. 243, 258, 259, 260). The section contains another Israelite exemplar, Ṭālūt, divinely chosen to rule the Israelites. Those who followed their prophet-king into battle ultimately became victorious. God thereby surfaces as guiding to ultimate success those who put their lives and wealth in his hands.

The idea of testing emerges clearly in the last section, where putting one's life and wealth on the line for God becomes a kind of test of people's sincerity and commitment to the new faith. Just as the Israelites were tested under Ṭālūt when they first appointed a king and emerged as a political force, so too will Muslims be tested. Although the deity's test takes the form of the charity and fighting injunctions in this section, it is overlaid with other kinds of tests from elsewhere in the sura. In section 1.1 the requested book becomes the first and general test for humanity as a whole, portrayed as God's response to the supplication in al-Fātiḥa. It is in this book that the injunctions occur, so the idea of the book as a test continues to be operative here as well. Hence there is a broad connection between the "tests" of sections 3 and 1. However, the connection does not stop there but is also present in the "test" of panel 2. The idea of the book as a test also overshadows section 2.3, where the deity's present-day test for the Children of Israel takes the form of the new book and the new prophet (vv. 87–91, 99–101).

Furthermore, the idea of testing is also present in each of the story sections, tying together the concepts of instruction and test. Thus, in the story of Adam (§1.3), God's command to the angels becomes a trial, which most of the angels pass but Iblīs fails. His prohibition against eating from the tree becomes a test for Adam and Eve, which they in turn fail. Similarly, in section 2.2 the history of the ancient Israelites is interlaced with trials. They include Pharaoh's oppression (v. 49), the calf (v. 51), the deity's command to kill themselves as penance for the worship of the calf (v. 54), his command to enter the village in humility (v. 58), the food he provides (vv. 57, 61), his covenant (v. 63), the Sabbath (v. 65), and the episode of the heifer and God's command to slaughter it (vv. 67–73). The story of the ancient sanctuary in section 3.1 is also replete with commands and trials. It begins with the deity trying Abraham, upon which God makes him a leader of humankind (v. 124). God's command to change the prayer direction also becomes a test to distinguish between those who follow the prophet and those who do not (vv. 142–50). Thus the story sections provide examples of command and test situations. The deity's guidance is thereby interlaced with real-life test situations in which adherence to the guidance is incumbent.

Conclusion

In a divine self-revelatory reading of Surat al-Baqara, God is placed at the focal point, and the sura is read for what it reveals about the deity. Although the text is rich in descriptions of God, the lens used here is a holistic one that explores the common denominator that ties the sura together as a unit rather than zooming in on the plethora of meanings in individual passages. The common denominator is established by means of the *Leitwort* "guidance," which appears in various grammatical forms throughout the text and is set apart by its special form and location within the sura's first inclusio, as well as by the word's relatively high concentration within the sura. Every time "guidance" or its derivatives occur, it is in relation to God, so Surat al-Baqara's common theme in the divine self-revelatory mode becomes "God as Guide."

The theme of God as Guide forms a through-line, or spine, for the depiction of God as it develops within the sura, a dominant attribute that holds this characterization together and makes God a singular, vivid protagonist who propels the narrative forward. Al-Baqara's three panels develop the deity's guiding role in different situations, beginning with God guiding humanity as a whole, followed by the Children of Israel, and ending with the Muslim community. Panel 1 portrays God as the ultimate master of guidance for humanity, from his primordial promise of guidance for Adam and Eve's progeny to his provision of the Qur'an as guidance for all of humankind in the present moment. Panel 2 illustrates the transcendence of divine guidance, its continuity, and its breadth by elaborating this theme in the context of the Children of Israel and their covenant. Panel 3 expounds the systematic, methodological nature of God's guidance by repeating and elaborating patterns similar to those depicted in relation to the Children of Israel, emphasizing that ancient Israelites and Muslims received similar ordinances. Moreover, reading these two panels together suggests that guidance is a special privilege, one that God allocates to selected communities at certain times within their history. God becomes the ultimate selector of the recipients of guidance, choosing humankind, the Children of Israel, and the Muslim community.

In turn, each of the panels contains three sections: story, instruction, and test. The stories portray a promise of guidance in the distant past, which foreshadows certain expectations associated with the coming of this gift. These expectations take the form of clearly delineated ordinances in the present moment, which exemplify substantive guidance. They are needed for the ensuing tests, which carry momentous consequences. The elaboration of God's role as guide in different contexts, past and present, from the simple commandments to the more detailed expositions, brings to the reader a thorough understanding of this aspect of the deity. When Surat al-Baqara's three panels are read together, God emerges as the ultimate, transcendent, systematic guide, the sender of prophets with concrete guidance, who ultimately guides the reader toward success.

6

Placing Humanity at the Focal Point

"Responsibility" as the Pedagogical Running Theme of Surat al-Baqara

When one explores Surat al-Baqara's chiastic structure, the patterns formed by the sura's thematic repetitions suggest that what holds the sura together as a unit can be summed up in one intriguing notion: responsibility. The arrangement of the themes of election, instruction, and test as they are repeatedly and consistently reiterated in every panel and all the story sections drives home the message that privilege invariably comes accompanied by special expectations and performance reviews. In terms of education and human development, this recurrent pattern suggests that Surat al-Baqara has a pedagogy of "responsibility" embedded within its structure, one that functions as a running theme. But how does this theme unfold within the sura's various panels? What are the distinctive features of this pedagogy if one places humanity at the focal point and reads the sura for its educational content? And do the smaller thematic figures that embellish the structure of Surat al-Baqara also contribute to this pedagogy? These are the concerns of this chapter.

The Progressive Structure

There is one last creative figure that can help to explain how Surat al-Baqara's pedagogy develops throughout the text: progression. This structure is similar to *iqtiṣāṣ*, which I defined in chapter 2 as "taking a word, expression, or idea from a certain context and repeating it in a different one, thereby carrying nuances and layers of meaning over to the new context." With regard to progression, Yairah Amit explains,

> The progressive structure serves not only to make order in the data sequence, but also to organize it so that, as well as having an aesthetic value, the text is given added meaning. Sometimes the progression serves to shed added light on the protagonists, and sometimes it reveals the writer's conceptual world. In every case it also addresses the reader. Moreover, its discovery, like other artistic devices, heightens the awareness of the text's crafting and styling. This is why searching for it and finding it enhances and enriches the reading.[1]

In light of these two descriptions, both *iqtiṣāṣ* and progression are rhetorical figures that involve repetitions of some kind with added meaning, whether they are repeated words, expressions, or ideas. The main difference between the two devices is in the implied forward movement of the progressive structure. In contrast, *iqtiṣāṣ* can also move backward into the text, such as when it layers meanings from sura 50 onto the earlier sura 40, as Jalāl al-Dīn al-Suyūṭī has recognized.[2] What makes *iqtiṣāṣ* distinctive is its synchronic, intertextual character, which goes hand in hand with the practice of reading the Qur'an over and over again. When this occurs, a text that is sequentially in a later position can function as the intertext of a text that is in a former position since someone performing a second reading will already have read the later text and thus have it as a reference when constructing meaning. *Iqtiṣāṣ* thereby casts a somewhat wider net than progression, and although it is not the same concept, progression can perhaps be viewed in very broad terms as a subgenre or subcategory of *iqtiṣāṣ*, even though there is no direct historical relationship between the two words.

There are advantages to using the term "progression" instead of making do with *iqtiṣāṣ* alone. First of all, using this term builds bridges between the Bible and the Qur'an, offering similar terminology for scholars to use when describing the genre "scripture" or even when further exploring "Abrahamic scripture" as a genre. "Progression" therefore is one more figure in the literary toolbox with which to explain the development of meaning within a text. Furthermore, the implied forward movement that forms part of the term's semantic range is well suited to demonstrating the way meaning develops from panel to panel throughout Surat al-Baqara. In a way, it goes hand in hand with the term "crescendo," which conveys rising emphasis in the realm of dynamics; also, when it comes to meaning, there is an explosion of ideas that accompanies the sura's mounting dynamics. "Progression" conveys this sense of rapid growth. The third advantage of using "progression" has to do with the subject matter of this chapter: the pedagogical reading of the sura. "Progression" implies development of some kind and is therefore well suited to the way the human brain learns. It is an appropriate description for the repetition and recycling of pedagogical content, a practice that reflects good pedagogic technique, such as when teachers review material from previous years or lessons before developing and expanding it with new material. In a way, the material in al-Baqara is similarly laid out since it gets recycled and developed in a cylindrical fashion. Therefore, "progression" reflects a sense of growth that is eminently suited to expressing al-Baqara's pedagogical features.

Progression in Surat al-Baqara

How is progression reflected in Surat al-Baqara and its pedagogy? This occurs in a number of interesting ways. First, al-Baqara's three panels display chronological progression in the way its election theme unfolds. Accordingly, panel 1 speaks of the election of all of humankind in the Adam and Eve story, set in the creation narrative of humanity in the primordial past. Panel 2 speaks of the election of the Children of Israel in the story of Moses and his followers in the wilderness, which is also set in the distant past, even though it is not as far removed as the election of the first human couple. Panel 3 is the most recent since it speaks of the election of the Muslim community with the coming of the prophet Muḥammad, who is much closer in time compared to Adam and Moses. Therefore, the theme of election progresses chronologically in time from panel to panel. In sum, each panel presents a phase in human learning. Each constitutes a synthesis of a particular phase in human education, and from a pedagogical perspective, prior panels act as a "revision" for subsequent ones. In this manner, panel 1 primes readers for panel 2, and both panels together prepare readers for the new material in panel 3.

Furthermore, instructional content also progresses throughout the sura as it is recycled from panel to panel. In panel 1 worship of God alone is the main instruction, in addition to a brief mention of belief, prayer, and charity. These instructions are expanded in panel 2 and then again in panel 3. For example, the idea of prayer initially occurs in panel 1, where it is briefly mentioned in verse 3, then it moves to panel 2, where it is expanded by the idea of prostration in verse 43, and finally it is repeated and augmented in panel 3 with the change in prayer orientation (vv. 142–50) and the fear prayer (vv. 238–9), among other things. This is one example among a multitude of instances that begin in the shortest panel (panel 1) and then are progressively expanded until they reach their most generous expression in the last and longest panel (panel 3). Therefore, the development of this material from panel to panel suggests that instructional content is characterized by progression.

The instructional content reaches epic proportions in al-Baqara's third panel, covering almost every aspect of the basic beliefs and practices of the Islamic covenant, including the five pillars (i.e., testimony of faith, ritual prayer, charity, fasting, and pilgrimage), marriage, divorce, inheritance, capital punishment, and war regulations. Almost every topic that is later expanded in the rest of the Qur'an has its beginnings here. It is this feature that makes Surat al-Baqara distinct from Surat al-Fātiḥa, despite the close lexical and ideational connection between the two. Indeed, al-Fātiḥa functions as a miniscule "revision" of the fundamentals established by older faith traditions, whereas al-Baqara moves away from what is shared into what is distinctly Islamic, such as the prayer orientation toward the Kaʿba, pilgrimage to Mecca, fasting during Ramadan, and divorce regulations. There is progression from al-Fātiḥa to al-Baqara, for whereas al-Fātiḥa is all about common grounds, al-Baqara builds on those foundations, laying out the fundamentals of Islam. The sura thereby launches the emerging faith tradition and teaches the Muslim community its first encompassing lesson.

In light of the above, one of the distinctive features of al-Baqara's pedagogy of responsibility is its timeless and progressive character. Beginning with Adam, as humanity journeys through time, instruction tends to increase and, by extension, also responsibility. This feature can apply individually in terms of the reader's personal learning curve or collectively as an emerging community grows and acquires the basics of its new faith tradition. It can even apply historically when one views humanity as an entire species developing over time. Therefore, within al-Baqara's educational framework, responsibility is something that progresses over time in accordance with human development.

It is possible to see the progressive character of Surat al-Baqara's pedagogy of responsibility only when taking a step back and looking at the sura from a distance. But what would happen if one took a closer look at each panel? Would one be able to uncover other features of this distinctive pedagogy and experience how it ties the sura together as a unit? To further explore al-Baqara's pedagogy of responsibility, I zoom in on the individual panels in the following analysis, placing humanity at the focal point and reading panel 1 for its education-related content.

Panel 1: Humankind (vv. 1–39)

Like all of al-Baqara, panel 1 also displays a pedagogy of responsibility composed of the elements of election, instruction, and test; however, they come layered with other meanings. As one ventures into the sura, the first section (§1.1, vv. 1–20) is the test that classifies humanity into three groups depending on their reception of the book. Only the first group is portrayed positively, responding with belief, prayer, and charity, the latter two activities being concrete tasks an individual can perform (v. 3). Nevertheless, belief also receives a concrete character since belief in "what was sent down to you," in "what was sent down before you," and in the "hereafter" is specified (v. 4). In this section, the test is "this book" (v. 2), commonly understood to be the Qur'an, which is also referred to as "what was sent down to you." As the sura reviews performance, this group is the only one that is characterized by success.

The individuals in the second group, the ungrateful *(kāfirūn)*, are portrayed as having a cover over their eyes, ears, and minds that renders any attempts to instruct them futile (v. 6–7). The word *khatama* (to seal), which is associated with the deity, carries undertones of finality with regard to their situation (v. 7). The hopelessness implied by this term underlines the pedagogical significance of the sensory and mental capacities.

The third group, those gone astray (*ḍāllīn*), has connections with the two preceding groups since they claim to believe in God and the Day of Judgment (v. 8), thereby resembling the first group (vv. 3–4). However, when they are required to believe "as the people believe," they decline, considering themselves above those whom they deem "fools" (v. 13). Since "as the people believe" refers back to the belief of the first group, they are shown to reject some or all scripture, sharing the fate of the ungrateful. Those gone astray are also connected to the ungrateful in the seeing, hearing, and thinking metaphor. Whereas the ungrateful are incapable of perceiving guidance (v. 7), those gone astray possess their faculties but seem unwilling to use them (v. 17), thereby running the risk of having their hearing and sight permanently removed from them (v. 20). By means of a parable (*mathal*) they are portrayed as relying on other people to guide them;[3] instead of lighting a fire in an active fashion, they ask others to do so for them (v. 17). The grammatical form of *istawqada*, the word used in connection with lighting, gives the action quasi-passive undertones, transferring agency to someone else.[4] The subject *seeks* to have the action done but without actually enaging in it and concluding it. This word can also denote trying or pretending to light a fire while not actively and sincerely lighting it. As a result, God takes away their light, leaving them in darkness, "deaf, dumb and blind" (v. 18).

The second parable similarly relies on the likeness of light, seeing, and hearing. Those gone astray are portrayed as being in the middle of a rainstorm and placing their fingers in their ears for fear of death (v. 19). Lightning almost blinds them; when it lights up their way, they walk, but when it gets dark, they stop walking (v. 20). Al-Biqāʿī explains the rainstorm as being the Qur'an since both the rainstorm and the Qur'an can function as tools of enlivenment.[5] Whereas the rainstorm can enliven the earth, sending forth vegetation (Q. 2:164), the Qur'an can enliven human beings, stimulating perceptions, minds, and hearts (Q. 6:122; 8:20-4). Whenever the Qur'an agrees with the notions of those gone astray, they are careful to follow it, but whenever it does not, they stand still, not having developed their faculty of perception (*baṣīra*). Although Burhān al-Dīn al-Biqāʿī (d. 885/1480) noted the life metaphor, he did not comment on the death metaphor, which can indicate ungratefulness (*kufr*) and the accompanying loss of God's grace (Q. 6:122). Thus fear of the loss of God's grace and of ending up in hell may motivate their mental and sensory inactivity.

The portrayals of the three groups of section 1.1 teach the importance of using one's eyes, ears, and mind in engaging scripture and discourage sitting passively back and depending on others to perform this task. The passages' strong monotheistic flavour is echoed in section 1.2, the beginning of which is signalled by a change in person. The deity now directly addresses humankind, instructing them to worship him so that they may become mindful (v. 21). This commandment dominates section 1.2, where humankind is invited to worship God and God alone, identified as the creator and referred to as "your rabbi" (*rabbakum*), recalling his description in al-Fātiḥa. Human beings are thereby encouraged to look to God as their ultimate teacher. The human search for knowledge is no longer bound within a particular cult or tradition but moves beyond such confines to whatever God may bring.

When sections 1.1 and 1.2 are read together, this particular brand of monotheism encourages studying scripture directly, using the eyes, ears, and mind, rather than relying exclusively on religious authorities to perform this activity. This directive is reinforced by the painful consequences associated with failing to comply: a fire fuelled by human beings and stones (v. 24). Its importance is further bolstered by its dominance of section 1.2, which is the "instruction" component of section 1, since it is the only commandment given here. As section 1.3 proceeds to take the reader back in time to the creation of the first human couple as vicegerents on earth, the introduction of the element of election into the panel points to adherence to monotheism as a primordial responsibility that accompanies this special privilege. This panel therefore develops the notion of monotheism introduced in al-Fātiḥa, setting it in a framework of responsibility. In effect, worship of God alone becomes everyone's responsibility. To be counted as successful with regard to fulfilling this responsibility, individuals need to use their eyes, ears, and hearts when accessing the book without giving undue authority to middlemen.

Just as monotheism and direct responsibility for the book emerge in sections 1.1 and 1.2 as features of al-Baqara's educational theory, the third section contributes other nuances to this pedagogy. Like all the story sections, this story has all three of the main components of al-Baqara's pedagogy of responsibility, which I have termed "election, instruction, and test." In effect, humanity is elected through the creation of Adam as vicegerent (v. 30). He is taught the names of all things, meriting the angels' obeisance (vv. 31–4). He and Eve are instructed to refrain from eating from the tree, and both fail the test (vv. 35–6). They are thereby doomed to earth, for which they were originally created (vv. 30, 36). Noteworthy are the words of repentance that Adam receives, which have the character of both instruction and test since they teach human beings how to deal with their inevitable errors (v. 37). The ultimate test becomes the one with eternal consequences: those who follow the deity's guidance should neither have fear nor grieve, and those who reject his guidance will have a sorry fate (vv. 38–9). As this section affirms al-Baqara's tutoring in responsibility, it also highlights the importance of knowledge and repentance from mistakes, providing a primeval example.

It is noteworthy that Adam is highly regarded as a prophet and a chosen one of God in the Qur'an, on par with figures such as Noah, Abraham, and Jesus (Q. 3:33). That he was unable to keep one simple commandment suggests that mishaps are unavoidable and do not necessarily detract from the overall evaluation of a person's performance. Adam, after all, was created for earth, yet he was placed in the Garden and managed to fulfil his destiny only after he erred and was gifted with words of repentance (vv. 36–8). His education was incomplete until he had learned how to deal with error, and only then was he ready to be placed on earth. It seems that error is the real test, repentance entailing the ability to learn from one's mistakes and move forward. Adam took responsibility for his mistake by repenting, his triumph signalled by God's forgiveness. In this regard, the story's pedagogy of responsibility comes layered here with schooling in dealing with error, suggesting that mistakes are to be expected and that repentance is the responsible choice when dealing with such mishaps.

Panel 2: The Children of Israel (vv. 40–123)

In this panel, too, the pedagogy that emerges is one of responsibility layered with a pedagogy of error. "Responsibility" permeates all three of its sections both in content and in the way that the panel is organized. In the first section, placing the instructions within the framework of the Israelite covenant reinforces the notion of covenantal responsibility (§2.1). This notion is also present in the second section, where the Israelites' founding narrative is again intertwined with their special covenant, the accompanying instructions, and reviewing their performance on various occasions (§2.2). The third section similarly suggests the notion of responsibility, as evident in its closing statement. It reminds the Israelites of God's blessings upon them and of the upcoming Day of Judgment, when all are responsible for themselves and none may intercede on behalf of another, exhorting them to safeguard themselves from the consequences of their own actions (vv. 122–3).

Similar to the story of Adam and Eve (§1.3), the founding narrative of the Children of Israel has its fair share of trials and tribulations that are interlaced with the motifs of error, punishment, and forgiveness (§2.2). The primordial precedent set by the first couple is continued in their children, for just as Adam and Eve disobeyed their commandment, were chastised, and were saved through repentance, so too did the Israelites flout the rules, get punished, and eventually receive forgiveness. There are a total of six consecutive stories in this narrative that elaborate the idea: the story of the calf (vv. 51–4), the request to behold God (vv. 55–6), entry into the city (vv. 58–9), food and drink in the wilderness (vv. 57, 60–1), the covenant and the violation of the Sabbath (vv. 63-6), and the story of the heifer, which does not contain outright disobedience but hesitancy and argumentation in obeying instruction (vv. 67–73).

As set by these six stories, the tone of section 2.2 is generally positive. In each case, the Children of Israel repent, receive their punishment, and eventually succeed. It is this characteristic that seems to earn them their name and special designation since the term "Jew" (*yahūd*) in the Qur'an is associated with the act of repenting or going back to God: they are *alladhīna hādū*, the "ones who have turned/repented [to God]" (Q. 2:62; 4:46, 160; 5:41, 44, 69; 6:146; 16:118; 22:17; 62:6). It also explains the curious puzzle of why God would select this particular people when their history, like that of other nations, shows so many failings. As in Adam's case, it may be this very characteristic that makes them worthy of being chosen as a people and privileged over all the people of the world (Q. 2:47, 122). Pedagogically, it seems to reinforce the notion that the real test is not of one's ability to keep ordinances faultlessly but of one's ability to repent and make good when one does inevitably break one or two. Responsibility thus entails responsibility for one's errors, among other things. Consequently, the continuing pattern of slip-ups and repentance affirms panel 1's pedagogy of error as a feature of al-Baqara's pedagogy of responsibility.

There is one more feature that becomes clearer in this panel: the pluralism embedded in Surat al-Baqara's pedagogy. Even though the Children of Israel are clearly a people distinct from the emerging Muslim community and their Ishmaelite ancestors, they too are elected by means of *ʿahd* (covenant), just like the Muslim community in panel 3. The use of this terminology in relation to the Children of Israel suggests that they are more or less equally blessed with this great privilege, indicating a plurality of election and therefore a multiplicity in this special favour. Moreover, the election of Adam and his descendants as vicegerents on earth reinforces the pluralism inherent in the al-Baqara portrayal of election since all of humanity becomes elected. Therefore, responsibility is not the purview of the Muslim community alone but also belongs to the Children of Israel and humanity in general, a notion that is reinforced by their respective panels, each also displaying an instruction and test section for the evaluation of performance. Therefore, there is pluralism inherent in al-Baqara's pedagogy of responsibility.

Panel 3: The Emerging Muslim Nation

Panel 3 displays some of the same pedagogical features as panels 1 and 2, but they become clearer here as one moves through the panel. The basic three elements are again displayed in the panel's structure, which begins with a story of election, followed by instruction and test sections. Election is located in the founding narrative of the city of Mecca and in the Ishmaelite covenant, which features Abraham and Ishmael and the promise of the prophet to come (§3.1). Although this story is set in the distant past, it has a physical manifestation in the present, as it is reenacted yearly and embodied through the performance of the pilgrim rituals. Evoking the past thereby conjures a social memory that is centred on this tangible presence and recurring celebration.[6] Both the concept of "social memory," or "collective memory," and the more recent concept of "cultural memory" have received increasing scholarly attention, particularly since the 1990s.[7] Social memory has a pedagogical dimension, for as it contributes to the formation of group identity, it also induces a sense of collective responsibility.[8] Although the physical presence of the ancient sanctuary helps to give substance to this memory, it is not a phenomenon that is reserved for the Muslim community alone. In panels 1 and 2 a similar social memory is invoked with the election narratives of humanity and of the Children of Israel, an approach that is not without interest in relation to contemporary scholarship surrounding Moses and cultural memory, such as the well-disseminated work of Jan Assman.[9] Like some of the recent approaches to ancient Israel's past, his work is concerned with its cognitive reception and meaning for communities in the present rather than with the historicity of the narratives or even their textuality. In the Qur'anic rendition, the word *udhkurū* (remember), which is repeated three times within the inclusio that frames the panel (vv. 40, 47, 122), clearly suggests social memory. When all three panels are seen together, a pattern emerges in which social memory plays a role in Surat al-Baqara's pedagogy of responsibility.

As one moves into the remaining sections of panel 3, other structures emerge that also have pedagogical ramifications. A noteworthy pattern is the alternation between practice and belief that covers sections 3.2 and 3.3, highlighting the link between these two elements. When set within a framework of responsibility, this linkage teaches that belief must always be accompanied by practice and that believers invariably carry special responsibilities.

However, there is more to the pedagogical content of the al-Baqara alternations, for they take on a special character in each of the two sections. In section 3.2 the instructional content seems to reflect an expectation of mishaps, recalling the "error" theme in panels 1 and 2 and directing the newly minted Muslim community to act responsibly when things go wrong. Thus there are more verses on divorce than on marriage, more on war than on peace, and more on misguided faith than on true belief. This feature is reflected in both the practice and the belief components of the alternation, each of which contributes its own nuance to Surat al-Baqara's pedagogy. The practice-related topics of section 3.2 are grouped together in five passages, which fan out from the subject of food (vv. 168–9, 172–3) and cover prayer, fasting, pilgrimage, charity, capital punishment, testamentary inheritance, divorce, war, alcohol, and gambling prohibitions. With regard to food, the Islamic tradition receives dietary restrictions that are consistent with those of its precursors; however, what stands out in the al-Baqara rendition is the way that allowances are made in cases when one is obliged to put aside such ordinances – an indication of the expectation that things will not go according to plan (v. 173). In the realm of the pillars of Islam, ritual prayers, fasting, and pilgrimage also show the same characteristic since in each passage the expectation of mishaps is evident. Indeed, if one is too scared of enemy attacks to pray in the usual manner, which involves bending and prostrations, one can do so while walking or on horseback

(vv. 238–9). Likewise, if one cannot fast due to difficulty, whether long-term or short-term, there are guidelines one can follow, such as feeding the indigent or making up the lost days in cases of sickness or travel (vv. 183–7). With regard to pilgrimage, the verses also provide accommodations if one is unable to complete the ritual, such as how to conduct the sacrifice and what to do if one has to shave one's hair before completing the requirements (vv. 195–203). So the theme of error in previous panels is elaborated here, inherently acknowledging and responding to the possibility of unexpected situations developing that are less than perfect.

Although practices such as prayer, charity, fasting, and even pilgrimage are well known from earlier faith traditions, there are some unusual regulations in al-Baqara, particularly regarding divorce, testamentary inheritance, and capital punishment, all of which similarly carry nuances of trial and hardship. Like the food laws, the theme of marriage and its unhappy sundering begins with a delineation of restrictions but this time regarding marriage partners and marital relations (vv. 221–3). The divorce theme begins with temporary separation (v. 226), followed by either reparation or divorce. Divorce regulations include things like alimony, waiting periods, and nursing mothers. Widows also receive guidelines, which similarly include waiting periods for remarriage (vv. 226–7, 237, 240–1). Thus the emerging Muslim community receives directions regarding the unhappy conclusion of a marriage, whether through divorce or demise.

The theme of what to do when things go wrong, which is so characteristic of the practice component of section 3.2, is also evident in the choice of the topics of capital crime and testamentary inheritance. Death can arguably be an unexpected trial, particularly if it is through murder or manslaughter but also if it is a natural occurrence. In these contexts, Surat al-Baqara provides guidance, such as calling for reparation or capital punishment in cases of homicide and for the leaving of a last will and testament when approaching death (vv. 178–82). Testamentary inheritance may come as a surprise to Muslims given the history and development of Islamic jurisprudence, which has opted for heirship. The classical schools of Islamic law do not always follow the letter of the

Qur'anic text but have made allowances for abrogating the legal content of its verses on the basis of hadith reports and other religious-legal tools.[10] In the case of testamentary inheritance, some have argued for the abrogation of these verses based on hadith, whereas others have based their nullification on the inheritance portions prescribed in Surat al-Nisā' (Q. 4:11–12).[11] It is noteworthy that the text in Surat al-Nisā' comes in the form of general guidelines that it consistently subordinates to the last will and testament (*waṣiyya*). As one can see, the interpretation of inheritance laws in Islamic jurisprudence is one example of the complexity of Islamic exegesis and how tradition is in conversation with the text of the Qur'an. In the al-Baqara inheritance laws, there is a strong warning against changing the will of the deceased, yet allowances are again made here for error, such as permitting a witness who fears injustice to intervene in order to change the bequeathor's mind before death (vv. 181–2). Thus the sura provides guidance for the difficult moments that attend the sad occasion of death.

Among all this diverse legislation, what probably catches one's attention most are the regulations that explain what to do when the calamity of war hits. The passages that deal with war in section 3.2 (vv. 190–3) begin as follows:

> Fight in the path of God those who are killing you, but do not commit aggression, for God does not love those who commit aggression. Kill them wherever you encounter them and expel them from the places where they have expelled you, for persecution is more grievous than killing, but do not fight them at the sacred sanctuary until they fight you there first, for such is the recompense of the ungrateful. But if they desist, then God is forgiving and merciful. Fight them so there is no more persecution and religion is for God alone, then if they desist, let there be no more aggression except against transgressors.

The first verse explains *when* Muslims may go to war, namely upon being physically attacked by another party; that is, they may engage only in a defensive war. The second verse describes *where* they may engage in fighting, with sanctuaries being excluded, which in Islamic law generally include mosques, churches, and synagogues. The third and fourth verses explain when to stop fighting, namely when the other party stops, and what happens *after* war has ended, instructing that there should be no further aggression, except against transgressors (e.g., war criminals). The verses also explain *why* war is allowed despite all the killing it involves, namely to preserve freedom of worship. Thus these verses provide a foundation for war legislation, or a "just war theory," guiding the Muslim community when peace falters and they are attacked by another party. Other verses elaborate this foundation, explaining things like what to do in case of taboos being breached and reaffirming the importance of freedom of worship (vv. 194–5, 216–17).

In light of the above, Surat al-Baqara's pedagogy of error is continued from panels 1 and 2 and elaborated in panel 3. The content of the practice components of the lengthy alternation covering section 3.2 suggests that these passages deal with the burning question of what to do when things go wrong. Whether one is in a relationship with God or with human beings, either communally one group to another or interpersonally in the most intimate of unions, the sura posits directions that help one to deal with mistakes, misfortune, and the unexpected. War, divorce, and even death are hemmed in by guidelines, leading the believer and the affected parties through these difficult moments. This question ties in with the founding narratives of humanity and ancient Israel, which provide examples of people who have successfully dealt with wrongdoing (§1.3, §2.2). When viewed in conjunction with the sura as a whole, the inevitable inclusion of error and difficult circumstances reinforces the connection within its educational framework between responsibility and dealing with the less than perfect, the suggestion being that what makes for good calibre human beings is not their flawlessness but how they handle themselves in their lowest moments.

The theme of slip-ups and difficult circumstances paves the way for the test component of panel 3, which comes right at the end of the sura in section 3.3. This section features three alternations superimposed on one another: a continuation of the previous belief-practice alternation from section 3.2, a new alternation between topics related to life and wealth, and a third alternation between story and injunction (see table 4.6). The alternation between the topics concerning life and wealth highlights the test character of this section since it suggests that the ultimate test of members of the the Muslim community is to place their lives and their wealth in the hands of God, either by fighting to defend freedom of worship or by almsgiving and other charitable spending. The story-injunction alternation also supports this theme by presenting ancient illustrations of God's character as master over life and death. The story of Ṭālūt, the first king of Israel, is particularly interesting since it places the first war in the Israelite tradition within a framework of the self-same Qur'anic war regulations (vv. 246–51). The narrative engages questions that are of interest within contemporary Biblical scholarship, such as holy war in ancient Israel and the rise of the ancient Israelite monarchy. There is no ethnic dimension in the Qur'anic narrative; rather, the reason for the Israelites going to war is that they have been evicted from their homes and separated from their children (v. 246). Here, too, war functions as a test or a trial that Israel has to overcome. It is noteworthy that the way Ṭālūt is portrayed in the Qur'an combines elements from several Biblical characters, suggesting that the Qur'an reads the Biblical narratives of Joshua, Gideon, and 1 Samuel 8–32 in parallel as featuring the self-same historical figure.[12] All these characters engage in war of some sort in the Hebrew Bible; thus the Qur'anic narrative is in conversation with the Bible and offers a new reading of war-related books and passages.

As for the basic belief-practice alternation: the practice passages of this final section address spending and fighting, and the belief elements support this theme, depicting God in ways that highlight his omnipotence, not only through stories but also through descriptions. In this regard, the throne verse (v. 255) instills a reliance on and trust in God, making it one of the most popular verses in the entire Qur'an among those recited in times of fear, anxiety, and misfortune. It inspires a sense of security and protection that can help people through their most difficult moments.

Pedagogy and Hermeneutics: The Role of *Ra'y* (Personal Judgment) in the Interpretation of the Qur'an

There is one more feature that the section 3.2 alternation contributes to Surat al-Baqara's distinctive pedagogy and that is relevant to contemporary discussions, more specifically the ongoing debates between reformists and traditionalists over how to interpret the Qur'an. This feature is contributed by the belief passages of section 3.2, which address scripture in a recurring pattern that has hermeneutical implications. Thus it is not only the practice passages of the alternation that give finer nuances to al-Baqara's pedagogy of responsibility but also the belief elements.

The belief-practice alternation covering section 3.2 contains four belief passages, all of which mention scripture in connection with its reception among humanity and thereby develop ideas from panel 1. Indeed, they seem to explain how *not* to read the Qur'an, repeating and expanding on the three groups of section 1.1: those mindful of God (*muttaqūn*), the ungrateful (*kāfirūn*), and the ones who are astray (*ḍāllūn*). All four belief passages connect to either group 2 or group 3 – both of which are charged with negative connotations. The central passage is the only one that elaborates the second group, the ungrateful, who cannot hear, speak, or see because they restrict themselves to the traditions of their predecessors instead of independently following the book as they are supposed to do (vv. 170–1). At this chiastic midpoint, those who prefer the ways of their forefathers instead of what God has sent down are likened to sheep who follow senseless sounds and callings – being "deaf, mute and blind" to meaning (vv. 170–1). In the realm of hermeneutics, this approach to ancestral traditions recalls traditionalist polemics against using one's personal judgment to interpret the Qur'an (*tafsīr bi'l-ra'y*) and the insistence on restricting interpretation to inherited traditions via the method of "interpretation by transmission" (*tafsīr bi'l-ma'thūr*). In both traditionalist exegesis and the negative Qur'anic depiction, the authority of the ancients is preferred to the exclusion of using one's own eyes, ears, and brain in connection with the book. As a matter of fact, the "interpretation by transmission" method is so named because of the chains of transmission that trace each interpretation, name by name, all the way back to one of the prophet's companions, to their immediate successors, or on rare occasions to the prophet Muḥammad himself. Authenticity is a key argument since these early interpretations preserve how the first generations understood the text. Within this framework, this limited group of early Muslims (*ahl al-ta'wīl*) alone has the authority to interpret the Qur'an. It is this method that feminists and other reformists are at such pains to expand and to enrich with new interpretations that better fit the text in a contemporary world.

Traditionalists are at odds with the concept of new interpretations, often responding either with the hadith "whosoever interprets the Qur'an using his personal judgment (*ra'y*) let him await his seat in the hell-fire"[13] or with reports of a similar nature. It is noteworthy that this hadith has its *Sitz im Leben* ("setting in life," or socio-historical context) within the late second and early third centuries of Islam during the disputes between the early rationalists, known as *ahl al-ra'y* (people of personal judgment, opinion, and reason), and the traditionalists, known as *ahl al-ḥadīth* (people of reports and traditions), in the realm of Islamic jurisprudence.[14] Nevertheless, this hadith and others like it have been so influential that the authors of almost every major commentary in the classical exegetical tradition have seen fit to explain why their interpretations do not fall into the blameworthy *ra'y* category. It seems that this restriction is at odds with the pedagogy of Surat al-Baqara.

The three remaining belief passages of section 3.2 all elaborate group 3, the ones who are astray, also critiquing their approach to the book (see table 4.5). The first such passage describes them as suppressing the book and accuses them of venerating their equals in the way God should be venerated (vv. 159–67). The verses thereby highlight the theological problems of this approach, illustrating its nonmonotheistic implications. Nevertheless, members of this group are not hopeless cases since they still have the ability to do right (v. 160).

The second such passage (vv. 174–7) again combines group 3 and the idea of suppressing the book, using some of the self-same vocabulary of panel 1 to describe the group's members, such as the expression "to purchase going astray at the price of guidance" (vv. 16, 175). Thus there can be no mistaking that these verses are describing and elaborating the same group. This passage also introduces the idea of differing over scripture (v. 176), which is picked up and expanded in the fourth and last of the belief passages of section 3.2. This finale again elaborates group 3, critiquing the contrast between its members' outwardly pleasing exterior and what is in their hearts, while directing the Muslim community not to slip up and follow them when they already have the clear verses of the book (vv. 204-14). The words *bayyināt* (clear signs, verses, proofs) (v. 209) and *āya bayyina* (clear sign, verse) (v. 211) underline the clarity of the verses, repeating the same word and description from verse 159, and incidentally also verse 185, which describes Ramadan as the month in which the Qur'an was sent down as *bayyināt* of guidance and discernment. This unusual choice of vocabulary in a persistent pattern supports the notion of using one's eyes, ears, and brain to interpret the book since it suggests that the verses are already clear and not necessarily in need of ancestral figures to clarify them. Thus the recurrent depiction of the book and its reception seems to support the hermeneutical endeavours of feminists and other reformists, if not always the substance of their interpretations.

In light of the above, the belief-practice alternation of section 3.2 organizes the belief-related material into four segments that repeat certain ideas in a carefully structured pattern. This arrangement draws attention to the connection between belief, the book, and how to approach it, suggesting a pedagogy of *ra'y* – an educational method that promotes reason and the use of personal judgment rather than diminishing it. Indeed, this pattern inherently teaches a hermeneutical method that encourages using one's faculties to interpret the Qurʾan, as opposed to depending only on inherited traditions. The meanings embedded in the sura's special patterns consequently have ramifications for the ongoing question of the use of *raʾy* versus the *maʾthūr* traditions within exegesis, a subject that has occupied Muslims for centuries. Thus, as Surat al-Baqara lays down the foundation of the book, it also suggests directions on how to read it, encouraging independent thinking and framing responsibility for actively engaging with the book as an aspect of its distinctive pedagogy.

In the realm of academia, it seems that Surat al-Baqara has an attractive pedagogy since it encourages intellectual curiosity and independent thinking. However, what are the implications for the corpus of exegetical traditions that have accumulated over the ages, including the *maʾthūr* traditions? Does this mean that they are to be ignored or discarded, or does modern literary theory with its preoccupation with reader-oriented approaches make room for them? It is noteworthy that these traditions have an important place within reader-response theory since they elucidate how the Qurʾan has been interpreted across history. This school of literary theory focuses on the reader and the reader's experience of the text and is sometimes termed "reception theory" when it addresses the reader or audience's reception of the text. Within this theoretical framework, the *maʾthūr* traditions represent a response from the first and early second centuries of Islam, whereas this monograph, for example, is a twenty-first century response. They can even be read together, for although each reading on its own is synchronic, if one examines them collectively or in conjunction with readings from other centuries, one can explore how meaning develops over time and thereby conduct a diachronic reading. Thus, within this rich and complex theoretical framework, the early corpus of traditions occupies a significant space. Even today, the meticulous analysis of the words and passages of the Qurʾan guarantees these classical commentaries their value and contribution as works of secondary scholarship in the study of the Qurʾan.

Bringing Together the Pedagogical and Divine Self-Revelatory Readings

Does the pedagogical reading connect to the divine self-revelatory reading illustrated in the previous chapter? In theory, they connect since the two readings have counterbalancing literary foci, which coincide with "God" and "humanity," who are the main protagonists or categories of protagonists within the text. Together, they are two sides of a whole in the divine-human relationship that the text depicts, beginning with al-Fātiḥa. But do the contents of the readings also connect? To begin with, the divine self-revelatory reading has one running theme that develops and is elaborated throughout the text: "God as Guide." As the reading develops from panel to panel, God becomes the ultimate, transcendent, universal guide, the sender of prophets and books as vehicles of guidance. Whereas this reading revolves around God, the pedagogical reading is concerned with the substance of the guidance, or what comes to humanity from this guiding deity. The two readings are thus connected by "guidance," which characterizes the deity and which is taken up by human beings in the form of pedagogical content for which they are responsible. Hence the pedagogy of responsibility.

However, there is more to this connection, for the distinctive characteristics of the guide are also reflected in the special qualities of the pedagogy. Accordingly, the transcendence of the guide is displayed in the social memory aspect of the pedagogy, which transcends past and present. Moreover, the universality of the guide is reflected in the pluralism of the educational theory and in its pedagogy of error since God guides everyone, irrespective of ethnicity and whether or not they have made mistakes. Similarly, the preeminence of the guide is evident in the cylindrical, progressive quality of the pedagogy and in the distinctive monotheism that encourages individuals to read the book for themselves and ponder its meanings. Thus the special traits of the guide are reflected in the finer nuances of the pedagogy.

Conclusion

As the sura's narrative structure unfolds and recurrent patterns become evident, they reveal pedagogies that are rooted in the very structure of the text and that tie together the sura's contents. Foremost among these is al-Baqara's pedagogy of responsibility, which is manifested in the motifs of election, instruction, and test. This trio of elements occurs repeatedly in all three of its panels and underlines the connection between privilege and responsibility, suggesting that being elected to a special position invariably comes with a set of instructions and expectations.

Nevertheless, there are other features embedded within this educational framework that are developed from panel to panel. They include a pedagogy of error, suggesting that human success does not depend on flawlessness but on the ability to repent and deal appropriately with human shortcomings and difficult circumstances. Another feature is its pluralism, for responsibility is not portrayed as the purview of the Muslim community alone but also belongs to the Children of Israel and humanity in general. Other features include the theory's use of social memory to enhance the sense of responsibility and its distinctive monotheism, which emphasizes an access to the divine word that is unfettered rather than mediated by ancestral traditions or religious authorities. Last but not least is the pedagogy's progressive, cylindrical character, for as educational content gets recycled from panel to panel, it is also expanded and developed, consistent with the way human learning works over time. Within this education-focused framework, Surat al-Baqara functions as the foundation of the Islamic covenant, as a kind of first, comprehensive lesson on the emerging faith tradition.

7

Windows into the Tradition

Al-Biqāʿī and al-Ṭabāṭabāʾī on Surat al-Baqara

Does one need to be a scholar well versed in the poetics of Qurʾanic narrative structure and modern literary theory in order to understand the organization of Surat al-Baqara, or is it possible to do so without all this complicated theory? What did people do before the discovery of oral structural markers and other organizational tools? After all, the history of Islamic scholarship is rich and varied, so it seems hardly credible that scholars across the ages did not study the Qurʾan's organization and come up with their own set of answers. Although these questions may never be fully answered, to get a sense of the different approaches within Islamic scholarship across the ages and the findings of those who did not have access to this intellectual background, I present two examples: one by a classical exegete and the other by a modern scholar, each set within its intellectual environment. I have chosen Burhān al-Dīn al-Biqāʿī (d. 885/1480) and Muḥammad Ḥusayn al-Ṭabāṭabāʾī (d. 1981) because of their exceptional contributions to approaching suras as whole units and because of the way they successfully navigated the underlying tensions of their time. This exposition therefore provides windows into the Islamic tradition, showcasing the two extracts and their historical contexts, which helps to explain past scholarly aversion toward holistic approaches and their sudden surge in popularity in modernity.

Al-Biqāʿī's Context: *Naẓm*, *Munāsaba*, and Historical Tensions

It is truly noteworthy that despite the classical Islamic tradition's remarkable scholastic achievements in almost every field of human endeavour, it has somehow managed to overlook a field as important as the poetics of narrative structure – at least in the sense of Surat al-Baqara's overall layout, if not necessarily with regard to smaller literary structures. Al-Biqāʿī's work stands out for this reason, for he alone has succeeded in producing a truly holistic commentary, looking for a single idea within each sura and exploring how suras are held together as distinct units. To be sure, his work is also singular in other ways, particularly his ardent defence of using the Bible to interpret the Qurʾan, which caused a heated debate in his day and age.[1] Even today, his legacy continues to inspire readers, and few can boast of similar acumen.

Yet is there truly nothing in the Islamic tradition that addresses the poetics of the Qurʾan's narrative structure, or can one perhaps find something buried deep in the recesses of history? The title of al-Biqāʿī's book, *Naẓm al-durar fi tanāsub al-āyāt wa'l-suwar* (Arrangement of Pearls: On the Correlation of Verses and Suras), alludes to two such related fields: *naẓm* (literally, "order, arrangement, organization") and *munāsaba* (literally, "suitability, correlation, connection").[2] Both are genres that address the Qurʾan's organization and coherence in some form or other, but they did not find continuous traction in the classical age. Although these terms have resurfaced in modernity, few are aware of the sectarian tensions surrounding them and how these tensions may have contributed to the curious lack of holistic approaches in the classical tradition. As I show below, al-Biqāʿī's successful navigation of these tensions makes his work all the more remarkable.

How can one know that al-Biqāʿī's references to *naẓm* and *munāsaba* really alluded to established genres rather than a figment of a modern imagination? The case for *naẓm* is clearer than the case for *munāsaba*, for although only a few works of the former type have survived the ravages of history, we know the titles and sometimes brief extracts of many more that are now lost – enough to constitute a genre. They include *Kitāb al-Naẓm* (The Book of Arrangement) by al-Ḥasan ibn Naṣr al-Jurjānī (d. 263/876),[3] *Iʿjāz al-Qurʾān fī naẓmih wataʾlīfih* (The Qurʾan's Inimitability in Its Arrangement and Composition) by Muḥammad ibn Zayd al-Wāsiṭī (d. 306/918), and four separate books that carry the title of *Naẓm al-Qurʾān* (The Arrangement of the Qurʾan) by Abū ʿAlī al-Ḥasan ibn ʿAlī ibn Naṣr al-Ṭūsī (d. 312/924), ʿAbd Allāh ibn Sulaymān ibn Abī Dāwūd al-Sijistānī (d. 316/928), Abū Zayd Aḥmad ibn Sahl al-Balkhī (d. 322/934), and Abū Bakr Aḥmad ibn ʿAlī ibn Bayghjūr[4] ibn al-Ikhshīd (d. 326/938) respectively.[5] Together, these lost books indicate that *naẓm* was an established genre quite early in Islamic history, so the loss of these books, along with the lack of interest in the genre, is a puzzle that deserves explanation.

To unravel this mystery, one must delve into the surviving works, searching for the earliest of them to see what could possibly have affected the development of the genre. Among the few compositions that have survived are the works of Abū Sulaymān al-Khaṭṭābī (d. 388/998),[6] Abū Bakr al-Bāqillānī (d. 403/1013),[7] ʿAbd al-Qāhir al-Jurjānī (d. 471/1078),[8] and Jār Allāh al-Zamakhsharī (d. 538/1144).[9] However, the earliest work is that of the influential ʿAmr ibn Baḥr al-Jāḥiẓ (d. 254/868),[10] which is lost but has been reconstructed to some extent from his other existing works. Insights on the historical development of the different genres can also be gleaned from the medieval literature on exegetical method, particularly the two major compendia of the Qurʾanic sciences: *Al-Burhān fī ʿulūm al-Qurʾan* (The Compelling Proof in the Qurʾanic Sciences) by Badr al-Dīn al-Zarkashī (d. 794/1391) and *Al-Itqān fī ʿulūm al-Qurʾan* (Mastering the Qurʾanic Sciences) by Jalāl al-Dīn al-Suyūṭī (d. 911/1505).[11] These multivolume books distill and summarize the various subjects and disciplines of exegesis, which prospective interpreters need to master – or which al-Zarkashī and al-Suyūṭī expect them to master. Much can be learned from the way these works present the material, what they include, and what they leave out. Both contain a chapter on *munāsaba* and discuss *naẓm* in their chapters on *iʿjāz* (the theory/doctrine of the Qurʾan's inimitability). Some of their contents overlap since al-Suyūṭī's book is heavily dependent on al-Zarkashī's and can even be considered an abridgement of it. However, al-Suyūṭī's work does contain some independent material, and since al-Suyūṭī postdated al-Zarkashī by more than a century, he is invaluable in pointing out intermediate developments, the most important of which is al-Biqāʿī's work. These books show how their authors approached the subject of the Qur'an's organization and coherence, incidentally reflecting some of the tensions surrounding the different genres. Understanding the historical tensions can help to clarify some of the contemporary dynamics at work between different approaches.

The *Naẓm* Genre

Of the two terms used to denote intra-textual coherence, *naẓm* is the older, predating *munāsaba* by decades, if not centuries. The earliest known work on *naẓm* is the well-attested, ninth-century al-Jāḥiẓ's *Naẓm al-Qur'an*, whereas al-Zarkashī attributes the first occurrence of *munāsaba* to the chief tenth-century Shāfiʿite jurist Abū Bakr Abd Allāh ibn Muḥammad Ziyād al-Nīsābūrī (or al-Naysabūrī) (d. 324/936), citing a somewhat obscure source for this information.[12] Al-Zarkashī curiously makes no mention of al-Jāḥiẓ or of *naẓm* in his section on *munāsaba* but takes care to ground *munāsaba* in his own school of jurisprudence: the Shāfiʿite school. Al-Suyūṭī, also Shāfiʿite in orientation, follows al-Zarkashī in citing the obscure source and similarly does not mention al-Jāḥiẓ or the idea of *naẓm* in his section on *munāsaba*, although he quotes al-Jāḥiẓ in a lengthy passage on the Qur'an's linguistic superiority in the introduction to a section on *iʿjāz*.[13] The puzzling disassociation between *munāsaba* and *naẓm*, in spite of the semantic and functional overlap between the two terms, may make sense in light of the sectarian dynamics of the time.

Al-Jāḥiẓ's surviving epistles offer glimpses into his motivation for writing the book and into the intellectual environment of his age, including the sectarian dynamics surrounding the idea of *naẓm*. He explains,

> I have written a book for you, in which I have exerted myself, and in which I have accomplished the utmost someone like me can accomplish in arguing for the Qur'an, and in responding to every contester. I have not left out any question for a Rāfiḍite, or a traditionalist, or a vulgariste,[14] or an overt unbeliever, or a careless hypocrite, or al-Naẓẓām's associates, or those who have appeared

> after al-Naẓẓām who claim that the Qurʾan was created, but that its composition is not an authoritative argument (*ḥujja*), and that it is a revelation, but that it is neither compelling proof (*burhān*) nor convincing, logical proof (*dalāla*).[15]

From the above, we can surmise that he wrote his book to defend the Qurʾan against several groups as part of a larger intellectual dispute on the subject of the Qurʾan's (un)createdness and authoritativeness as a religious-legal argument. It would seem that al-Jāḥiẓ equates the Qurʾan's proponents with the ones who use its composition to argue for its createdness and who uphold its authoritativeness – in contradistinction to the other groups mentioned above. The nature of the dispute is clearer for some groups than for others since al-Jāḥiẓ's book has not survived in its entirety, and neither have al-Jāḥiẓ's other works or the works of his opponents. However, what remains provides some insights, gained by exploring the dialectical relationship between al-Jāḥiẓ's *naẓm* and the discourses of the other groups.

Al-Jāḥiẓ is well known for his connection to the Muʿtazilite school of theology, of which he is a major thinker. Adherents of this school referred to themselves as *ahl al-tawḥīd wa'l-ʿadl* (people of monotheism and justice), due to the school's emphasis on these two theological principles. In terms of practice – specifically law – most Muʿtazilites adhered to the Ḥanafī school of jurisprudence since this school resonated with Muʿtazilite rationalist leanings; indeed, both the theological school and the legal school are generally classified as "rationalist" in contemporary scholarly works. Abū Ḥanīfa al-Nuʿmān ibn Thābit (d. 150/767), the Ḥanafī school's eponym, is well known for his use of *raʾy* – hence the the school's designation of *ahl al-raʾy*. In their use of reason and personal judgment, these "rationalists" differ from the more tradition-oriented *ahl al-ḥadīth*, among whom adherents of al-Zarkashī's Shāfiʿite school may be ranked. This group seems to be what al-Jāḥiẓ points to with the words "traditionalist" (*ḥadīthī*) and "vulgariste" (*ḥashwī*). The first word, *ḥadīthī*, refers either to "traditionists," who are actively engaged in the study, transmission, collection, or production of hadith, or more generally to "traditionalists," who support their work and hold the opinion that the law must rest squarely on it.[16] Traditionists are therefore highly skilled individuals who can navigate the complex hadith corpus, with its varying versions of reports, chains of transmission, and levels of authenticity, whereas traditionalists include a much broader variety of people. The second word, *ḥashwī*, is particularly derogatory, being derived from *ḥashwat al-nās* (the lowest or most uncritical people), which may be directed at Ḥanbalites in particular or traditionalists in general.[17] Aḥmad Ibn Ḥanbal (d. 241/855) responded to the term quite vehemently and identified the source of the appellation as the *aṣḥāb al-ra'y* (those who use personal judgment, those whose opinions carry weight), whom he claimed were lying and were themselves the *ḥashwiyya*.[18] As one can see, the modern tensions between reformists and traditionalists have a long history, even if today the matter is not as simple as rivalry between different schools.

With ancient traditionalists, the main theological point of contention was likely the doctrine of *khalq al-Qur'ān* (createdness of the Qur'an) since they claimed it was uncreated, whereas al-Jāḥiẓ used the idea of *naẓm* to underline the Qur'an's physical, created qualities. He portrayed the Qur'an as follows: "The Qur'an … is a body and a voice, has composition, arrangement (*naẓm*), performance, divisions, and a created, self-sufficient existence, independent of others, heard in the air, seen on paper, detailed and connected, [characterized by] assembly and dispersion, can be added to or diminished, can cease to exist or remain in existence: [it can do] everything that a physical body is capable of doing, or that describes a body. Everything which is thus characterized is physically created, not metaphorically so or [created] according to the extension of linguists."[19]

Thus al-Jāḥiẓ used *naẓm* to indicate an aspect that the Qur'an shared with created bodies, and he may therefore have caused some negative reaction from adherents of the doctrine of uncreatedness. The disbelief with which his claims were met still resonates today, as can be noted in the sarcastic additions reiterated by contemporary scholars: "A body which has the option of changing shape into a man, or into an animal or female."[20] The association of *naẓm* with the doctrine of the createdness of the Qurʾan and its use as an argument for the doctrine may explain traditionalists' dissatisfaction with it – an uneasiness that may have trickled down to their contemporary counterparts as well.

Al-Jāḥiẓ's theological school, the Muʿtazilite school, is well known for its adherence to the doctrine of createdness, a group to which Ibrāhīm al-Naẓẓām (d. between 220/835 and 230/845) also belonged.[21] Although al-Jāḥiẓ had this doctrine in common with al-Naẓẓām (and many others), he rejected his *ṣarfa*, a theory entailing not that the Qurʾan is inimitable in and of itself but that God turns away any who attempt to emulate it. Both al-Naẓẓām's and al-Jāḥiẓ's ideas arose in the context of discussions on the Muʿtazilite doctrine of inimitability.[22] Although both scholars adhered to the doctrine, they differed in its interpretation. Thus al-Jāḥiẓ's exposition of the Qurʾan's *naẓm* argues for its compositional inimitability and against *ṣarfa*.[23]

Similar to al-Jāḥiẓ, many later Sunnis adhered to the doctrine of inimitability and rejected *ṣarfa*.[24] In particular, al-Bāqillānī's *Iʿjāz al-Qurʾān* (The Qurʾan's Inimitability) went a long way to promoting the theory, as can be noted in the way both al-Suyūṭī and al-Zarkashī praise the book.[25] However, the Mālikite al-Bāqillānī does not give sufficient credit to his Muʿtazilite predecessors but – as is often the case when sectarian rivalries come into play – attempts to belittle their accomplishments, even when he is copying from them.[26] Thus *naẓm* found an entrée into Sunni discourse through the doorway of the theory of the inimitability of the Qurʾan.

The particular Rāfiḍite views with which al-Jāḥiẓ was in conversation are harder to gauge. The term *rāfiḍī* was applied to early Imāmī Shia,[27] and al-Jāḥiẓ has a letter on the topic,[28] but he does not mention views of the Qurʾan that could be construed as offensive. However, in his letter on the createdness of the Qurʾan (*fī khalq al-Qurʾān*), he mentions the Rāfiḍites in the context of persons who restricted the doctrine to createdness in an allegoric sense, as opposed to the physical reality.[29] The desire to propound this distinction may have formed some of his motivation.

More substantial insights may be gained from early Imāmī exegesis: Meir Bar-Asher has analyzed the work of several pre-Buwayhid exegetes, all of whom were active after al-Jāḥiẓ but who reflect the views of certain Imāmī Shia current in his time.[30] This correlation is all the more credible on account of the traditionalist character of their interpretations since they generally relied exclusively on the transmitted traditions of their predecessors and were not comfortable voicing their own opinions unless bolstered by a transmitted tradition. This method of interpretation has survived in the form of the present-day *tafsīr bi'l-ma'thūr* (exegesis by transmission) and may itself have been the bone of contention – just as it is in some reformist and feminist circles today. It places the transmitted traditions in a dominant position over the Qur'anic text, thereby subordinating its meaning to that of the traditions. As can be surmised, *tafsīr bi'l-ma'thūr* prevailed within Sunni circles as well, especially after the publication of Ibn Jarīr al-Ṭabarī's (d. 310/923) monumental *Jāmiʿ al-Bayān ʿan taʾwīl āy al-Qurʾān* (The Comprehensive Elucidation of the Interpretation of the Qur'an), in which he collected the various interpretations of early exegetical authorities, each complete with a chain of transmission.[31] Accordingly, the dynamics between al-Jāḥiẓ's *naẓm* discourse and Rāfiḍite *tafsīr bi'l-ma'thūr* may also have existed in connection with Sunni *tafsīr bi'l-ma'thūr*, such as the work of ʿAbd Allāh ibn Wahb al-Miṣrī (d. 197/812), who predeceased al-Jāḥiẓ by half a century or so.[32] However, prior to al-Ṭabarī, the preoccupation with chains of transmission does not seem to have been as dominant a feature of Sunni exegesis.

The controversy between *ahl al-ḥadīth* and *ahl al-ra'y* is primarily a legal one, and it is in the context of law that the rivalry between the two methods and their privileged texts becomes more visible. Here, it takes on the character of a power struggle between traditionalists, who relied on prophetic and other traditions (i.e., hadith) for authority, and rationalists, who gave precedence to the Qur'an and had no qualms refuting a tradition if it conflicted with the Qur'an – no matter how strongly traditionists bolstered it with chains of transmission going all the way back to the prophet.[33] In this context, al-Jāḥiẓ's *naẓm* discourse takes on a new dimension since it implicitly argues for the Qur'an's superiority vis-à-vis the corpus of hadith traditions. A clear, well-organized Qur'an, in which the relation of verses to one another provides context and contributes to meaning, is more difficult to manipulate than an ambiguous, atomistic one, whose verses are independent of one another and which relies on the traditions provided by the traditionists for meaning. The last group that al-Jāḥiẓ mentions here, those who consider the Qur'an a revelation but neither a compelling proof nor a convincing logical proof, carries hints of this controversy since the words *burhān*, *dalāla*, and even *ḥujja* carry legal (and theological) connotations.

Is law related to theology? In other words, is there a possible connection between legal disputes over the authoritativeness of the Qur'an vis-à-vis the Sunna (Tradition), which comprises the hadith corpus, and theological disputes over the createdness or uncreatedness of the Qur'an? And if so, does this connection somehow explain why the genre of *naẓm* – and, by extension, a clear, well-organized Qur'an – was somehow perceived as threatening? After all, traditionalists' insistence on the Qur'an's uncreatedness in the face of all odds – they were even briefly subjected to an inquisition of sorts[34] – is rather surprising from a modern perspective, where the issue seems inconsequential. However, an uncreated Qur'an underlines its ambiguity, whereas a created Qur'an is more accessible to minute scholarly analysis and intellectual enterprise – in fact, *ra'y*. An uncreated Qur'an is reminiscent of God since God is similarly uncreated, thereby highlighting the sacred text's mystery and incomprehensibility to the human brain and, as a result, the need for the transmitted *ma'thūr* traditions to interpret it. Needless to say, this dispute recalls early Christian discussions about the createdness and uncreatedness of Jesus Christ, who from a Christian perspective is similarly uncreated and somehow divine. Of course, in both the Islamic and the Christian traditions, there is a lot more to these theological positions that fine-tune them and reconcile them with the monotheism that is so distinctive of these faiths. However, in both traditions, the elevation of their respective "uncreated" being or object gives it an air of mystery and takes it out of reach of the common person, making room for exegetical and other intermediaries. Therefore, the importance that this theological position gives to the *ma'thūr* traditions as vehicles for understanding the Qur'an may explain traditionalist attachment to it. This importance also extends to the realm of law, where the theory of the uncreatedness of the Qur'an similarly bolsters traditionalist interpretations of the scripture and the authoritativeness of the traditionalist corpus of hadith and *āthār* (reports that go back to a companion of the prophet or an immediate successor). Here, too, a mysterious and incomprehensible Qur'an stands in need of prophetic and other traditions to explain it.[35] So traditionalist positions in theology and law go hand in hand, theology elevating the Qur'an to the point of incomprehensibility, which leaves jurists free to establish the dominance of the hadith corpus.[36] Hence the two reasons for traditionalist dissatisfaction with the *naẓm* genre – the theological and the religious-legal – are connected and part of the same worldview.

Is this perhaps why al-Jāḥiẓ saw the need to defend the Qur'an? Did he write *Naẓm al-Qur'ān* to assert the scripture's authoritativeness in the face of those who contested it? Given the centrality of law in his day – perhaps any day – this enterprise seems to be rather ambitious. Can this one book, or even the ensuing genre, really accomplish this feat? Whether or not it did so in its time, defending the Qur'an seems to have been the raison d'être of the book, perhaps even of the genre. Moreover, since the genre is founded on the assumption that the Qur'an is well organized, even rhetorically superb, it inevitably makes an implicit argument for the book's comprehensibility and thereby indirectly undermines any attempt to establish the dominance of traditionists and their traditions in the legal realm. This intellectual heritage may also explain some of the present-day tensions between reform-oriented holistic and tradition-oriented atomistic approaches to the exegesis of the Qur'an. Vestiges of this ancient rivalry are perhaps also at work in some of the criticisms that contemporary traditionalists and hadith experts level against feminists and other reformists, such as accusations of being

"Qur'an-only" feminists, either because they recognize the preeminence of the Qur'an vis-à-vis the hadith corpus or because their work is centred on the Qur'an.[37]

In spite of the early tensions, *naẓm* made its way into the medieval literature, where it was employed by several leading scholars, as demonstrated by the prevalence of the term in both existing and lost titles of books of this genre. The term had multiple meanings, varying in application from single words or sentences to whole suras and even to general stylistic and rhetorical features of the Qur'an. For example, in the work of al-Khaṭṭābī, al-Bāqillānī, al-Jurjānī, and al-Zamakhsharī, *naẓm* can refer to rhetorical aspects and word-meaning relationships, which can narrow the scope of *naẓm* to the way single words or expressions are chosen and arranged within their immediate context rather than drawing attention to the way suras are organized into whole units.[38] However, in some of the self-same works, *naẓm* can also refer to broader aspects of organization, such as in al-Bāqillānī's analysis of Surat Ghāfir and Surat Fuṣṣilat in his book on the inimitability of the Qur'an, *I'jāz al-Qur'an*. He points out the connections between their meanings and identifies a central theme for both:[39] "the necessity of the Qur'an being a proof, and the indication of its miracles" (*luzūm ḥujjat al-Qur'ān wa'l-tanbīh 'alā mu'jizātih*).[40] Al-Bāqillānī clearly indicates that it is a central theme, stating that from the beginning to the end, these suras are based on it.[41] This scholar evidently did not limit himself to rhetorical aspects and word-meaning relationships but produced what are the earliest extant examples of treating suras as whole units. Hence, in the classical Islamic literature, the *naẓm* genre of literary investigations encompassed holistic concerns, in addition to word-meaning relationships, whole verses, and general stylistic features of the Qur'an, which were more prevalent.

It is noteworthy that al-Bāqillānī wrote in the context of the theory of the Qur'an's inimitability, which underlines its marvelous, even mysterious, qualities and therefore does not conflict with traditionalist discourses regarding the theory of uncreatedness. Moreover, the common theme that he identifies for Ghāfir and Fuṣṣilat suggests that the Qur'an is a miracle (*mu'jiza*) and thereby reinforces the theory of inimitability (*iʿjāz*); indeed, the two words are even derivatives of the same etymological root (*ʿ-j-z*). Although not a Shāfiʿite, al-Bāqillānī belonged to another traditionalist school: the Mālikite school of jurisprudence, which has rationalist elements, as all traditionalist schools have come to incorporate over time. It seems that explorations of *naẓm* in the context of inimitability were deemed unexceptional within traditionalist circles as well, even if couched in different language. After all, inimitability does not conflict with ambiguity but may even reinforce the notion.

In light of the above, medieval scholars understood *naẓm* to refer to various aspects of the Qurʾan's organization, composition, and general style, in addition to treatments of suras as whole units. The idea of *naẓm* has an early connection to Muʿtazilite theories of *khalq* and *iʿjāz* and developed into a distinct genre. However, whereas *iʿjāz* theory was absorbed into the Sunni tradition and had many proponents, the theory of createdness elicited hefty opposition and became a hallmark of the *ahl al-tawḥīd waʾl-ʿadl*. Consequently, in medieval and some contemporary Sunni literature, discussions of *naẓm* seem invariably to appear in the context of *iʿjāz*. As a result of this history, scholars within al-Biqāʿī's intellectual environment who chose to embark on new explorations of *naẓm* were at risk of being viewed as Muʿtazilites and thereby eliciting righteous indignation or a more hefty response.

The *Munāsaba* Genre

The earliest known monograph on *munāsaba* is *Al-Burhān fī munāsabāt tartīb āy al-Qurʾan* (The Compelling Proof in the Suitability of the Arrangement of the Qurʾan's Verses) by Abū Jaʿfar ibn al-Zubayr al-Gharnāṭī (d. 708/1308).[42] This short, one-volume work is mentioned by al-Zarkashī, al-Suyūṭī, and al-Biqāʿī, and it is the only known monograph on the topic in his time. Thus the first monograph on *munāsaba* seems to postdate the one on *naẓm* by approximately four and a half centuries. Nevertheless, al-Zarkashī indicates that it was recognized as a Qurʾanic science prior to that monograph, attributing its origins to the aforementioned Shāfiʿite Abū Bakr al-Nīsābūrī, albeit via the obscure

Abū al-Ḥasan al-Shahrabānī (d. 936/1486). He quotes al-Nīsābūrī: "He used to say while sitting on the chair, when a verse was recited to him: 'Why was this verse placed beside this one? What is the wisdom in placing this sura next to that sura?' He used to rebuke the scholars of Baghdad for their lack of the science of *munāsaba*."[43]

However, despite al-Nīsābūrī's presumed interest in *munāsaba*, he has no known book on the subject; the only known monograph prior to al-Zarkashī is that of Ibn al-Zubayr. Moreover, al-Biqāʿī does not mention this incident at all, perhaps because he considers it historically unreliable. Other than al-Zarkashī's oblique reference, there does not seem to be any evidence to support al-Nīsābūrī's concern for the organization of the Qurʾan. This statement may indicate more about sectarian rivalries and the attempt to establish a Shāfiʿite pedigree for the science than about actual historical origins.

It is unclear whether *munāsaba* was recognized as the name of an independent Qurʾanic science prior to al-Zarkashī, even though he mentions that the well-known Fakhr al-Dīn al-Rāzī (d. 607/1210) took a decided interest in it.[44] The term does not appear in the quotation al-Zarkashī attributes to al-Rāzī, who uses the words *tartībāt* (arrangements) and *rawābiṭ* (connections) instead: "The most delicate of the Qurʾan's niceties are in its arrangements and connections."[45] Oddly, the word *naẓm* is also noticeably absent – as it is from the entirety of al-Zarkashī's discussion on *munāsaba*. However, it is present in the passage that both al-Biqāʿī and al-Suyūṭī choose to reiterate in order to indicate the importance that al-Rāzī gave to *munāsaba*:

> Whosoever ponders the niceties of the organization (*naẓm*) of this sura [al-Baqara], and the beauty of its ordering will know that just as the Qurʾan is inimitable due to the quality of its vocabulary and the nobility of its meanings, it is also inimitable because of its organization (*naẓm*) and ordering. It is possible that the ones who said: "It is inimitable because of its style," meant this, except that I have seen the majority of commentators turn away from these

niceties, not interested in these secrets. Concerning this matter, the issue is nothing more than what is expressed in the words: "Eyesight makes the image of the star appear small; the fault of diminutiveness is that of the body part not that of the star."[46]

Even more curiously, in al-Rāzī's statement, the word *munāsaba* does not appear at all, but *naẓm* occurs twice. One may wonder why it is that al-Rāzī does not mention *munāsaba* in these memorable quotes that scholars have used to attribute an interest in the science to him, even though he does mention *naẓm.* It seems that in al-Rāzī's day, *munāsaba* had not been established as a genre of writing or even as a Qurʾanic science. Rather, *munāsaba* gained its technical sense mainly through the efforts of al-Zarkashī. He placed it in a category of its own, a distinction he did not accord to *naẓm*, despite *naẓm* similarly having a monograph that set it apart – in fact, several monographs attesting to its dissemination as a genre. He thereby not only privileged *munāsaba* but also disassociated *munāsaba* from *naẓm*, mentioning the latter only within his section on *iʿjāz.* Perhaps *naẓm* had become too broad a concern, covering rhetorical aspects as well, so a narrower term was needed. Or perhaps sectarian rivalries came into play. It is difficult to know, and both developments or some other factors may have contributed.

Munāsaba was cultivated by only a few medieval scholars, among whom al-Rāzī is the most prominent early exegete. Al-Rāzī's method is best described as linear-atomistic since he only consistently links each verse to the subsequent one.[47] Thus al-Rāzī does not approach suras as a whole per se, even though he does display an interest in coherence. Furthermore, Ibn al-Zubayr's book, the one and only early monograph on the science, deals only with the immediate links between suras, focusing on verses at the end of a sura and the beginning of the next, not on internal connections within a sura. It too is linear-atomistic and does not approach suras as whole units. Therefore, among the exegetes who predate al-Zarkashī, there do not seem to be any works on which one can base equating *munāsaba* with a holistic concern. Unlike *naẓm*, the *munāsaba* genre addressed only the immediate linear connections between suras and sometimes passages. This history may explain why al-Biqāʿī found the *munāsaba* genre insufficient, despite its connections to his own school, locating his work in both *munāsaba* and the more contentious *naẓm.*

Al-Biqāʿī lived several centuries after the height of the disputes over createdness or uncreatedness of the the Qurʾan – the infamous *miḥna* (inquisition) of 833–48 CE. By his time, things had settled down in favour of uncreatedness in the Sunni tradition and createdness in the Shiʿi tradition, which absorbed Muʿtazilite ideas. The question had quickly lost its appeal within the Muslim psyche, even if the *maʾthūr* traditions proved to be a mainstay of Muslim exegesis, both Sunni and Shiʿi, each with its own set of early authoritative figures. The intense struggles between proponents of reason (*raʾy*), on the one hand, and revelation in the form of hadith and the *maʾthūr* traditions,[48] on the other hand, led to the affirmation of both within Islamic history, particularly its legal tradition. The schools that survived were those that managed to incorporate both reason and revelation into their theoretical framework. It is as if every group made its contribution and left a legacy behind – rationalists upholding a role for independent thinking and traditionalists preserving prophetic and other traditions that may otherwise have been lost to posterity. Although the *naẓm* genre may initially have developed as a rationalist discourse and *munāsaba* as a traditionalist one, each made its contribution to the Islamic exegetical tradition. In a way, al-Biqāʿī is an heir to both these legacies.

It is to al-Biqāʿī's credit that he managed to combine both genres into a single composition – that is, if one can consider *munāsaba* a genre. The title of his work, *Naẓm al-durar fī tanāsub al-āyāt wa'l-suwar* (Arrangement of Pearls: On the Correlation of Verses and Suras), is a clear indication of his creative bridge building since it contains both *naẓm* and the *munāsaba* derivative *tanāsub.* His initiative is remarkable given that he was himself a staunch Shāfiʿite. In fact, his multivolume compendium was so influential as to have caused al-Suyūṭī – also Shāfiʿite – to summarize the topic, albeit leaving the controversial word *naẓm* out of the title and retaining the *munāsaba* derivative in *Tanāsuq al-durar fī tanāsub al-suwar* (Correlation of Pearls: On the Correlation of Suras).[49]

Nevertheless, despite the occurrence of *naẓm* in the title, al-Biqāʿī takes care to ground his work in the science of *munāsaba* and does not classify it as an investigation into *naẓm*. He mentions Ibn al-Zubayr's book, in addition to al-Zarkashī's and the work of other prominent Sunni scholars, referring to their favourable evaluation of the Qurʾanic science. He thereby positions himself well within the scholarship of his own school and sect.[50]

Vestiges of the ancient rivalry can be detected in the measures al-Biqāʿī takes to defend his work from criticism. He mentions his most daunting obstacles and subsequently neutralizes them. The first is a tradition attributed to the famous ʿAbd Allāh ibn ʿAbbās (d. 68/687), via al-Ṭabarī, which classifies exegesis into four categories: "a kind known to the scholars, a kind known to the Arabs, a kind no one is excused from being ignorant of it, and a kind which is known only to God: Whosoever claims to know it is lying."[51] The second is a statement by a prominent scholar prohibiting (*ḥarām*) Qurʾan interpretation without knowledge or the ability to talk about its meanings, thus restricting it to qualified scholars, a statement that he considers to carry the authority of consensus. Al-Biqāʿī renders these traditions harmless by positioning his work in the "scholars" category, which he classifies as "good" according to the consensus.[52] Thus, rather than functioning as obstacles, these traditions bolster his authority to interpret.

In addition to these rather generic measures, al-Biqāʿī uses another defence that is somewhat more specific to his own particular brand of inquiry. He links his book to the work of another famous Shāfiʿite jurist and exegete – ʿAbd Allāh ibn ʿUmar al-Bayḍāwī (d. 685/1286 or 716/1316) – portraying his work as a successor to al-Bayḍāwī's.[53] The latter is known to have relied heavily on another Muʿtazilite author, al-Zamakhsharī, offering a cleaned-up version of his book with its contentious Muʿtazilite elements removed.[54] This connection seems to indicate that al-Biqāʿī was well aware of his own work's Muʿtazilite connections and was not ashamed of them but instead wished to set a precedent – one that was widely accepted and well respected within his own school. Thus, rather than be accused of Muʿtazilite tendencies, he becomes a staunch proponent of Sunnism and sufficiently well versed in Shāfiʿite doctrine to sift through Muʿtazilite knowledge and reformulate it for Shāfiʿite consumption. That he evokes al-Bayḍāwī's example supports this stance.

However, al-Biqāʿī has one more argument to offer detractors, just in case they are still struck by the novelty of his book and are unable to digest it. He describes a dream he had at ten years old, in which he saw the angel Gabriel and the prophet Muḥammad riding two horses, and suggests that his work was facilitated by the blessings of this dream.[55] Innovative content should therefore not be considered "lying" but understood to carry quasi-divine sanction. Thus al-Biqāʿī employs a number of measures to dissuade would-be critics, deploying the *munāsaba* genre, Shāfiʿite precedents, a dream, and his own stature as a scholar to navigate the tensions surrounding *naẓm* and successfully promote his work. His tactics were largely successful, and his work was well received within the Sunni faction of the scholarly community, as can be noted in the fact that it was praised by al-Suyūṭī, who appropriated and rewrote it in his own separate composition.

Al-Biqāʿī's Approach

In terms of method, al-Biqāʿī emulates the work of Abū al-Faḍl al-Bijāʾī (d. 865/1459), whom he quotes as follows:

> The whole, beneficial matter of determining the verse connections (*munāsabāt*) for the entire Qurʾan is that you look for the sura's objective (*gharaḍ*), determine the primary content this objective demands, and ascertain the categories in which the primary content meets the required goal, either closely or loosely. When the words flow in the primary content, look to how they are followed by the listener's exposure to the laws and his other needs which

> require eloquent clarification. The healing of afflictions alleviates the trouble of reflecting upon it. This is the whole matter governing the determining of connections between all the Qur'an's parts. If you do this, God willing, you will ascertain the arrangement method (*naẓm*) in detail, between each of the verses and each of the suras.[56]

The passage quoted by al-Biqāʿī suggests that al-Bijāʾī's method revolves around identifying a central idea, various preliminary components, and the relationship between them. Whereas al-Bijāʾī describes the central idea as an objective (*gharaḍ*), al-Biqāʿī uses a different term with a similar meaning, *maqṣūd*, and expands his predecessor's method by pointing out that the objective of every sura is contained in its name.[57] Both methods treat suras as whole units, moving beyond the connections between one verse and the next, and investigate the connections between larger groupings, identifying a central theme. As noted earlier, he uses Surat al-Baqara's two names, "the heifer" and the "the radiant" (al-Zahrāʾ), and he employs the term "guidance" in connection with each of these themes – in the first passage speaking of "guidance to be followed in everything it says" and in the second passage using the phrase "lights up the path of guidance."[58] Therefore, although his suggested central theme is not my proposed "God as Guide," it does carry hints of it. Even though al-Biqāʿī does not know anything of the *Leitwort* or identify a similar device in the sura, he seems to have intuitively used it in his explanation of the sura's central theme.

Although al-Biqāʿī identifies a central theme in the beginning of his treatment of Surat al-Baqara, he also has a summary of the sura at the end of his exposition:

> The secret of the pinnacle[59] sura's arrangement in this sequence is that May He Be Glorified and Exalted [God] commenced with the classification of people who carry the faith, just as the foundations carry the pinnacle. The initial intent was then established by means of mentioning the closest part of the pinnacle to the minds

of the practitioners. So he said, addressing all the types of people with which he had commenced: "O humankind! Worship your lord ..." [al-Baqara 21]. He then continued until the matter was clearly established. So he mentioned His benevolence, may He be glorified, to the people who are commanded to worship: the blessing of having created for them everything that is in existence, a blessing with which He had honoured their forefather Adam, may prayers and peace be with him. Then he specified Arabs and their followers, pointing out His benevolence towards them during the discussion and censuring of the Children of Israel. Every little while, May He Be Glorified and Exalted confirms the matter of His lordship and worship of Him alone without mentioning any ordinances except for what the Children of Israel have deviated from. He mentioned the matter as an act of benevolence towards the Arabs and a censuring of the Children of Israel for leaving it, but not because He intended it for itself. Once they were purified, rose higher and became ready for the various kinds of knowledge, He spoke to them, elevating them by changing the vantage point from that of lordship to that of divinity: "Your god is one god, there is no god but He ..." [al-Baqara 163]. When they received this high honour, He instructed them in the purifying religious observances and cleansed them with their clarifying spirit. So He mentioned the primary devotional activities, both fundamental and subsidiary, the five pillars and the associated activities, and what follows of the dietary, drink, and marriage restrictions and other matters of interest. They thereby became prepared – for these are the noble deeds which draw one closer to the majestic one. So He said to them, elevating them to the mystery of His exalted presence, mentioning the One named by all the names: "There is no God but He, the Alive, the Care-Giver" [al-Baqara 255]. However, since according to the people, whoever reaches the highest station of freedom must return to the level of servitude, He mentioned some suitable activities for them. So He urged them to perform things which mostly revolve around benevolence, which is

> the station of those who know. Then He mentioned the example of spending, which is one of the building blocks of the sura, after He mentioned the station of reassurance, implying that this is the situation of the reassured one. He encouraged it, pointing that there is no hope in arriving at the goal except through renouncing all worldly things. He repeatedly urged goodness in food, without which there is no survival in any case. He forbade usury in very strong terms, indicating that one should be satisfied with the least provision, and forbade absolute increase for the elite and everything that is unlawful for the general public. He guided to the behaviours of a religion which necessitates trusting in God, entails sincere confidence, and results in support from God, may He be glorified and exalted, and which lead to it. The prophet (pbuh) passed away while he was garbed in it. May He Be Glorified and Exalted structured it in a threefold manner, basing it on an introduction to establish His matter and ending it with a warning against taking it lightly. He added the third part because it is the last and carries the blessing of finality for having conclusively reinforced believing in everything within the sura. He finished with pointing out that the foundation of this is the effort against transgressors and stubborn ones. Dependency in this should be on the sovereign lord and king of humanity. This is the way of the ones who have wisdom, guidance, and behave appropriately, while God, may He be glorified and exalted, is the one who leads to success and the right answers.[60]

Al-Biqāʿī's analysis of Surat al-Baqara differs widely from my own. He does not clearly demarcate the sura's structure by identifying sections or explore how the sura's various parts develop its central theme. He also does not set out to perform a divine self-revelatory reading or a pedagogical reading. Nevertheless, there are some broad similarities. For example, his words indicate a tripartite structure and a sense of progression, even though the progression takes on a mystical character. He points to three verses, the first of which mentions "lord/legislator" (*rabb*), the second "God/divinity" (*ilāh*), and the third some divine names. He thereby indicates a mystical progression in knowing God: first as lord, second as divinity, and third via his attributes. This concept hints at the idea of divine self-revelation, albeit a progressive one rather than a single dominant theme such as "God as Guide." Al-Biqāʿī also identifies a tripartite pattern of introduction, warning, and reinforcement, which carries hints of pedagogy. Thus, although al-Biqāʿī's treatment of Surat al-Baqara is markedly different from mine, it contains hints of divine self-revelation, pedagogy, and a tripartite composition.

Al-Ṭabāṭabāʾī's Context: Modernity and the Reemergence of Holistic Approaches

Al-Ṭabāṭabāʾī's timeframe differed substantially from al-Biqāʿī's. Whereas the first thirteen centuries of vigorous Islamic scholarship yielded few multivolume holistic treatments of the Qurʾan – I have found only one – the twentieth century saw the production and proliferation of several such works. The impetus for these modern exegetical experiments can be located within the nineteenth- and twentieth-century reform movement in Muslim societies. One of the earliest reformers was Jamāl al-Dīn al-Afghānī (d. 1897), an ardent advocate of pan-Islamic unity. Although he was of Iranian, Shiʿi background, his views found traction within Sunni circles, particularly in the case of Muḥammad ʿAbduh (d. 1905) in Egypt, a reformer whose name stands out for his approach to the Qurʾan, among other things.[61] ʿAbduh's ideas are similar to those of Sir Sayyid Ahmad Khan (d. 1898) in India since both take a critical approach to the hadith and other traditions and detach the interpretation of the Qurʾan from their restrictions.[62] Like al-Afghānī, they advocated the use of reason and took an interest in modern science. ʿAbduh in particular was not averse to looking, for example, toward the rationalist heritage of the Muʿtazilites, using the work of the Muʿtazilite al-Zamakhsharī when writing his own commentary.[63] These reformers, among others, called for new Qurʾanic interpretations better suited to the changing needs of the time and promoted a disentanglement of Qurʾanic interpretation from tradition.[64] They thereby opened the door for new hermeneutical methods, creating an intellectual environment more conducive to sensitive new – or in this case, not so new – approaches.

Although these reforms created the conditions in which the new approaches could thrive, it was nevertheless the efforts of individual exegetes that led to their materialization in the twentieth century. Mustansir Mir is one of the earliest scholars to have drawn attention to this phenomenon,[65] examining the works of several such scholars, including al-Ṭabāṭabāʾī. These scholars are located in different parts of the Muslim world, for Ashraf ʿAlī Thanwī (d. 1943), Ḥamīd al-Dīn al-Farāḥī (d. 1930), and Amīn Aḥsan Iṣlāḥī (d. 1987) are from India, whereas Sayyid Quṭb (d. 1966) and Muḥammad ʿIzzat Darwaza (d. 1964) are from Egypt.[66] They are also of different sectarian orientations, al-Ṭabāṭabāʾī being Iranian and Shiʿi, like his predecessor al-Afghānī. All six share a broadly similar analytical approach since they divide suras into sections and then establish links between these sections. The term *naẓm* is again in evidence, particularly in the work of Iṣlāḥī, the most holistic of them all. Whereas Quṭb uses the term *miḥwar* (literally, "axis, pivot") to refer to the central idea, al-Farāḥī and Iṣlāḥī use the term *ʿamūd* (literally, "column, pillar"), and al-Ṭabāṭabāʾī uses *gharaḍ* (objective, purpose, intention), recalling the language of al-Bijāʾī and al-Biqāʿī.

Although these six authors are particularly well known in contemporary scholarship through the work of Mir,[67] there are others who are worthy of mention and whose works shed light on some of the motivation behind the modern interest in holistic approaches. These include ʿAbd al-Mutaʿāl al-Ṣaʿīdī (d. 1971),[68] who relies heavily on al-Biqāʿī, and Muḥammad Fārūq al-Zayn,[69] both of whom use *naẓm* in the title of their books. Following in the footsteps of al-Bijāʾī, whose words he reiterates, al-Ṣaʿīdī also uses the word *gharaḍ* when referring to the central theme, whereas al-Zayn prefers *miḥwar*, similar to Quṭb. Al-Zayn's is a much larger work than al-Ṣaʿīdī's since, in addition to addressing the central theme of a sura, he briefly explains each individual verse, tying his explanation to the preceding verses. As in the classical works, the *munāsaba* terminology has also resurfaced, even if it is not as prevalent as *naẓm.* For example, Muḥammad ʿAbd Allāh Drāz (d. 1958) uses this term to refer to linear connections when advocating for approaching suras as whole units in his work on Surat al-Baqara.[70] Recalling al-Biqāʿī, he uses *maqṣid* (objective, purpose, intention, meaning) to refer to the objectives of the sura.

Thus there is a revival of interest in holistic treatments of the Qurʾan, some even employing the classical *naẓm* and *munāsaba* terminology. Several expressions are used in modernity to refer to common themes, including *miḥwar*, *ʿamūd*, and the more traditional *gharaḍ* and *maqṣid*. The first two terms highlight the central theme's structural dimension, whereas the last two lend it purpose-oriented nuances.

The use of classical terminology underscores the connections between modern and classical works, suggesting that the modern holistic approaches developed out of the classical Islamic tradition. However, a case can also be made for external influencing factors. This notion is particularly true of al-Ṣaʿīdī, who explains that his book is a response to some European scholars who faulted the Qurʾan's organization and considered it disjointed. He mentions Thomas Carlyle (d. 1881) and Reinhart Dozy (d. 1883) by name but does not cite specific references or give further information about them.[71] Carlyle's dictum on the Qurʾan is well known and has been reiterated by several scholars: "I must say, it is as toilsome reading as I ever undertook. A wearisome confused jumble, crude, incondite; endless iterations, long-windedness, entanglement; most crude, incondite; – insupportable stupidity, in short! Nothing but a sense of duty could carry any European through the Koran."[72]

Carlyle was not unsympathetic to Islam or to Muḥammad, which makes this evaluation so particularly severe. It is also not the only such unflattering assessment, and it is conceivable that they could easily have provoked investigations into coherence. Al-Ṣaʿīdī was also unsatisfied with some of the existing Muslim apologetics who claimed a divine book need not follow the patterns of human compositions, and he saw the need for a more compelling argument. Thus, in the case of al-Ṣaʿīdī at least,

Orientalist critique formed a powerful incentive. Al-Zayn also mentions Orientalist critique as motivation but not exclusively so, pointing out that some Muslims also have difficulties understanding the Qurʾan's internal connections, and he puts the blame partly on excessive preoccupation with certain traditions.[73] In general, there is a dialogic relationship between Orientalist critique and holistic approaches since holistic approaches are in an apologetic relationship to Orientalist critique, which responds in part to Muslim claims of the Qurʾan's inimitability and linguistic superiority.

In connection with Orientalist response, one should also mention the work of John Wansbrough (d. 2002), which has had a considerable amount of scholarly attention.[74] Similar to the "atomistic" approaches, his theory has a fragmenting character and is in a dialogic relationship to the coherence-related approaches; he places the final composition and compilation of the Qurʾan from individual fragments within the late second or early third century of Islam. He notes that the Qurʾan "is characterized by variant traditions, but also in passages of exclusively paraenetic or eschatological content, ellipsis and repetition are such as to suggest not the carefully executed project of one or of many men, but rather the product of an organic development from originally independent traditions during a long period of transmission."[75]

Wansbrough's theory has been heavily criticized; for example, the historian Fred Donner points out some of the shortcomings of transposing the conclusions of Biblical criticism onto the Qurʾan.[76] However, the most decisive evidence against Wansbrough's theory is the early manuscripts dating to the first two centuries of Islam. Foremost among these texts is the Codex Ṣanʿāʾ 20–33.1, a complete Qurʾan manuscript from the grand mosque in the city of Ṣanʿāʾ, which has been dated on the basis of carbon-14 testing and other evidence to originate well within the first Islamic century.[77] Although this information may not have been available to Wansbrough, Muḥammad Muṣṭafā al-Aʿẓamī has pointed to several dozen first-century manuscripts in various libraries around the world.[78]

Although the changing intellectual environment and the activities of the reformers played a significant role in the current preoccupation with holistic approaches, the Qurʾan's text may also have provided some encouragement. Al-Zarkashī, for example, mentions verse 11:1 in support of *munāsaba*, which describes the Qurʾan as "a book of which the verses are judiciously expressed and then expounded from one who is wise and an expert on all things." Mustansir Mir and Asma Barlas quote an even more intriguing passage, hostile to fragmentation, which delivers a powerful warning against dividing the Qurʾan into bits and pieces for consumption: "Say: 'I am indeed one who warns clearly and without ambiguity,' – (Of just such wrath) have we revealed concerning the ones who fragment – those who have turned the Qurʾan into bite-sized pieces. Therefore, by your Lord, we shall call them to account for their deeds" (Q. 15:89–93).

These verses, among others, suggest a hermeneutic that is geared more toward comprehensive treatments than toward atomism. Indeed, Qurʾan 15:89–93 contains a warning against atomism, expressed in very strong language. It is no accidedent that feminists and reformists reiterate this passage since it bolsters their case for holistic interpretation. The Qurʾan, like other scriptures, does not come with a manual on how to read it, but it does include verses that can act as general guidelines. If one searches for such instructions, the above verses are among the most suggestive. It is the reformist impulse and the changing intellectual environment that have led to their being taken more seriously in modernity.

The above authors all approach the sura as the Qurʾan's basic unit, looking within its boundaries for coherence. However, there are others who have taken a different approach, looking to the Qurʾan as a whole. These authors are convinced that a sura's multiple topics may not necessarily be related as themes but may share more general, overarching characteristics that unify them. These attributes can include the physical and spiritual unity of the suras' general form, as expressed in rhythms and rhymes, in addition to their message, which exemplifies the teachings of Islam to humankind. These authors include Muṣṭafā Ṣādiq al-Rāfiʿī (d. 1937), Muḥammad Rashīd Riḍā (d. 1935), Muḥammad Rajab Bayyūmī (d. 2011),[79] Muḥammad al-Ghazālī (d. 1996),[80] and Ḥasan Ḥanafī,[81] the latter two being well known for using the word "thematic" in connection with their approach. It is also within these latter approaches that one can locate the bulk of current feminist readings of the Qurʾan, like those of Amina Wadud and Asma Barlas.

Al-Ṭabāṭabāʾī's Approach

In light of the above, al-Ṭabāṭabāʾī's modern context varies greatly from that of al-Biqāʿī since the reformist impulse and harsh Orientalist critique contributed to a sudden need to explore the Qurʾan's organization and how suras are held together as whole units. When it comes to this particular aspect of Qurʾan exegesis, the Shiʿi context did not greatly differ from its Sunni counterpart, modernist exegesis often being characterized by a rapprochement between the two major Islamic sects. Both the Sunni and the Shiʿi contexts display critique of the traditional approaches in their environment and a desire for new interpretations that were more responsive to the needs of the time, as can be noted, for example, in the works of Ayatollah Mahmud Taleqani (d. 1980), Ali Shariati (d. 1977), and Mortaza Motahhari (d. 1979).[82] Unlike al-Biqāʿī, al-Ṭabāṭabāʾī did not have to go to extreme measures to defend his work since his intellectual milieu was more conducive to new approaches, particularly when coming from someone as learned as al-Ṭabāṭabāʾī. As a matter of fact, he does not explain his approach to suras as whole units, even though he describes his method at length in relation to philosophical and mystical approaches, among other things.[83] Rather, he identifies his project as a work of *tafsīr*, which he defines as "clarifying the meaning of the verses of the Qurʾan and uncovering their objectives and their signification" (*bayān al-āyāt al-qurʾāniyya waʾl-kashf ʿan maqāṣidihā wa-madālīlihā*), thereby inherently highlighting *verses*, not suras.[84] That he approaches suras as whole units in the introduction and conclusion of his exposition of suras suggests that doing so had become a matter of course for him,[85] even a well-accepted and expected feature of Qurʾan interpretation by that time. Of course, one should keep in mind, that Twelver Shiʿi theology went the rationalist way and was therefore not historically opposed to Muʿtazilite theology but even adopted elements of it. Nevertheless, that al-Ṭabāṭabāʾī does not care to even explain the holistic aspect of his work suggests that he considered it too commonplace to be worthy of special attention.

He begins his treatment of Surat al-Baqara with a short introduction:

> Since the sura descends in a piecemeal fashion, no single purpose unites it, except that most of it informs about one collective aim: clarifying the worship that is owed to God, may He be glorified – that His servant believes everything He has sent down through the words of His prophets, without differentiating between revelation and revelation, messengers and messenger, or otherwise. Then comes the censuring of the ungrateful and hypocrites and reproaching the people of the book for inventing divisions in the religion of God and the differentiation between his prophets. It concludes with the clarification of several ordinances, such as the changing of the prayer direction, the pilgrimage, inheritance and fasting ordinances, and otherwise.[86]

Although Ṭabāṭabāʾī's treatment is markedly different from my analysis, there are also some broad parallels. He begins with the idea of belief, which recalls the main monotheistic message identified in panel 1 of al-Baqara. He proceeds with the idea of censure, which seems to be a reference to panel 2, where the Children of Israel are reproached. And he concludes with the ordinances, which dominate panel 3. Thus the tripartite character of Ṭabāṭabāʾī's description seems to link with the tripartite structure that I have identified for the sura.

Conclusion

In light of the above, the Islamic tradition has an established history of exploring the Qurʾan's organization using the terms *naẓm* and *munāsaba* to refer to such lines of investigation, with *naẓm* in particular developing into a genre. Tensions with rationalists contributed to traditionalist disaffectation with the genre in premodernity; however, holistic approaches experienced a rise in popularity in the twentieth century. Consequently, al-Biqāʿī seems to be the only well-known classical exegete to take up the challenge and engage with suras as whole units, whereas there are many such individuals in modernity. Within this modern context, al-Ṭabāṭabāʾī stands out not only for his successful ability to blend tradition with modernity but also because his work demonstrates the breadth of proliferation of holistic approaches across the Muslim world, covering both Sunni and Shiʿi exegesis.

Al-Biqāʿī, al-Ṭabāṭabāʾī, and other classical and modern exegetes display their interest in the Qurʾan's organization by exploring central themes, section demarcation, and internal connections of suras as whole units. However, they do not generally investigate the shapes and figures that a sura's layout takes. Thus their study of the poetic dimension of the Qurʾan's narrative structure does not normally extend to the sura as a totality but is limited to smaller literary structures and other rhetorical features, as seen in the more atomistic and linear-atomistic works of al-Khaṭṭābī, al-Jurjānī, and al-Zamakhsharī, among others. More than anything, past and present holistic approaches demonstrate a developing interest in the sura as a unity rather than revealing sophisticated techniques to analyze the aesthetics and hermeneutics of the Qurʾan's compositional schema.

Nevertheless, despite the lack of modern literary theory and comprehensive poetic analysis, the two examples that I have chosen – the commentaries of al-Biqāʿī and al-Ṭabāṭabāʾī – display parallels with my understanding of Surat al-Baqara as a whole: al-Biqāʿī's use of the word "guidance" recalls the central theme of the divine self-revelatory reading, expounded in chapter 5. And there are some other broad similarities between my analysis of structure and that of these great exegetes. Both scholars identify a tripartite composition. Moreover, al-Biqāʿī's analysis has hints of progression, divine self-revelation, and pedagogy, and al-Ṭabāṭabāʾī's has thematic parallels. Thus the broad, general structure of the sura as identified in this work roughly coincides with the observations of some of the Islamic tradition's major exegetes, suggesting that it is possible to arrive at a broad general sense of the sura without access to modern analytical methods. Furthermore, the results affirm the uniqueness and value of these exetical traditions and the contributions that contemporary literary theory and other developing disciplines can make to our understanding of the Qur'an.

Conclusion

Crescendo: The Poetics of al-Baqara's Narrative Structure

Can one sum up the poetics of Surat al-Baqara's narrative structure in a single word, capturing what makes the ṣura so distinctive and even etches it with the ebb and flow of the emotive experience? If it were possible to accomplish this feat, my choice would be the word "crescendo," hinted at throughout this book. This small piece of vocabulary conveys two things: nuances of the acoustic realm in which the text is performed and at the same time the sura's distinctive dynamics, which permeate its structure and layer its meanings with heightened anticipation and the finality of closure. This phenomenon is therefore worthy of further consideration.

As we have seen, Surat al Baqara's narrative structure is delineated by its rhetorical figures, which also have aesthetic dimensions. These figures are composed of either verbatim or thematic repetitions that work together to organize the sura, arranging its contents in distinct patterns and embellishing its subunits with creative designs. This method of composition stresses certain portions of text and de-emphasizes others, imbuing the sura with changing intensities. In the world of sound, such subtleties resemble the dynamics of musical compositions, which are expressed in variations of volume, alleviating the boredom of an otherwise monotone piece. I call this aspect of poetics "the dynamics of Qur'anic narrative structure." This avenue of aesthetic expression deals with variations in emphasis that accompany established poetic figures, particularly those that have uneven and incremental patterns, such as al-Baqara's inclusios (framing devices), chiasms (alternations in reverse order), and alternations (in the same order).

Surat al-Baqara's structure is outlined twice, once by its verbatim repetitions and a second time by its thematic figures. Its *verbatim* devices consist of seven inclusios that clearly indicate thematic borders in al-Baqara, symmetrically layering the sura with a sense of balance, while highlighting the middle portion. Their placement within the sura in a nonmonotone yet symmetrical fashion imbues the narrative structure with aesthetic appeal.

Thematic reiterations also contribute to the sura's poetic character. Each of al-Baqara's three panels is again divided into three sections, which correspond to the three general characters of story, instruction, and test, meaning that the sura has three story sections, three instruction sections, and three test sections. The story sections revolve around the idea of election and portray the primeval origins of guidance, so they are also inherently election sections. The instruction sections include themes of food, pilgrimage, prayer, patience, dealing with death, withholding scripture, fasting, marriage, and divorce. These sections thereby intricately weave together various foundational aspects of the Islamic faith tradition's beliefs and practices. The test sections deal with the testing of faith that invariably accompanies the privilege of election and special instruction. These nine units are laid out in alternating fashion but in reverse order, thereby indicating a chiastic structure. This form of composition is well known in ancient literatures that are of the oral variety or that have an oral history since it helps in the process of memorization.

In addition, there are two methods of emphasizing text, one for the verbatim figures and another for the thematic figures. With regard to the inclusios, repetitions provide emphasis, and when the length of the verbatim repetitions increases, emphasis also increases. As for the thematic repetitions, the bigger the space allotted to a thematic unit, the more its particular theme is emphasized. It follows that as space increases or decreases, emphasis rises and falls, layering the sura with a dynamics of emphasis.

The sura's panels and rhetorical devices are generally of an escalating character, contributing to a sense of rising expectations and fulfilment, like narrative versions of musical crescendos. The panels swell from one to the next, as indicated by their increasing length. The last panel is by far the longest and covers more than the length of the first two panels combined, meaning that the former panels function as a kind of buildup to it. Furthermore, this rhetorical augmentation is reflected in the sura's thematic composition, just as music may accompany the words of a song. The sura's narrative begins with humankind and the creation of Adam, proceeds with a longer panel on the Children of Israel, and peaks with the election of the Muslim community in the last panel. The chronological ordering of these three groups based on their election adds to the sense of expectancy. The appointment of the Muslim community by means of the Abrahamic and Ishmaelite covenant, which is even more ancient than the Israelite one, heightens the sense of upsurge by implying that the coming of this particular prophet and this particular community has been long in the making.

Both the sura's verbatim and thematic figures display similar patterns of mounting emphasis, while conversely possessing an inbuilt symmetrical quality that provides balance. In the thematic realm, there are two chiasms at work in the general layout of the sura: the tripartite, incremental chiasm, which gives the sura its rising, crescendo-like qualities; and the less pronounced, even topical ring construction, which layers the sura with a semblance of balance and contributes not only to the augmentation but also to the sense of finality at the end of the sura. Although the use of a single structural chiasm is not uncommon in ancient world literature, the layering of two of these blanket devices so that they interact with one another is somewhat atypical. The interplay between these two chiasms contributes to the intricacy of the sura's internal dynamics.

The repetitive shifting between story and injunction in the final section is probably the most interesting of the sura's alternations. The stories mimic the tripartite structure of Surat al-Baqara and Surat al-Fātiḥa, whose first two elements gradually increase in size and whose last element forms the peak and has a threefold character. If one imagines this figure in the musical realm, it resembles a rise in volume, followed by an increase in tempo to heighten expectations. The tripartite, flaring structure of al-Fātiḥa and al-Baqara is echoed in the construction of the three short story segments of the sura's final section, contributing to the sense of upsurge that is so distinctive of musical crescendos.

However, there is more that makes this particular alternation so interesting: its thematic composition mimics Surat al-Baqara's panel construction. The first story segment (v. 243) has a multitude of unaffiliated human beings as the central protagonist, recalling panel 1 of Surat al-Baqara, which addresses humanity as a whole. The second story segment (vv. 246–53) has the first king of Israel as the central protagonist, recalling panel 2 of Surat al-Baqara, which similarly addresses the Children of Israel. And the third story segment (vv. 258–60), which consists of three short stories, has Abraham as the central protagonist in two of them, recalling panel 3 of Surat al-Baqara. The two stories featuring Abraham (vv. 258, 260) sandwich between them a story with an unaffiliated human being as the central protagonist (v. 259), recalling the first of this alternation's stories and providing a sense of closure. Thus the short story segments mimic Surat al-Baqara's thematic composition, drawing the reader's attention to this structure and affirming it in the listener's aesthetic imagination. Moreover, the recurring pattern of a gradual increase in intensity leading up to a threefold finale adds to the sense of climax at the end.

Like the sura's thematic layout, the verbatim repetitions that frame its major parts also exhibit rising emphasis, even as they are inherently balanced. The sura's inclusios are laid out symmetrically but display augmentation. All the inclusios are visibly incremental, relaying emphasis to the end of the enclosed unit. Each inclusio is thereby a minute crescendo, with the final repetition functioning as the climax not only for the literary figure but also thematically for the text it frames since it underlines a main message in the text. Moreover, when viewed collectively, the inclusios together form a kind of large-scale, sweeping crescendo. They too serve as a buildup to the epilogue (vv. 284–6), which functions as the peak. As in a musical crescendo, there is a steady increase in intensity that leads to a sudden stop. Compared to the simple, two-repetition frame known from other literature, the sophisticated al-Baqara inclusios have a much more complex and layered dynamic, which skilfully builds anticipation and provides termination.

The al-Baqara structuring devices are unusual in the history of such compositions, particularly in the way both the thematic and the verbatim ones contribute to a sense of amplification and closure, infusing the sura with the ebbs and flows of an internal dynamic. Although chiastic structures, internal broken chiasms, and uneven alternations are not unknown in ancient literatures, what is uncommon is the layering of these devices, systematically one over the other, in complex figures that work together to organize the sura and heighten the emotive experience. Moreover, complex, consecutive, incremental inclusios are rare; indeed, in my study of the Book of Psalms and other writings, I have not come across a single one. The al-Baqara inclusios are unusually and consistently incremental; the way the finale captures elements from the entire sura and provides closure is striking. Rather than treating the seven inclusios as independent, the epilogue weaves them together into a single, poetic masterpiece. Thus, although it is possible and necessary to dismantle the sura into its component units and to identify the individual building blocks, one should keep in mind that these rhetorical devices work together in sophisticated ways, forming new and complex figures of their own.

Final Remarks

How do Surat al-Baqara's structure and my innovative divine self-revelatory and pedagogical readings contribute to understanding the Qurʾan? The sura's location in the beginning of the book, immediately following upon the short Surat al-Fātiḥa, makes al-Baqara the gateway to understanding the divine message. Indeed, its formation as a response to the supplication in al-Fātiḥa frames the Qurʾan as a relationship comprised of a prayer by humanity and a divine answer. Since al-Baqara is the first in the series of suras that formulate this answer, it is the foundation for understanding subsequent suras. Its excessive length and disparate, seemingly disjointed topics also underline the need to unravel its mysteries before delving further into the Qurʾan. Thus a major step toward understanding the entire scripture is to comprehend al-Baqara's internal organization and how to read it in ways that retain a grasp on the sura as a whole.

Yet despite the sura's importance and the various scholarly investigations of the sura across the ages, there has been no clear-cut answer to the riddle of al-Baqara's internal organization, particularly its structure and the common themes that hold it together as a unit. Although several scholars have proposed solutions, most academics working in the area of Islam remain unconvinced. Some of the difficulties associated with answering these questions are due to the sura's unusual composition, the repetitive character of its many disparate topics, and the curious, escalating nature of its literary devices. The text's piecemeal history and nonchronological ordering also make a strong argument for disjointedness since the process of revelation took more than twenty years and the final composition is not organized according to the order of revelation. The form and history of the text are probably the strongest argument for the lack of a clear, coherent, compositional schema and the reason why scholars have not sought to overcome the challenges of al-Baqara's internal structure more avidly.

In addition to the Qur'an's form and history, tensions between rival scholarly factions within Islamic history led to disenchantment with holistic approaches and a preference for atomistic interpretations that were more flexible and supportive of the existing religious-legal tradition. Nevertheless, in modernity, changing circumstances have contributed to a desire for new exegetical approaches that are better suited to the needs of the time. As a result, the contemporary exegetical tradition is experiencing a developing interest in holistic treatments of the Qur'an, particularly from Islamic feminists and other modernists who seek to change the tradition from within.

To provide an answer to the riddle of Surat al-Baqara, I have posited several methodological premises, thereby outlining the theoretical foundation upon which this study stands. I have also explored the connections between these premises and those of other classical and contemporary approaches, including the approaches of women, as well as how these premises interact with the broader context of the Abrahamic scriptural heritage. All of this research has led to a reading method that is literary, synchronic, reader-oriented, intertextual, and holistic.

The approach taken here is literary in two respects: it uses literary theory, and it is preoccupied with certain poetic devices that pertain to the sura's structure. Literary theory has made it possible to experiment with new reading methods, namely the divine self-revelatory and the pedagogical readings, which are based on the assumption that what a reader is looking for when reading scripture is knowledge of the divine and pedagogical content on how to live one's life. The divine self-revelatory reading sets God at the focal point, reading the text for what it reveals about the deity and exploring the deity's image, or "voice," as the central protagonist within it. The pedagogical reading is antithetically related to the divine self-revelatory reading since it forms a contrasting or counterbalancing literary focus. Now the human being is placed at the centre, and the text is read for its pedagogical lessons for the individual. Each of these two readings is used to identify a central theme that forms the spine around which the interpretation flows. These readings thus have structural undertones: they illustrate that Surat al-Baqara is organized in ways that reflect both divine self-revelation and the communication of pedagogical content from the divine. In other words, they suggest that the sura's unusual configuration can be explained by its arrangement in accordance with what best meets the objectives of scripture.

This study's second literary feature – its focus on specific poetic devices – is concerned with certain repetitions in special patterns that help to identify al-Baqara's structure. The underlying basis for this approach is the text's oral dimension due to its social context, a feature that does not diminish its visual, written qualities. Rather, it highlights the oral nature of both the text's performance in the liturgy and its dissemination across the ages, an orality that requires oral structuring devices that can be heard and that do not depend on being seen. An active listener should be able to discern the sura's structure without visual aids, necessitating the use of well-established techniques with which the listener is familiar – that is, a listener practised in the art of listening. Here, five devices are essential: the inclusio, the *Leitwort* (a special keyword), *iqtiṣāṣ* (a cohesive device), chiasm, and alternation. All these figures are repetitions of one kind or another, which an active listener can hear during the text's oral performance. All of them are well known from the Bible and other ancient texts and have been extensively studied by scholars in other disciplines. For ancient listeners, these repetitions signalled ordering of some kind, such as the end of a subunit of text, the beginning of a new one, or even just the tying of a text together into a coherent composition.

Although the new readings and their common themes make a contribution to the understanding of Surat al-Baqara, the value of this approach moves beyond the strict confines of Qurʾanic studies and into the interdisciplinary realm. Its interdisciplinary contribution can be noted in the way it builds bridges between the methodologies used within Qurʾanic and Biblical studies, such as the theories of Mikhail Bakhtin, poetics, and the differentiation between synchronic and diachronic approaches. It has also demonstrated common methodological ground between Qurʾanic studies and literary theory by exploring the application of terms such as "author-oriented," "reader-oriented," "intertextuality," and "reception theory" within Qurʾanic studies.

The interdisciplinary character of this work has facilitated a detailed listing and exhaustive analysis of the various oral structuring devices at play in the narrative structure of sacred texts. This overview may provide prospective scholars with new perspectives, tools, and terminology with which to analyze Qurʾanic narrative structure – tools that move beyond the currently popular ring composition. It shows that there may be several devices at work simultaneously, some augmenting and others balancing, thereby providing the text with a distinctive internal dynamic. This monograph thus underlines the possibility that studying the poetics of narrative structure can contribute to a better understanding of the Qurʾan. Moreover, it introduces the notion of dynamics, which imbue the text with changing intensities due to variation in emphasis. This feature, as it is presented in this monograph, is new in the study of sacred texts, moving beyond the various poetic devices previously identified by Biblical scholars.

This monograph provides a theoretical and methodological foundation for the study of the Qur'an's pedagogies, in addition to its poetics. Indeed, the two new readings may have prospects in Qur'an scholarship: it is possible to apply the divine self-revelatory and the pedagogical readings to other suras, which may provide useful insights. These readings use an essentially literary framework to help identify the narrative structure and pedagogy of the sacred text, thereby avoiding problematic theological premises that may conflict with the belief systems of various faith traditions. The use of a literary approach builds common grounds for Qur'an interpretation so that both Muslims and adherents of other faiths and persuasions may feel at ease approaching the text and engaging a variety of surrounding scholarships and discourses.

The new readings also help to focus attention on the educational aspect of the Qur'an, identifying the various pedagogies at work, such as its inherent pedagogy of responsibility. The stories in Surat al-Baqara – the founding narratives of humanity and ancient Israel – suggest that what makes great human beings is not their flawlessness but how they handle themselves in their lowest moments and how they deal with their mistakes. Thus the pedagogy of responsibility comes intertwined with a pedagogy of error that points the way to repentance as a key feature of this educational theory.

Another feature that characterizes Surat al-Baqara's pedagogy is its inherent pluralism and the use of social memory to evoke a sense of responsibility. Its progressive character is also noteworthy, suggesting that responsibility increases in accordance with human development. However, the most interesting feature for feminists and contemporary reformists is its monotheistic nuances, which suggest that it is the responsibility of individuals to read the book for themselves, using their eyes, ears, and minds, instead of depending on intermediaries. Rather than asserting the ambiguity of the Qur'an and, by extension, the need for authoritative interpretations, this sura describes the verses as clear (*bayyināt*), critiquing those who rely exclusively on ancestral traditions without engaging with the revealed text on their own (vv. 171–2). This feature is therefore in conversation with traditionalist polemics against the use of personal judgment (*raʾy*), particularly the way they restrict exegesis to the corpus of inherited (*maʾthūr*) traditions, the sura thereby inherently supporting *raʾy*. Indeed, the sura suggests that it is not only the right of individuals to read and interpret the Qurʾan for themselves but also their responsibility.

Surat al-Baqara introduces the foundations of the emerging faith tradition, the basic elements of the Islamic covenant. In form, function, and location within the Qurʾanic canon, it therefore acts as the gateway into the Qurʾan, the Muslim community's first comprehensive lesson. So, although all the factors enunciated here have value, the biggest contribution of this monograph is that it brings together all these insights to answer the question posed at the outset regarding the nature of Surat al-Baqara's compositional schema and the rationale and poetics of its structure. This monograph identifies the layout, running themes, and organizational aesthetics of al-Baqara, the first of the long Medinan suras and the introduction to the Qurʾan. Within the liturgy and in private worship, whenever the Qurʾan enters the soundscape, a listener conversant with the poetics of narrative structure is better able to grasp its meanings as they unfurl in the course of the recitation. As its bits and pieces come together, the listener is in a position to experience the text on multiple levels; the unfolding image of the deity, the budding pedagogy, and the interweaving themes are all brought into relief by the ebb and flow of the emotive experience. As the words spread in the air and are shaped into meaning, the aesthetic imagination decodes the rise and fall of intensity produced by the compounded dynamics of the al-Baqara crescendo.

Appendix

Holistic Approaches in Biblical Studies

To locate the Qurʾan and "holistic" approaches to its interpretation within a larger historical context, I present the following excursus on relevant approaches to the Bible. Unlike in the field of Qurʾanic studies, the term "holistic" is well-established in the study of the Bible, signifying approaches that treat the Bible as a coherent, integrated text, as opposed to a conglomeration of source documents. One of the earliest scholars to have used it is Moshe Greenberg, who places it in the title of his article "Ezekiel 17: A Holistic Interpretation."[1] It appears in other studies as well, such as Jacob Hoftijzer's "Holistic or Compositional Approach? Linguistic Remarks to the Problem."[2] However, some authors seem reluctant to use it, such as Rolf Rendtorff, who instead employs the phrase "as a whole," as in his chapter title "The Pentateuch as a Whole."[3] Interestingly, "holistic" is applied to Rendtorff's chapter by John L. McLaughlin.[4] The term is also applied to one of two broad general approaches to the Bible, as in the work of Aulikki Nahkola, who contrasts "holistic" treatments and those that stress the heterogeneous nature of the Biblical texts.[5]

To gain some idea of these approaches, a brief look at their history and development may prove useful. Both trends can be located within the broad, general area of literary approaches to the Bible. Nonholistic methods generally fall under the term "Biblical criticism" and have taken on a historical character. Nahkola has pointed out that Biblical criticism was centred on the double-narrative phenomenon in the Hebrew Scriptures and has explored the connection between the work of each scholar and the intellectual environment in which it was conceived.[6]

One of the earliest names associated with the rise of Biblical criticism is Baruch (Benedict) Spinoza (d. 1677), who is sometimes accorded the epithet "father of Biblical criticism." He commented on the occurrence of double narratives, explaining their inconsistencies as being the result of collation from different sources, thereby challenging the traditional claims of Mosaic authorship and the integrity of the Bible.[7] Spinoza's observations clashed with existing ideas of scriptural authority and dogmatic exegesis since he saw reason as the only proper foundation for human religion. Spinoza lived in the intellectual environment of the late Renaissance and early Enlightenment, an epoch preoccupied with reason and scientific methodology. His approach did not differ much from that of a natural scientist since he observed and documented the repetitions as though they were natural phenomena and the Bible were a profane text.

Countering Spinoza, Richard Simon (d. 1712) and Jean Astruc (d. 1766) attempted to preserve the authority of scripture, while explaining the double-narrative phenomenon. Whereas Astruc hypothesized that Moses used documents in his compilation of Genesis, Simon proposed that it was put together by inspired editors, who used Moses's own work in addition to other documents from the Israelite archives for the creation of the Pentateuch.[8] Although these two writers regained some measure of authority for the Biblical text, they similarly attributed double narratives to the book's composition from multiple sources, thereby contributing to the perception of the Biblical text as fragmented or incoherent with regard to composition.

Subsequent scholarship further strengthened the connection between parallel narratives and multiple sources, particularly the work of Julius Wellhausen (d. 1918), who presented a full treatment of doublets and a coherent theory for their presence in the Hebrew Scriptures. Whereas Wellhausen stressed the written nature of the documents, Hermann Gunkel (d. 1932) focused on the oral character of composition, explaining the double narratives as resulting from permutations due to oral intervention.[9] His approach was elaborated by many subsequent scholars, some of whom used folklore studies to explain the repetitions. These two approaches have become important features of Biblical scholarship today and underline the composite nature of the Biblical text.

Patricia Tull has pointed out relevant aspects of the intellectual environment from the mid-eighteenth to the early twentieth century, particularly the preoccupation with the notion of originality sometimes referred to as "influence theory." Critics who considered "originality" to be the true indicator of an author's genius searched texts for "influences," thereby incidentally privileging the earlier "influencing" texts. Tull connects this concern with the Enlightenment spirit of independence and the associated distrust of tradition. This separation from human tradition and institutions is applied to the classical Biblical prophets, whose "original" sayings Wellhausen attempted to isolate from their subsequent scribal accretions by romantically portraying the prophets as solitary individuals acting as God's mouthpieces.[10]

"Influence theory" falls in the general category of author-oriented approaches, which are concerned with uncovering the meaning that an author intended for a text. Today, there is a stronger emphasis on the role of the reader in the creation of meaning, the reader now being considered an active participant in the process. This change is sometimes expressed by the catchy phrase "death of the author," which was originally the title of an article by the literary theorist and philosopher Roland Barthes. The shift from author- to reader-oriented approaches is also reflected in the modern holistic approaches, which treat the Bible as a whole text, independent of origins.

Nahkola has pointed to the diversity of holistic approaches, loosely identifying two groups. The first is represented by Umberto Cassuto, Samuel Sandmel, Moses Hirsch Segal, and Roger Norman Whybray, who reject Wellhausen's theory and emphasize authorial intent.[11] The second group includes Robert Alter and David Damrosch, who exemplify a new literary criticism.[12] This trend has emerged as a major force in the study of the Hebrew Scriptures over the past decades, partly due to the efforts of Alter, whose work has been described as the "watershed" of the literary approaches to the Bible; whereas prior to the publication of his book there were some sporadic attempts at literary investigations, afterward there was a marked increase, suggesting a movement. It is perhaps the strength of this latter trend that caused some authors to suggest a paradigm shift more than a decade ago; however, few would go so far today.

The Biblical and the Qurʾanic holistic approaches share some commonalities: both are predicated on the notion that there is more to the text when it is studied as a whole than when its component parts are looked at in isolation. They also share an exuberance for and enthusiastic appreciation of each text's literary qualities. If Robert Alter has done much to bring attention to the Bible's literary artistry, the work of Sayyid Quṭb is a prime example of similar accomplishment with regard to the Qurʾan.[13]

The holistic approaches are also not devoid of interaction with their intellectual environment but are in conversation with the fragmenting approaches and have an apologetic dimension that functions as a defence against the undermining of the integrity and authority of scripture. Although holistic approaches can display a criticism of the fragmenting ones, the nature and degree of criticism can vary. The Qurʾanic coherence-related approaches are often accommodating of the fragmenting ones – the modern Muḥammad al-Ghazālī (d. 1996), for example, even claiming that his interpretation "does not replace atomistic interpretation; rather it completes it, and is to be considered an effort to be joined to the [previous] appreciable efforts."[14] In contrast, Mustansir Mir and Amīn Aḥsan Iṣlāḥī (d. 1997) seem to take a more critical stance, the former even quoting a Qurʾanic verse hostile to fragmentation. The Biblical literary approaches can be disapproving of the fragmenting ones, some even disparagingly terming them "excavative" scholarship.[15] However, scholars such as Robert Cohn are more accommodating and have pointed out that the literary approaches do not stand alone but are supported by the other critical methods.[16]

There are some parallels between the Biblical and Qurʾanic holistic and coherence-related approaches. Both can often be located under the literary umbrella, even though there are more authors in the Biblical field who identify their approach as literary than there are in the Qur'anic field. Within their respective intellectual environments, both also occasion some tension with the fragmenting approaches. Whereas the fragmenting, "atomistic" approaches to the Qur'an were often those of religious orthodoxy or Orientalism, the fragmenting approaches to the Bible were not generally religious and were often conducted by historians or Biblical critics. However, practitioners of both Qur'anic and Biblical holistic and coherence-related approaches were successful in negotiating an intellectual environment that was inclined toward fragmentation, gaining recognition and establishing their methods within it.

Glossary

ALTERNATION: a rhetorical device that consists of the repetition of words, ideas, or themes in the same order.

CHIASM (CHIASMUS): a rhetorical device that consists of the repetition of words, ideas, or themes in an inverted order.

COHERENCE: a quality that makes a text semantically meaningful for the reader. It is often concerned with linear connections between passages.

DIACHRONIC: a quality that denotes a preoccupation with how a text or its interpretation changes over time.

DIVINE SELF-REVELATORY READING: a reading in which God or another divine being is placed at the focal point and the text is read for what it reveals about the deity.

INCLUDITUR: a unit of text enclosed by an inclusio.

INCLUSIO: a bracketing device that consists of a repeated word, phrase, or verse located close to the beginning and end of a text, forming a frame for the enclosed unit.

INFLUENCE THEORY: a preoccupation with the notion of originality that is often associated with the eighteenth and nineteenth centuries but is still current today. Earlier texts were privileged as the older, original, and "influencing" texts.

INTERTEXTUALITY: a relationship of texts to one another that contributes to shaping their meanings.

IQTIṢĀṢ: a compositional device that ties together disparate elements of a text. It entails taking a word, expression, or idea from a certain context and repeating it in another, thereby creating intertextual nuances and layers of meaning. It is this intertextual quality that distinguishes it from the *Leitwort* and the inclusio.

HOLISM: the view that the whole is more than the sum of its parts. When applied to the Qur᾿an, it supposes that there is an added value when a sura is viewed as a whole rather than looked at in a linear-atomistic, verse-by-verse fashion. This added value can take the form of a central theme.

LEITWORT: a leading keyword repeated verbatim throughout a text, often in various grammatical forms, imbuing a text with a distinctive character. This device is distinguished from the inclusio by its profusion and its dispersion throughout the text.

ORAL TYPESETTING: the use of oral techniques, such as repetition and the vocative, to segment, unify, highlight, and otherwise organize a text.

PEDAGOGICAL READING: a reading in which human beings are placed at the focal point and the text is read for its pedagogical content.

PROGRESSION: a rhetorical structure that denotes a progressing sequence within a text.

SYNCHRONIC: a quality that denotes a preoccupation with a text or its interpretation at a certain time, without reference to the historical context or changes that occur over time.

Notes

INTRODUCTION

1 Bell, *Introduction*, 82.
2 Ibid., 71–2.
3 Nicholson, *Literary History*, 161.
4 See Neuwirth, *Studien zur Komposition*.
5 Nöldeke, *Geschichte des Qorans.*
6 Zahniser, "Major Transitions," 26, quotation translated from the German by Zahniser. For the original German, see Neuwirth, "Vom Rezitationstext," 98. Neuwirth further suggests that Medinan suras "cease to be neatly structured compositions, but appear to be the result of a process of collection that we cannot yet reconstruct." Neuwirth, "Sūra(s)," 174.
7 Sadeghi and Goudarzi, "Ṣanʿāʾ 1," 8. See also von Bothmer, "Neue Wege der Koranforschung."
8 Sells, "Literary Approach." See also Neuwirth, *Scripture*.
9 Rippin, "Qurʾān as Literature."
10 See, for example, Geiger, *Was hat Muhammad?*; Wellhausen, *Prolegomena zur ältesten Geschichte* and *Das arabische Reich*; and Nöldeke, *Geschichte des Qorans*.
11 Günther, "O People of the Scripture!"; Brown, ed., *Three Testaments.*
12 See, for example, Ford and Pecknold, eds, *Promise*; and Smith, "How Religious Practices Matter."
13 See, for example, the al-Baqara-inspired synoptic reading of the Biblical books of Joshua, Judges 6–8, 1 Samuel 1–7, and 1

Samuel 8–31 as parallel accounts revolving around the same historical personage. Reda, "Qurʾānic Ṭālūt."

14 Robbins, *Exploring*, 1–2.

15 Ibid.

16 Bakhtiar, *Sublime Qurʾan*; ʿAlī, *Meaning of the Holy Qurʾan.*

17 Bakhtiar, *Sublime Qurʾan*, vol. 1, xii.

CHAPTER ONE

1 It is also possible to translate the Arabic *iqraʾ* as "read out loud, recite"; however, "read" is more prevalent. See, for example, the translation in Guillaume, *Life of Muhammad*, 106.

2 See, for example, Olsen, "What Is Poetics?"

3 Mir, *Coherence in the Qurʾan*, 99, and "Sūra as a Unity," 217; Barlas, *"Believing Women" in Islam*, 18; Wadud, *Qurʾan and Woman*, 1–5.

4 See Mir, *Coherence in the Qurʾan*, 99.

5 Wadud, *Qurʾan and Woman*, 1–5.

6 Barlas, *"Believing Women" in Islam*, 18. See also Ricoeur, *Hermeneutics*, 212–13. Ricoeur does not discuss the Qurʾan specifically but refers to text in general, although his work is of great significance for the study of the Bible. He states, "A text is a whole, a totality. The relation between whole and parts – as in a work of art or in an animal – requires a specific kind of 'judgment' … For all these reasons there is a problem of interpretation not so much because of the incommunicability of the psychic experience of the author, but because of the very nature of the verbal intention of the text. This intention is something other than the sum of the individual meanings of the individual sentences. A text is more than a linear succession of sentences. It is a cumulative holistic process." Ibid., 211–12. The original article appeared as Paul Ricoeur, "The Model of the Text: Meaningful Action Considered as a Text," *Social Research* 38, no. 3 (1971): 548–9.

7 Iṣlāḥī, *Tadabbur-ī Qurʾān*.

8 The genre of classical Qurʾan commentary is generally atomistic,

with a few notable exceptions. For the commentaries used by Geissinger, see her *Gender and Muslim Constructions*, 17–25.

9 For more on the occurrence of the term "holistic" in Biblical studies and the distinction between fragmenting and holistic approaches, see the appendix.

10 Barlas, *"Believing Women" in Islam*, 18. See also Ricoeur, *Hermeneutics*, 212–13.

11 Iṣlāḥī, *Tadabbur-ī Qurʾān*; al-Ṣaʿīdī, *Al-Naẓm al-fannī*; Thanwī, *Bayān al-Qurʾān*; Darwaza, *Al-Tafsīr al-ḥadīth*; Quṭb, *Fī ẓilāl*; al-Ṭabāṭabāʾī, *Al-Mīzān*; al-Ghazālī, *Naḥwa tafsīr mawḍūʿī* and *Al-Maḥāwir al-khamsa*; al-Zayn, *Bayān al-naẓm*.

12 Drāz, *Al-Nabaʾ al-ʿaẓīm*; Smith, "Structure of Surat al-Baqarah"; Farrin, "*Surat al-Baqara*."

13 Ibn Taymiyya, *Muqaddima*; al-Zarkashī, *Al-Burhān*; al-Suyūṭī, *Al-Itqān*; al-Dhahabī, *Al-Tafsīr wa'l-mufassirūn*.

14 Soroush, *Qabz o bast-e*.

15 Al-Ṭabarī, *Jāmiʿ al-bayān*.

16 See, for example, the linguistic problems of al-Ṭabarī's list of interpretations for Qurʾan 4:3. Reda, "Al-Niswiyya al-islāmiyya."

17 Al-Ṭabarī, *Jāmiʿ al-bayān*, vol. 1, 8–12.

18 Ibn Taymiyya, followed by others, directs the exegete to use *tafsīr bi'l-maʾthūr* if *tafsīr al-Qurʾān bi'l-Qurʾān* proves too tiresome, using the words *faʾin aʿyāk(h) dhālik* (if this tires you [him] out). Ibn Taymiyya, *Muqaddima*, 93–105. Compare also al-Zarkashī, *Al-Burhān*, vol. 2, 175–6; and al-Suyūṭī, *Al-Itqān*, vol. 4, 174. Thus nuances in the words of these scholars imply that finding internal connections within the Qurʾan is an arduous or difficult task, necessitating the use of the *maʾthūr* traditions. In contrast, the modern Muḥammad Ḥusayn al-Dhahabī (d. 1977), when repeating the same idea based on Ismāʿīl Ibn Kathīr (d. 774/1373), omits the word *aʿyāk(h)*. Al-Dhahabī, *Al-Tafsīr wa'l-mufassirūn*, vol. 1, 72. His omission reflects the modern interest in the *tafsīr al-Qurʾān bi'l-Qurʾān* method.

19 Rājiḥ, ed., *Mukhtaṣar tafsīr Ibn Kathīr*; al-Ṣābūnī, ed., *Mukhtaṣar*

tafsīr Ibn Kathīr; Mubārakfūrī, *Al-Miṣbāḥ al-munīr* (an English translation of which is available) and *Tafsīr Ibn Kathīr*.

20 Al-Jāḥiẓ and Muḥammad, *Naẓm al-Qurʾān*; al-Jurjānī, *Asrār al-balāgha*; al-Zamakhsharī, *Al-Kashshāf.* For more on al-Zamakhsharī, see al-Jindī, *Al-Naẓm al-Qurʾānī*. Claude Gilliot and Pierre Larcher spell Jindī's name "Jundī," in keeping with classical pronunciation. Gilliot and Larcher, "Language and Style." I have chosen to spell it "Jindī," in keeping with how this Egyptian surname is commonly pronounced today since this person is a twentieth-century scholar.

21 ʿAbd al-Raḥmān (Bint al-Shāṭiʾ), *Al-Tafsīr al-bayānī*.

22 Ibid., 13.

23 For more, see the work of Abu Zayd, such as "Dilemma."

24 Mir, "Qurʾān as Literature"; Johns, "In Search of Common Ground."

25 Kandil, "Schwure," 48. See also Neuwirth, "Images and Metaphors"; and Ibrahim, "Oaths in the Qurʾan."

26 I am indebted to Ayman El-Desouky for his insights on the subject of world literature, among other things. El-Desouky, "Between Hermeneutic Provenance," 16–17.

27 Quoted in ibid., 14. See also Frye, *Northrop Frye on Religion*, vol. 4, 22.

28 El-Desouky, "Between Hermeneutic Provenance," 15.

29 Ibid., 12. See also El-Desouky, "*Naẓm*, *iʿjāz*, Discontinuous Kerygma." In chapter 7, I explore the literary genre of *naẓm al-Qurʾān* (arrangement of the Qurʾan) and its relationship to the theory of inimitability (*iʿjāz*). The genre *naẓm* dealt with literary aspects of the Qurʾan and was used to argue for that certain extra something that made the Qurʾan inimitable and, by extension, for its divine provenance.

30 El-Desouky, "Between Hermeneutic Provenance," 15.

31 Although the phenomenon of silent reading was not entirely unknown in late antiquity, it became widespread only in the late eighteenth century. See Jajdelska, *Silent Reading*.

32 See Nelson, *Art of Reciting*. The term *Sitz im Leben* refers primarily to the early historical context and social setting of Biblical texts and, by extension, to their function and "original" purpose. Here, I use it to refer to the Qur'an's early socio-historical setting in the liturgy. Of course, its deployment for other purposes is likely to have also been oral.

33 See Günther, "Muḥammad, the Illiterate Prophet."

34 Muslim ibn al-Ḥajjāj, *Ṣaḥīḥ Muslim: Kitāb ṣalāt al-musāfirīn wa-qaṣrihā, bāb istiḥbāb taṭwīl al-qirā'a fī ṣalāt al-layl,* hadith no. 772.

35 See Leemhuis, "From Palm Leaves."

36 Useem, "In Islam"; Rasmussen, "Qur'an" and *Women*.

37 Gade, "Taste, Talent."

38 El-Desouky, "Between Hermeneutic Provenance," 17. See also Pulitano, "Writing in the Oral Tradition."

39 See, for example, Dundes, *Fables of the Ancients?*

40 See, for example, Bannister, *Oral-Formulaic Study*.

41 See, for example, Pregill, "Hebrew Bible and the Quran."

42 El-Desouky, "Between Hermeneutic Provenance," 20–1.

43 Kadi and Mir, "Literature and the Qur'ān," 205–13.

44 See, for example, Cuypers, *Composition* and *Banquet*.

45 Parunak, "Oral Typesetting."

46 Barthes, "Death of the Author."

47 Rippin, "Qur'an as Literature."

48 Ibid., 44.

49 Neuwirth, "Referentiality and Textuality," 143–5, and "'Oral Scriptures' in Contact."

50 Hidayatullah, *Feminist Edges*, 146–9.

51 See, for example, Bakhtiar, *Moral Healing*.

52 Madigan, "Themes and Topics," 79–80.

53 Rahman, *Major Themes*; Sherif, *Guide*; Jomier, *Great Themes*; Abdel Haleem, *Understanding the Qur'an*.

54 See, for example, Barth, *Christliche Verständnis* and *On Religion*.

55 See Pannenberg, *Offenbarung als Geschichte*.

56 See Talmon, "Revelation in Biblical Times."
57 See, for example, Laney, "God's Self-Revelation"; and Kim, "Who Is Yahweh?" William A. Dyrness has identified several instances of divine self-revelation in Genesis and Exodus in *Themes*, 27–38.
58 For example, compare Qur'an 20:12–16, 27:8–9, 7:143, and 2:84.
59 See Mills, *Images of God*.
60 Barazangi does not describe her work as feminist; however, feminism is a broad-ranging field and incorporates different movements and ideologies. Her work is feminist in the sense that it advocates equal rights for women in religious education and knowledge production.
61 Nahkola, *Double Narratives*, 55–7. See also Cassuto, *Documentary Hypothesis*, 255–318, originally published in Hebrew in 1941; and Wellhausen, *Prolegomena zur Geschichte Israels*, first published in 1878 and enlarged in 1883.
62 Al-Biqāʿī, *Naẓm al-durar*, vol. 1, 11, previously edited and published by Al-Sayyid Sharaf al-Dīn Aḥmad (Haydar Abad: Dāʾirat al-Maʿārif al-ʿUthmāniyya, 1968).
63 It is noteworthy that the orthodox Bakhtin wrote in an Eastern, soviet environment and mainly in the context of Russian novels. The legitimacy of appropriating his ideas in a Western, Biblical environment has been questioned. For a brief overview of some of these critiques, see Green, *How Are the Mighty Fallen?* 28–9. See also Green, *Mikhail Bakhtin*. The work of Bakhtin has not often been used in the study of the Qur'an; however, his ideas have been discussed in connection to Scriptural Reasoning, a practice that bridges the Bible and the Qur'an. See Quash, "Heavenly Semantics."
64 Bakhtin, *Dialogic Imagination*, 426. See also Green, *How Are the Mighty Fallen?* 24.
65 Green, *How Are the Mighty Fallen?* 26.
66 Green quotes Holquist as follows: "The dialogue between organ-

ism and environment must take place in a constant *experimentation* on the part of the situated subject." Ibid., 26, emphasis in original. See also Holquist, "Bakhtin and Beautiful Science," 222.

67 Green, *King Saul's Asking*, 2–11.

68 A.R. Pete Diamond also uses Bakhtin's ideas, approaching Yahweh as a literary construct with a distinct voice. Diamond, "Interlocutions." Lyle Eslinger's approach is perhaps also pertinent since he too presents Yahweh as a literary character among other characters in the Saul narrative. Eslinger, "Viewpoints," reprinted in J. Cheryl Exum, ed., *The Historical Books* (Sheffield, UK: Sheffield Academic Press, 1997).

69 Green, *How Are the Mighty Fallen?* 25–6.

70 See, for example, al-Zarkashī, *Al-Burhān*, vol. 1, 40, 49.

71 Lawson, "Duality, Opposition and Typology."

72 Jung attributes the idea to the Greek philosopher Heraclitus (d. 475 BCE). Jung, *Collected Works*, vol. 7, 71, para. 111.

73 Lawson, "Duality, Opposition and Typology."

74 For a summary of her findings, see Geissinger's conclusion in *Gender and Muslim Constructions*, 275–80.

75 Wadud, *Qur'an and Woman*, 1–10.

76 Esack, *Qur'an*, 2.

77 Al-Sharqāwī, "Usus al-ʿilāqa bayna."

78 See Reda, "From Where?" 120–2.

79 For the distinction between Muslim feminism and Islamic feminism, see Badran, *Feminism in Islam*, 242–53.

80 Mattson, *Story of the Qur'an*.

CHAPTER TWO

1 Some numbering conventions do not count the *basmala* as part of the sura, which would result in a six-verse count. For more, see Neuwirth, "*Sūrat al-Fātiḥa*."

2 No sura is as widely recited within Muslim life, and it has even been likened to a "microcosm" of the scripture, or *umm al-Qur'an*.

Ibid., 180. Neuwirth has also drawn attention to al-Fātiḥa's connection to Surat al-Ḥijr, highlighting its liturgical importance. Ibid., 170–5, 180.

3 For more, see Ayoub, "Prayer of Islam."

4 Stewart, "Sajʿ in the Qurʾān," reprinted in Colin Turner, ed., *The Koran: Critical Concepts in Islamic Studies: Style and Structure*, vol. 3, 74–111 (London: RoutledgeCurzon, 2004).

5 Zwettler, "Mantic Manifesto." This article has generated a lively conversation, of which the latest installment is Shahid, "Sūra of the Poets."

6 Cuypers, *Composition.*

7 Al-Jurjānī, *Asrār al-balāgha*. See also Murād, *Naẓariyyat al-naẓm*; al-Ẓahhār, *Athar istikhdām naẓariyyat al-naẓm*; and al-Jindī, *Naẓariyyat ʿAbd al-Qāhir*.

8 See al-Suyūṭī, *Al-Itqān*, vol. 3, 249–89, 353–5. *Badīʿ* can also be translated as "Branch of Arabic rhetoric, dealing with figures of speech and (in general) the art of beautiful style." Wehr, *Hans Wehr Dictionary*, 57.

9 Abdel Haleem, *Understanding the Qurʾān*, 161.

10 Wehr, *Hans Wehr Dictionary*, 896. See also al-Zabīdī, *Tāj al-ʿarūs*, vol. 9, 338b; and Ibn Manẓūr al-Ifrīqī al-Miṣrī, *Lisān al-ʿarab*, vol. 7, 73b, 74b, 76b. The juridical meaning, "like for like retaliation," is probably the most widely used today.

11 Al-Suyūṭī, *Al-Itqān*, vol. 3, 264.

12 Bakhtiar, *Sublime Qurʾan*, vol. 2, 701–2, translates Qurʾan 29:27 as follows: "And We bestowed Isaac and Jacob on him and We assigned to his offspring prophethood and the Book. We gave him his compensation in the present. And, truly, in the world to come he will be, certainly, among the ones in accord with morality." And in ibid., vol. 2, 557, she translates Qurʾan 20:75 as follows: "And whoever approaches Him as one who believes, who, surely, did as the one in accord with morality, then, for those, they are of lofty degrees."

13 In his second example, Qurʾan 34:36 is used to explain the idea

of "*muḥḍarīn*" in Qur᾽an 37:57, and in his third example, Qur᾽an 50:21, 4:41, 2:143, and 24:24 are used to explain the idea of "*ashhād*" in Qur᾽an 40:32. In al-Suyūṭī's last example, Qur᾽an 7:44 and 80:34 are used to explain two variant readings of *yawm al-tanād(d)* in Qur᾽an 40:32.

14 There are two possible roots for this word: the geminate *n-d-d*, as in Qur᾽an 80:34, and the final weak *n-d-w*, as in Qur᾽an 7:44.

15 Müller, *Die Propheten*, 200.

16 Parunak, "Transitional Techniques," 526. See also Brogan, "Concatenation."

17 The word *rabb* is more commonly rendered as "Lord" or "Master" in English. It also has pedagogical nuances and can be translated as "nurturer," "cherisher," "sustainer," "chief," "leader," "owner," "teacher," or "religious authority." I have chosen "educator" to highlight the pedagogical nuances that are not adequately communicated when translating it as "Lord" or "Master." The word occurs in several Semitic languages, such as Arabic, Hebrew, and Aramaic. For more on the meaning of this word in the Qur᾽an, see Reda, "From the Canadian Sharia Debates," 82–5.

18 Wansbrough, *Qur᾽anic Studies*, 47.

19 Al-Andalusī, *Al-Baḥr al-muḥīṭ*, vol. 1, 35; al-Ṭabarsī, *Majma῾ al-bayān*, vol. 1, 23. Salwa El-Awa has pointed out that Arabic grammar and rhetoric generally assign repetitions the functions of *tawkīd* (emphasis) and/or *iṭnāb* (positive verbosity). El-Awa, "Repetition," 577n3.

20 Ṭanṭāwī, *Al-Tafsīr al-wasīṭ*, vol. 1, 19.

21 Abdel Haleem, "Grammatical Shift."

22 Pope, *Song of Songs*, 297.

23 The two occurrences of "it is You" (*iyyāka*) are separated by "we worship" (*na῾bud*), and the two occurrences of "way" (*ṣirāṭ*) are separated by "right" (*mustaqīm*).

24 *῾Ālamīn*, translated here as "everyone in the world," is more often translated as "worlds" or even "realms." Although both "realms" and "worlds" are good translations, I have chosen "everyone in

the world" because the other Qur'anic occurrences generally refer to people, not to the contents of the entire universe. Compare Qur'an 2:47, 131, 251; 3:33, 42, 96, 97, 108; 5:20, 28, 115; 6:45, 71, 86, 90, 162; 7:54, 61, 67, 80, 104, 121, 140; 10:10, 37, 104; 15:70; 21:71, 91, 107; 25:1; 26:16, 23, 47, 77, 98, 109, 127, 145, 164, 165, 180, 192; 27:8, 44; 28:30; 29:6, 10, 15, 28; 32:2; 37:79, 87, 182; 38:87; 39:75; 40:64, 65, 66; 41:9; 43:46; 44:32; 45:16, 36; 56:80; 59:16; 68:52; 69:43; 81:27, 29; and 83:6.

25 It is important to note that Christianity in ancient Arabia was different from Christianity today and even went by a different name, *naṣrāniyya* (Nazarene belief). See De Blois, "Nasrānī (Ναζωραιος)."

26 For more, see Reda, "From the Canadian Sharia Debates," 80–7.

27 Al-Suyūṭī, *Tanāsuq al-durar*, 40–1; al-Biqāʿī, *Naẓm al-durar*, vol. 1, 32; Ṭanṭāwī, *Al-Tafsīr al-wasīṭ*, vol. 1, 27.

28 Al-Rāzī, *Al-Tafsīr al-kabīr*, vol. 2, 58; al-Ṭabāṭabāʾī, *Al-Mīzān*, vol. 1, 55; al-Ṭūsī, *Al-Tibyān*, vol. 1, 97; al-Alūsī, *Rūḥ al-maʿānī*, vol. 1, 143. Some commentators have also interpreted the last two groups as Jews and Christians.

29 ʿAbduh, *Tafsīr al-manār*, vol. 1, 125; Quṭb, *Fī ẓilāl*, vol. 1, 31, 42–6.

30 Al-Biqāʿī, *Naẓm al-durar*, vol. 1, 40. In the realm of the Bible, Meir Steinberg has commented that Biblical repetitions can have an "expansion or addition" form or function, recalling al-Biqāʿī's notion of *ijmāl*. Sternberg, *Poetics of Biblical Narrative*, 390–1.

31 Al-Suyuṭī, *Tanāsuq al-durar*, 40–1.

32 Ibid., 40n15.

33 For a brief synopsis of Ricoeur's typology of Biblical literary poetics and their relation to Qur'anic discourse, see Robbins and Newby, "Relation," 28–9.

34 Ibid., 26–9.

35 Ibid., 29–32.

36 Ibid., 32–42.

37 Ricoeur, *Essays*, 75–7.

38 Jomier, *Great Themes*, 28–36. Jaques Jomier has even attempted a structural analysis of Qur'an 16:3–18.

39 On rhymed prose, see Stewart, "Saj' in the Qur'ān."

40 Lawson, "Duality, Opposition and Typology."

CHAPTER THREE

1 Arjomand, "Constitution of Medina," 562.

2 Ibn Hishām, *Al-Sīra al-nabawiyya*, vol. 2, 111.

3 Evans, Brogan, and Halsall, "Epanalepsis."

4 Moulton, *Literary Study*, 69–79, 528–30.

5 Fogle and Brogan, "Envelope."

6 Müller, *Die Propheten*, 200–1.

7 Rendsburg, "Literary Devices," 20.

8 Ibid.

9 The text of the prophecy is as follows: "*the one with the power to vanquish the Dark Lord* approaches … born to those who have thrice defied him … *born as the seventh month dies* … and the Dark Lord will mark him as his equal, but he will have power the Dark Lord knows not … and either must die at the hand of the other, for neither can live while the other survives … *the one with the power to vanquish the Dark Lord will be born as the seventh month dies*." Rowling, *Harry Potter and the Order of the Phoenix*, 741, emphasis added. It is noteworthy that the text framed in this fashion is a spoken prophecy, which has the inherent qualities of transcendence and ephemerality, like a timeless voice coming out of another realm. This usage may suggest the suitability of inclusios for divine speech and oral, mantic communication within popular perceptions and culture. In this prophetic speech, the repetition also summarizes and underlines the most important point that the bracketed text makes.

10 Parunak, "Oral Typesetting," 158.

11 Quoted and translated in Saleh, *Formation of the Classical*, 134–5.

12 For an example, see Kessler, "Inclusio in the Hebrew Bible," 49n7.

13 Ibid., 45, 49nn7–8.
14 Friedman, Doughtie, and Brogan, "Incremental Repetition."
15 Al-Ṭabāṭabāʾī, *Al-Mīzān*, vol. 1, 266.
16 Grossberg, "Disparate Elements," 97. See also Dahood, *Psalms I*, vol. 1, 5.
17 Al-Biqāʿī, *Naẓm al-durar*, vol. 1, 236.
18 Zahniser, "Major Transitions," 32.
19 Robinson, *Discovering the Qurʾan*; Mir, "Sūra as a Unity," 215–16. For an overview of Robinson's work, see El-Awa, *Textual Relations*, 22–4.
20 See also Qurʾan 3:96.
21 This translation of *Islām* best reproduces the Arabic meaning. *Islām* is a grammatical form of the root *s-l-m* (Form IV), a root that in its basic form has the meanings of "wholeness," "peace," "well-being," and "safety" (Form I). The more common translation, "submission," is more representative of the grammatical form *istislām* (Form X), which is very different from *Islām*. Whereas the latter gives the word a quasi-passive meaning in the sense of seeking to have an action accomplished by turning the agency to someone else, the former imparts a sustained causative nuance. Therefore, "submission" does not accurately reproduce the causative sense of *Islām*, which is better translated as "wholeness making," "peacemaking," "well-being making," and "safety making." For example, the notion of making whole one's devotions to God (literally making whole one's face or direction to God) implies this sustained causative action (Q. 3:20; 31:22). For more, see Reda, "'Good' Muslim," 243–6.
22 Al-Biqāʿī, *Naẓm al-durar*, vol. 1, 267.
23 Al-Ṭabāṭabāʾī, *Al-Mīzān*, vol. 1, 328. His explanation is supported by the differences in wording: whereas the first injunction was associated with "wherever you are," the second and third injunctions are associated with "from where you have come," perhaps indicating Mecca.
24 Al-Andalusī, *Al-Baḥr al-muḥīṭ*, vol. 2, 541–3; al-Alūsī, *Rūḥ al-*

maʿānī, vol. 1, 155; Quṭb, *Fī ẓilāl*, vol. 1, 257; Ṭanṭāwī, *Al-Tafsīr al-wasīṭ*, vol. 1, 545.

25 The first of these verses (v. 284) carries echoes of verses 20, 29, 33, 77, 106, 107, 109, 116, 117, 148, 164, 255, 259, and 271, whereas the second one (v. 285) recalls verses 2, 4, 21, 22, 30, 31, 34, 53, 58, 83, 87, 93, 98, 101, 105, 109, 113, 121, 126, 136, 144, 145, 146, 161, 163, 173, 177, 182, 192, 199, 210, 214, 218, 225, 226, 235, 248, 252, 253, and 255, and the last one (v. 286) draws on verses 44, 79, 134, 141, 202, 225, 233, 237, 249, 250, and 281. Robinson, *Discovering the Qurʾan*, 221–3.

26 Zahniser, "Major Transitions," 33.

27 Robinson, *Discovering the Qurʾan*, 210–11.

CHAPTER FOUR

1 Brogan and Halsall, "Chiasmus."

2 Kessler, "Inclusio in the Hebrew Bible," 45, 49nn7–8.

3 Farrin, "*Surat al-Baqara*." See also Farrin, *Structure and Qurʾanic Interpretation.*

4 Farrin, "*Surat al-Baqara*," 29–30. I have simplified his suggested themes.

5 Hamza Zafer has addressed the notion of election from a different perspective: that of communalism, communal boundaries, and salvific communities. He has termed verses 104–52 the "Ummah" pericope, for its communalism-related content. For this valuable work, see Mahmood (Zafer), "Qurʾān's Communal Ideology."

6 For other lexical and thematic elements of al-Baqara's Adam and Eve story and their echos throughtout the sura, see Klar, "Through the Lens."

7 The Arabic word *mathal* has no exact euquivalent in English. It is the cognate of the Hebrew *mashal*, which is most often translated as "proverb," "parable," or even "comparison." I have chosen to translate it as "parable" in order to capture the meaning of a comparison that is used for the purpose of instruction in moral and spiritual truth.

CHAPTER FIVE

1 Quṭb, *Fī ẓilāl*, vol. 1, 28.
2 Robinson, *Discovering the Qur'an*, 203; Farrin, "*Surat al-Baqara*," 30.
3 Buber, "Leitwortstil."
4 Alter, *Art of Biblical Narrative*, 92.
5 Al-Biqāʿī, *Naẓm al-durar*, vol. 1, 24, emphasis added.
6 Ibid., emphasis added.
7 For more on the Qur'anic portrayal of the ancient Israelite covenant (both the *ʿahd* and *mīthāq* terminology) and its relationship to the Ten Commandments, see Günther, "O People of the Scripture!"
8 Robinson, *Discovering the Qur'an*, 213.

CHAPTER SIX

1 Amit, "Progression," 28.
2 Al-Suyūṭī, *Al-Itqān*, vol. 3, 264.
3 The Qur'anic *mathal* (parable) is not necessarily a story but rather a comparison for instruction in moral and spiritual truth.
4 For more on the nuances of this grammatical form, see Reda, "'Good' Muslim," 243–6.
5 Al-Biqāʿī, *Naẓm al-durar*, vol. 1, 49–51.
6 Peterson, "Social Memory."
7 Brian, Jaisson, and Mukherjee, "Introduction," 7, figure 1.
8 Poole, "Memory, Responsibility, and Identity."
9 See Assman, *Das kulturelle Gedächtnis* and *Moses der Ägypter*. The latter caused some controversy, to which he responds in *Die Mosaische Unterscheidung*. See also Assman, *Religion und kulturelles Gedächtnis*.
10 See, for example, Reda, "From Where?" and "Al-Niswiyya al-islāmiyya." This latter paper explores how the principle of consensus (*ijmāʿ*) is also used to "drop" certain Qur'anic regulations.
11 See, for example, the discussion in al-Zarkashī, *Al-Baḥr al-muḥīṭ*, vol. 5, 262–72.

12 See Reda, "Qur'ānic Ṭālūt."
13 Al-Tirmidhī, *Al-Jāmi' al-ṣaḥīḥ: Kitāb tafsīr al-Qur'ān, bāb mā jā'a fī aladhī yufassir al-Qur'ān bi-ra'yih*, hadith nos 2950–2.
14 Reda, "From Where?"

CHAPTER SEVEN

1 For more on al-Biqā'ī's singular approach to exegesis as applied in the area of using the Bible to interpret the Qur'an, see Saleh, *In Defense of the Bible*, "Muslim Hebraist," and "'Sublime in Its Style.'"
2 See also Mir, *Coherence in the Qur'an*, 3.
3 Parts of this book have been preserved in Aḥmad ibn Muḥammad al-Tha'labī's (d. 427/1035) commentary. See Saleh, *Formation of the Classical*, 250.
4 There seems to be some confusion as to the spelling of this non-Arabic name, which occurs as Manjūr (Audebert, *Al-Ḫaṭṭābī*, 61), Ma'jūr (Vadet, "Ibn al-Ikhshīd"), and Bayghjūr (Thomas, "Ibn al-Ikhshīd," 221–3; al-Dhahabī, *Siyar a'lām al-nubalā'*, vol. 15, 218).
5 Audebert, *Al-Ḫaṭṭābī*, 193–4.
6 Al-Khaṭṭābī, *Bayān*.
7 Al-Bāqillānī, *I'jāz al-Qur'ān*. See also Yāsīn, *Dirāsat al-Bāqillānī*.
8 Al-Jurjānī, *Asrār al-balāgha* and *Kitāb dalā'il al-i'jāz*.
9 On al-Zamakhsharī's approach to *naẓm*, see al-Jindī, *Al-Naẓm al-Qur'ānī*.
10 Al-Jāḥiẓ and Muḥammad, *Naẓm al-Qur'ān*.
11 Al-Suyūṭī, *Al-Itqān*; al-Zarkashī, *Al-Burhān*.
12 Al-Zarkashī, *Al-Burhān*, vol. 1, 36. See also Audebert, *Al-Ḫaṭṭābī*, 58–9, 193–4.
13 Al-Suyūṭī, *Al-Itqān*, vol. 4, 5–6.
14 Translation of *ḥashwī* as "vulgariste" by Halkin, "Ḥashwiyya," 2.
15 Al-Jāḥiẓ, *Rasā'il*, vol. 2, 218–19.
16 I follow Wael Hallaq in distinguishing between traditionists and traditionalists. See Hallaq, *Origins*, 74.

17 See al-Jāḥiẓ's criticism of Aḥmad ibn Ḥanbal in al-Jāḥiẓ, *Rasāʾil*, vol. 2, 222–5.

18 Ibn Abī Yaʿlā, *Ṭabaqāt al-Ḥanābila*, vol. 1, 36.

19 Al-Jāḥiẓ and Muḥammad, *Naẓm al-Qurʾān*, 58; al-Jāḥiẓ, *Rasāʾil*, vol. 2, 221.

20 Ḥaddād, *Naẓm al-Qurʾān*, 4.

21 On Sunni anti-Muʿtazilite polemics, see Ibn Taymiyya, *Muqaddima*, 79-86; and al-Suyūṭī, *Al-Itqān*, vol. 4, 213.

22 Joseph van Ess also notes that this doctrine was brought up by the Muʿtazilites. Van Ess, "Verbal Inspiration?" 189. For more on inimitability, see Martin, "Inimitability."

23 Saʿd ʿAbd al-ʿAẓīm Muḥammad has pointed out that al-Jāḥiẓ accepts some aspects of *ṣarfa* but that his views differ substantially from those of al-Naẓẓām. Al-Jāḥiẓ and Muḥammad, *Naẓm al-Qurʾān*, g (*jīm*). Others have been less objective in their criticism; for example, Yūsuf Durra Ḥaddād describes al-Naẓẓām as the "Satan" of the dialectical theologians and alleges that al-Jāḥiẓ was "disturbed" in his views of *ṣarfa.* Thus, even among proponents of *naẓm*, Muʿtazilites and some of their ideas have elicited hostilities.

24 *Ṣarfa* was not limited to some Muʿtazilites but can also be found among Shia and Sunnis, as Kermānī notes in *Gott ist schön*, 246–7.

25 Al-Suyūṭī, *Al-Itqān*, vol. 4, 3; al-Zarkashī, *Al-Burhān*, vol. 2, 90.

26 Yāsīn, *Dirāsat al-Bāqillānī*, 71–2.

27 Kohlberg, "Al-Rāfiḍa or al-Rawāfiḍ."

28 Al-Jāḥiẓ, *Rasāʾil*, vol. 2, 237–45.

29 Ibid., vol. 2, 219.

30 Bar-Asher, *Scripture*.

31 For the differences between pre-Buwayhid Imāmī exegesis and al-Ṭabarī's approach, see ibid., 74.

32 Ibn Wahb, *Al-Jāmiʿ*.

33 For more, see Reda, "From Where?"

34 For more on this inquisition (*miḥna*), see Nawas, "Miḥna."

35 Saleh, "Ibn Taymiyya."

36 It is noteworthy that the earlier project to demote the Qurʾan and establish the Sunna as a judge over it was met with limited success, necessitating an alternative way of framing the Sunna's preeminence. This earlier endeavour is best summerized by the principle "the Sunna is a judge over the Qurʾan and abrogates it" (*al-sunna qāḍiyya ʿalā al-Qurʾān wa-nāsikha lah*); however, it was met with some discomfort, even from staunch traditionists, who came up with the notion of the Sunna "explaining" the Qurʾan instead. Reda, "From Where?" 126–31.

37 See, for example, Brown, *Hadith*, 243–51.

38 Mir, *Coherence in the Qurʾan*, 11–16.

39 Al-Jindī, *Al-Naẓm al-Qurʾānī*, 222; al-Bāqillānī, *Iʿjāz al-Qurʾān*, 8–15.

40 Al-Bāqillānī, *Iʿjāz al-Qurʾān*, 9.

41 Ibid.

42 See Ibn al-Zubayr al-Gharnāṭī, *Al-Burhān*.

43 Al-Zarkashī, *Al-Burhān*, vol. 1, 36.

44 Ibid., vol. 1, 35–6. For occurrences of *munāsaba* in al-Rāzī's *Al-tafsīr al-kabīr*, see Lagarde, *Index du Grand Commentaire*, no. 2479.

45 Al-Zarkashī, *Al-Burhān*, vol. 1, 36.

46 The reference contains two occurrences of *naẓm* but none of *munāsaba.* Al-Suyūṭī, *Al-Itqān*, vol. 3, 323; al-Biqāʿī, *Naẓm al-durar*, vol. 1, 6–7. For occurrences of *naẓm* in al-Rāzī's *Al-tafsīr al-kabīr*, see Lagarde, *Index du Grand Commentaire*, no. 2564.

47 Mir, "Sūra as a Unity," 211–12.

48 It was in part thanks to the hermeneutics of Taqī al-Dīn Aḥmad ibn Taymiyya (d. 728/1328) that the *maʾthūr* traditions came to be regarded as quasi revelation. Saleh, "Ibn Taymiyya."

49 Al-Suyūṭī, *Tanāsuq al-durar*.

50 Al-Biqāʿī, *Naẓm al-durar*, vol. 1, 5–6.

51 Ibid., vol. 1, 4. The mention of al-Ṭabarī as the source of this tradition is noteworthy. The same tradition with al-Ṭabarī as the

source is also to be found in Ibn Taymiyya, *Muqaddima*, 115. Al-Biqāʿī does not mention Ibn Taymiyya in his introduction, but he mentions al-Zarkashī; however, even though al-Zarkashī uses this tradition, he does not connect it to al-Ṭabarī but to a different source. Al-Zarkashī, *Al-Burhān*, vol. 2, 164–70. Al-Biqāʿī does not mention al-Zarkashī's source. Perhaps al-Biqāʿī expected his biggest critics to come from the proponents of al-Ṭabarī's method of interpretation – exegesis by transmission – which is why he attributed this tradition to him. Ever thorough, al-Suyūṭī, who came after al-Biqāʿī, also mentions the same tradition, attributing it to al-Ṭabarī but indicating that there are other sources for it as well. Al-Suyūṭī, *Al-Itqān*, vol. 4, 188–93.

52 Al-Biqāʿī, *Naẓm al-durar*, vol. 1, 5.

53 Ibid.

54 Andrew Lane has critiqued the Muʿtazilite nature of al-Zamakhsharī's commentary. Lane, *Traditional Muʿtazilite*, 76–85, 107–13, 141–8.

55 Al-Biqāʿī, *Naẓm al-durar*, vol. 1, 5.

56 Ibid., vol. 1, 11. Al-Ṣaʿīdī repeats al-Bijāʾī's words as the "rule" for finding verse connections but does not attribute them to al-Bijāʾī. Al-Ṣaʿīdī, *Al-Naẓm al-fannī*, 31.

57 Al-Biqāʿī, *Naẓm al-durar*, vol. 1, 12. For more on sura names, see Neuwirth, "Sūra(s)," 166.

58 Al-Biqāʿī, *Naẓm al-durar*, vol. 1, 24.

59 *Sanām* is literally the hump of the camel, which I translate here as "pinnacle." Al-Biqāʿī equates Surat al-Baqara's relation to the Qurʾan with the hump's relation to the camel, which he describes as the highest part of the animal. Ibid., vol. 1, 563.

60 Ibid., vol. 1, 563–4.

61 J.J.G Janssen also describes ʿAbduh's religious attitude as "rationalist." He sums up ʿAbduh's method as follows: "The nucleus of Abduh's exegetical system – if the word 'system' may properly be used in this respect – is his hesitation in accepting material

from outside the Koran itself as meaningful towards its interpretation." Janssen, *Interpretation*, 20, 25.

62 For more on Sir Sayyid Ahmad Khan, see Lawrence, *Qur'an*, 143–50.

63 For more on al-Zamakhsharī, see Lane, "Working within Structure" and *Traditional Muʿtazilite*.

64 See Abu Zayd, *Reformation of Islamic Thought*, 27–9.

65 Mir, "Sūra as a Unity."

66 Mir cites Thanwī, *Bayān al-Qurʾān*; al-Farāḥī, *Majmūʿah-yi Tafāsīr-i Farāḥī*; Iṣlāḥī, *Tadabbur-ī Qurʾān*; Quṭb, *Fī ẓilāl*; and Darwaza, *Al-Tafsīr al-ḥadīth.*

67 Mir, "Sūra as a Unity."

68 Al-Ṣaʿīdī, *Al-Naẓm al-fannī.*

69 Al-Zayn, *Bayān al-naẓm*.

70 Drāz, *Al-Nabaʾ al-ʿaẓīm*.

71 For more on Dozy, see Inayatullah, "Reinhart Dozy."

72 Carlyle, *Heroes*, 59. Arthur John Arberry (d. 1969) quotes Carlyle in an abbreviated form drawn from a quotation attributed to H.A.R. Gibb. Arberry, *Holy Koran*, 36.

73 Al-Zayn mentions the "occasion of revelation material" at some length and repeats Abū Ḥāmid al-Ghazālī's (d. 505/1111) four factors that prevent understanding the Qurʾan: a preoccupation with accurate pronunciation, an attachment to a particular school of jurisprudence, some major sin or wrongdoing, and the restriction of the meaning of the Qurʾan to the *maʾthūr* traditions, considering anything else to be sinful *raʾy.* Al-Zayn, *Bayān al-naẓm*, vol. 1, 15–17.

74 See, for example, Rippin, "Literary Analysis of the Qurʾān."

75 Wansbrough, *Qurʾanic Studies*, 47.

76 Donner, *Narratives of Islamic Origins*, 29, 35–61. For more on fragmenting approaches to the Bible, see the appendix.

77 The exact date is somewhat unclear, carbon-14 testing showing it to originate between 657 and 690 CE. Hans-Caspar Graf von

Bothmer prefers a later date of 710–715 CE on the basis of some illustrations, explaining that it can take years to finish writing and illustrating a manuscript. Von Bothmer, "Neue Wege der Koranforschung," 45.

78 Aʿẓamī, *History of the Qurʾānic Text*, 315–18.

79 El-Awa, *Textual Relations*, 1.

80 See al-Ghazālī, *Al-Maḥāwir al-khamsa*.

81 Ḥanafī, "Method of Thematic Interpretation."

82 Amirpur, "Changing Approach," 337–8.

83 Al-Ṭabāṭabāʾī, *Al-Mīzān*, vol. 1, 4–14.

84 Ibid., vol. 1, 4.

85 For a brief summary of his approach, see Mir, "Sūra as a Unity," 214–15.

86 Al-Ṭabāṭabāʾī, *Al-Mīzān*, vol. 1, 43.

APPENDIX

1 Greenberg, "Ezekiel 17."

2 Hoftijzer, "Holistic or Compositional Approach?"

3 Rendtorff, "Directions in Pentateuchal Studies."

4 John L. McLaughlin, *Old Testament Abstracts*, no. OTA21-1998-JUN-717.

5 Nahkola, *Double Narratives*, 54; for the holistic approaches, see 54–72, and for the fragmenting approaches, see 6–54. I am deeply indebted to the work of Nahkola for his overview of the different approaches, which I review here.

6 More specifically, he has looked at "how Biblical criticism is indebted to conceptual models and its intellectual context." Nahkola, *Double Narratives*, 4. See also his entire introduction, ibid., 1–5.

7 Spinoza, *Tractatus Theologico-Politicus*.

8 Simon, *Histoire Critique*; Astruc, *Conjectures*.

9 See Gunkel, *Schöpfung und Chaos*.

10 Tull, "Intertextuality," 66–8.

11 Cassuto, *Documentary Hypothesis*, 255–318, originally published

in Hebrew in 1941; Sandmel, *Hebrew Scriptures*; Segal, *Pentateuch*; Whybray, *Making of the Pentateuch.*

12 Alter, *Art of Biblical Narrative*; Damrosch, *Narrative Covenant*.

13 Boullata, "Sayyid Quṭb's Literary Appreciation."

14 Al-Ghazālī, *Naḥwa tafsīr mawḍū ʿī*, back cover.

15 See, for example, Polzin, *Samuel and the Deuteronomist*, 3; Alter, *David Story*, ix.

16 Cohn, "On the Art," 14.

Bibliography

ʿAbd al-Raḥmān, ʿĀʾisha (Bint al-Shāṭiʾ). *Al-Tafsīr al-bayānī li'l-Qurʾān al-karīm*. 7th ed. Cairo: Dār al-Maʿārif, n.d.

Abdel Haleem, Muhammad. "Grammatical Shift for Rhetorical Purposes: Iltifāt and Related Features in the Qurʾān." *Bulletin of the School of Oriental and African Studies* 55, no. 3 (1992): 407–31.

– *Understanding the Qurʾan: Themes and Style.* London: Tauris, 1999.

ʿAbduh, Muḥammad. *Tafsīr al-manār*. Vol. 1. Cairo: Al-Hayʾa al-Miṣriyya al-ʿĀmma li'l-Kitāb, 1990.

Abu Zayd, Nasr Hamid. "The Dilemma of the Literary Approach to the Qurʾan." *Alif* 23 (2003): 8–47.

– with the assistance of Katajun Amirpur and Mohamad Nur Kholis Setiawan. *Reformation of Islamic Thought: A Critical-Historical Analysis*. Hague, Amsterdam: WRR and Amsterdam University Press, 2006.

ʿAlī, ʿAbdullah Yūsuf. *The Meaning of the Holy Qurʾan*. 4th ed. Brentwood, MD: Amana, 1991.

Alter, Robert. *The Art of Biblical Narrative.* New York: Basic Books, 1982.

– *The David Story.* London: W.W. Norton and Company, 1999.

Alūsī, Abū al-Faḍl Shihāb al-Dīn al-Sayyid Maḥmūd al-. *Rūḥ al-maʿānī fī tafsīr al-Qurʾān al-ʿaẓīm wa'l-sabʿ al-mathānī*. Vol. 1. Beirut: Dār Iḥyāʾ al-Turāth al-ʿArabī, n.d.

Amirpur, Katajun. "The Changing Approach to the Text: Iranian Scholars and the Quran." *Middle Eastern Studies* 41, no. 3 (2005): 337–50.

Amit, Yairah. "Progression as a Rhetorical Device in Biblical Literature." *Journal for the Study of the Old Testament* 28, no. 3 (2003): 3–32.

Andalusī, Abū Ḥayyān Muḥammad ibn Yūsuf al-Gharnāṭī al-. *Al-Baḥr al-muḥīṭ fī al-tafsīr.* 11 vols. Beirut: Dār al-Fikr, 2005.

Arberry, Arthur John. *The Holy Koran: An Introduction with Selections*. London: George Allen and Unwin, 1953.

Arjomand, Saïd Amir. "The Constitution of Medina: A Sociological Interpretation of Muhammad's Acts of Foundation of the *Umma*." *International Journal of Middle East Studies* 41, no. 4 (2009): 555-75.

Assman, Jan. *Das kulturelle Gedächtnis: Schrift, Erinnerung und politische Identität in frühen Hochkulturen.* Munich: Verlag C.H. Beck, 1992. Translated as *Cultural Memory and Early Civilization: Writing, Remembrance, and Political Imagination* (Cambridge, UK: Cambridge University Press, 2011).

– *Die Mosaische Unterscheidung oder der Preis des Monotheismus.* Munich: Carl Hanser Verlag, 2003. Translated as *The Price of Monotheism* (Stanford, CA: Stanford University Press, 2010).

– *Moses der Ägypter: Entzifferung einer Gedächtnisspur.* Munich: Fischer Taschenbuch, 1998. Translated as *Moses the Egyptian: The Memory of Egypt in Western Monotheism* (Cambridge, MA: Harvard University Press, 1997.

– *Religion und kulturelles Gedächtnis.* Munich: Verlag C.H. Beck, 2000. Translated as *Religion and Cultural Memory: Ten Studies* (Stanford, CA: Stanford University Press, 2006).

Astruc, Jean. *Conjectures sur les Mémoires originaux dont il paroit que Moyse s'est servi pour composer le Livre de la Genèse.* Brussels: Fricx, 1753.

Audebert, C.F. *Al-Ḫaṭṭābī et l'inimitabilité du Coran: Traduction et introduction au Bayān I'jāz al-Qur'ān.* Damascus: Institut Français de Damas, 1982.

Ayoub, Mahmoud. "The Prayer of Islam." In *The Koran: Critical Concepts in Islamic Studies: Translation and Exegesis*, vol. 4, ed. Colin Turner, 14–24. London: RoutledgeCurzon, 2004.

A'ẓamī, Muḥammad Muṣṭafā al-. *The History of the Qur'ānic Text.* Leicester, UK: Islamic Academy, 2003.

Badran, Margot. *Feminism in Islam: Secular and Religious Convergences.* London: Oneworld, 2009.

Bakhtiar, Laleh. *Moral Healing through the Most Beautiful Names: The Practice of Spiritual Chivalry.* Chicago: Institute of Traditional Psychoethics and Guidance, 1994.

– *The Sublime Qur'an: Original Arabic and English Translation.* 2 vols. [Chicago]: Library of Islam, 2010.

Bakhtin, Mikhail. *The Dialogic Imagination: Four Essays.* Ed. Michael Holquist. Transl. Caryl Emerson and Michael Holquist. Austin: University of Texas Press, 1981.

Bannister, Andrew G. *An Oral-Formulaic Study of the Qur'an.* Lanham, MD: Lexington Books, 2014.

Bāqillānī, Abū Bakr Muḥammad ibn al-Ṭayyib al-. *I'jāz al-Qur'ān.* Ed. Aḥmad Saqr. Cairo: Dār al-Ma'ārif, 1963.

Bar-Asher, Meir. *Scripture and Exegesis in Early Imāmī Shiism.* Leiden: Brill, 1999.

Barazangi, Nimat Hafez. *Woman's Identity and the Qur'an: A New Reading.* Gainsville: University Press of Florida, 2004.

Barlas, Asma. *"Believing Women" in Islam: Unreading Patriarchal Interpretations of the Qur'an.* Austin: University of Texas Press, 2002.

Barth, Karl. *Das Christliche Verständnis der Offernbarung: Eine Vorlesung.* Munich: Chr. Kaiser Verlag, 1948.

– *On Religion: The Revelation of God as the Sublimation of Religion.* Trans. Garrett Green. London: T.&T. Clark, 2006.

Barthes, Roland. "Death of the Author." 1967. Reprinted in *Modern Literary Theory*, 4th ed., ed. Philip Rice and Patricia Waugh, 185–9. London: Arnold, 2001.

Bell, Richard. *Introduction to the Qur'ān.* Edinburgh: Edinburgh University Press, 1953.

Bentley, David. *The 99 Beautiful Names of God for All the People of the Book.* Pasadena, CA: William Carey Library, 1999.

Biqāʿī, Burhān al-Dīn Abū al-Ḥasan Ibrāhīm ibn ʿUmar, al-. *Naẓm al-durar fī tanāsub al-āyāt wa'l-suwar*. Ed. ʿAbd al-Razzāq Ghālib al-Mahdī. Vol. 1. 3rd ed. Beirut: Dār al-Kutub al-ʿIlmiyya, 2006.

Bothmer, Hans-Caspar Graf von. "Neue Wege der Koranforschung." *Universität des Saarlandes Magazinforschung* 1 (1999): 33–46.

Boullata, Issa J. "Sayyid Quṭb's Literary Appreciation of the Qurʾān." In *Literary Structures of Religious Meaning in the Qurʾān*, ed. Issa J. Boullata, 354–71. Richmond, UK: Curzon, 2000.

Brian, Éric, Marie Jaisson, S. Romi Mukherjee. "Introduction: Social Memory and Hypermodernity." *International Social Science Journal* 62, nos 203–4 (2011): 7–18.

Brogan, T.V.F. "Concatenation." In *The New Princeton Encyclopedia of Poetry and Poetics*, ed. Alex Preminger and T.V.F. Brogan, 231. Princeton, NJ: Princeton University Press, 1993.

Brogan, T.V.F., and Albert W. Halsall. "Chiasmus." In *The New Princeton Encyclopedia of Poetry and Poetics*, ed. Alex Preminger and T.V.F. Brogan, 183–4. Princeton, NJ: Princeton University Press, 1993.

Brown, Brian Arthur, ed. *Three Testaments: Torah, Gospel, and Quran*. Lanham, MD: Rowman and Littlefield, 2012.

Brown, Jonathan. *Hadith: Muhammad's Legacy in the Medieval and Modern World.* Oxford: Oneworld, 2009.

Buber, Martin. "Leitwortstil in der Erzählung des Pentateuchs." In *Die Schrift und ihre Verdeutschung*, 211–38. Berlin: Schocken, 1936.

Carlyle, Thomas. *Heroes, Hero-Worship and the Heroic in History.* London: Chapman and Hall, 1899.

Cassuto, Umberto. *The Documentary Hypothesis and the Composition of the Pentateuch*. Trans. Israel Abrahams. Jerusalem: Magnes Press, Hebrew University, 1961.

Cohn, Robert L. "On the Art of Biblical Narrative." *Biblical Research* 31 (1986): 13–18.

Cuypers, Michel. *The Banquet: A Reading of the Fifth Sura of the Qurʾan.* Miami, FL: Convivium, 2009.

– *The Composition of the Qur'an: Rhetorical Analysis.* Trans. Jerry Ryan. London: Bloomsbury Academic, 2015.

Dahood, Mitchell. *Psalms I.* 3 vols. Garden City, NY: Anchor Bible, 1966.

Damrosch, David. *The Narrative Covenant: Transformation of Genre in the Growth of Biblical Literature.* San Francisco, CA: Harper and Row, 1987.

Darwaza, Muḥammad ʿIzzat. *Al-Tafsīr al-ḥadīth.* 12 vols. Cairo: Dār Iḥyāʾ al-Kutub al-ʿArabiyya, 1962-64.

De Blois, François. "Nasrānī (Ναζωραιος) and Hanīf (εθνικός): Studies on the Religious Vocabulary of Christianity and of Islam." *Bulletin of the School of Oriental and African Studies* 65, no. 1 (2002): 1–30.

Dhahabī, Muḥammad Ḥusayn al-. *Al-Tafsīr wa'l-mufassirūn.* Vol. 1. 8th ed. Cairo: Maktabat Wahba, 2003.

Dhahabī, Muḥammad ibn Aḥmad ibn ʿUthmān al-. *Siyar aʿlām al-nubalāʾ.* Vol. 15. Ed. Shuʿayb al-Arnaʾūṭ and Ḥusayn al-Asad. Beirut: Muʾassasat al-Risāla, 2001.

Diamond, A.R. Pete. "Interlocutions: The Poetics of Voice in the Figuration of YHWH and His Oracular Agent Jeremiah." *Interpretation: A Journal of Bible and Theology* 62, no. 1 (2008): 48–65.

Donner, Fred. *Narratives of Islamic Origins: The Beginnings of Islamic Historical Writing.* New Jersey: Darwin, 1998.

Drāz, Muḥammad ʿAbd Allāh. *Al-Nabaʾ al-ʿaẓīm: Naẓarāt jadīda fī al-Qurʾān, taqdīm ʿAbd al-ʿAzīz al-Maṭʿanī.* Cairo: Dār al-Qalam li'l-nashr wa'l-tawzīʿ, 2008.

Duderija, Adis, ed. *The Sunna and Its Status in Islamic Law: The Search for a Sound Hadith.* New York: Palgrave Macmillan, 2015.

Dundes, Alan. *Fables of the Ancients? Folklore in the Qur'an.* Lanham, MD: Rowman and Littlefield, 2003.

Dyrness, William A. *Themes of the Old Testament.* Downers Grove, IL: InterVarsity, 1979.

El-Awa, Salwa. "Repetition in the Qurʾān: A Relevance Based

Explanation of the Phenomenon." *Islamic Studies* 42, no. 4 (2003): 577–93.
– *Textual Relations in the Qur'ān: Relevance, Coherence and Structure*. London: Routledge, 2006.
El-Desouky, Ayman. "Between Hermeneutic Provenance and Textuality: The Qur'an and the Question of Method in Approaches to World Literature." *Journal of Qur'anic Studies* 16, no. 3 (2014): 11–38.
– "Naẓm, iʿjāz, Discontinuous Kerygma: Approaching Qur'anic Voice on the Other Side of the Poetic." *Journal of Qur'anic Studies* 15, no. 2 (2013): 1–21.
Esack, Farid. *The Qur'an: A User's Guide.* Oxford: Oneworld, 2005.
Eslinger, Lyle. "Viewpoints and Points of View in 1 Samuel 8–12." *Journal for the Study of the Old Testament* 26 (1983): 61–76.
Evans, Robert O., T.V.F. Brogan, and Albert W. Halsall. "Epanalepsis." In *The New Princeton Encyclopedia of Poetry and Poetics*, ed. Alex Preminger and T.V.F. Brogan, 361–2. Princeton, NJ: Princeton University Press, 1993.
Farāḥī, Ḥamīd al-Dīn al-. *Majmūʿah-yi Tafāsīr-i Farāḥī*. Trans. Amīn Aḥsan Iṣlāḥī. Lahore: Anjuman-i Khuddāmu'lqur'ān, 1973.
Farrin, Raymond K. *Structure and Qur'anic Interpretation: A Study of Symmetry and Coherence in Islam's Holy Text.* Ashland, OR: White Cloud, 2014.
– *"Surat al-Baqara*: A Structural Analysis." *Muslim World* 100, no. 1 (2010): 17–32.
Fogle, Stefan F., and T.V.F. Brogan. "Envelope." In *The New Princeton Encyclopedia of Poetry and Poetics*, ed. Alex Preminger and T.V.F. Brogan, 360–1. Princeton, NJ: Princeton University Press, 1993.
Ford, David F., and C.C. Pecknold, eds. *The Promise of Scriptural Reasoning.* Oxford: Blackwell, 2008.
Friedman, Albert B., Edward Doughtie, and T.V.F. Brogan. "Incremental Repetition." In *The New Princeton Encyclopedia of Poetry and Poetics*, ed. Alex Preminger and T.V.F. Brogan, 581–2. Princeton, NJ: Princeton University Press, 1993.

Frye, Northrop. *Northrop Frye on Religion*. Vol. 4. Ed. Alvin A. Lee and Jean O'Grady. Toronto: University of Toronto Press, 2000.

Gade, Anna M. "Taste, Talent and the Problem of Internalization: A Qur'anic Study in Religious Musicality from Southeast Asia." *History of Religions* 41, no. 4 (2002): 328–68.

Geiger, Abraham. "Was hat Muhammad aus dem Judenthume aufgenommen?" PhD diss., Königlich-Preussischen Rhein-Universität, Bonn, 1833.

Geissinger, Aisha. *Gender and Muslim Constructions of Exegetical Authority: A Rereading of the Classical Genre of Qur'an Commentary*. Leiden: Brill, 2015.

Ghazālī, Muḥammad al-. *Al-Maḥāwir al-khamsa li'l-Qur'ān al-karīm.* Cairo: Dār al-Ṣaḥwa, 1989.

– *Naḥwa tafsīr mawḍūʿī li-suwar al-Qur'ān al-karīm.* Cairo: Dār al-Shurūq, 1992.

Gilliot, Claude, and Pierre Larcher. "Language and Style of the Qur'ān." In *Encyclopaedia of the Qur'an*, vol. 3, ed. Jane Dammen McAuliffe, 109–35. Leiden: Brill Academic, 2006.

Green, Barbara. *How Are the Mighty Fallen? A Dialogical Study of King Saul in 1 Samuel*. London: Sheffield Academic, 2003.

– *King Saul's Asking*. Collegeville, MN: Liturgical Press, 2003.

– *Mikhail Bakhtin and Biblical Scholarship: An Introduction.* Atlanta: Society of Biblical Literature, 2000.

Greenberg, Moshe. "Ezekiel 17: A Holistic Interpretation." *Journal of the American Oriental Society* 103, no. 1 (1983): 149–54.

Grossberg, Daniel. "The Disparate Elements of the Inclusio in Psalms." *Hebrew Annual Review* 6 (1982): 97–104.

Guillaume, Alfred. *The Life of Muhammad: A Translation of Ishāq's Sīrat Rasūl Allāh with Introduction and Notes by A. Guillaume.* London: Oxford University Press, 1955.

Gunkel, Hermann. *Schöpfung und Chaos in Urzeit und Endzeit.* Göttingen: Vandenhoeck und Ruprecht, 1895.

Günther, Sebastian. "Muḥammad, the Illiterate Prophet: An Islamic

Creed in the Qurʾan and Qurʾanic Exegesis." *Journal of Qurʾanic Studies* 4, no. 1 (2002): 1–26.

– "O People of the Scripture! Come to a Word Common to You and Us (Q. 3:64): The Ten Commandments and the Qurʾan." *Journal of Qurʾanic Studies* 9, no. 1 (2007): 28–58.

Ḥaddād, Yūsuf Durra. *Naẓm al-Qurʾān wa'l-kitāb.* Beirut: n.p., [1960].

Halkin, A.S. "Ḥashwiyya." *Journal of the American Oriental Society* 54, no. 1 (1934): 1–28.

Hallaq, Wael. *The Origins and Evolution of Islamic Law.* Cambridge, UK: Cambridge University Press, 2005.

Ḥanafī, Ḥasan. "Method of Thematic Interpretation of the Qurʾan." In *The Qurʾan as Text*, ed. Stefan Wild, 195–211. Leiden: Brill, 1996.

Hidayatullah, Aysha. *Feminist Edges of the Qurʾan.* Oxford: Oxford University Press, 2014.

Hoftijzer, Jacob. "Holistic or Compositional Approach? Linguistic Remarks to the Problem." In *Synchronic or Diachronic? A Debate on Method in Old Testament Exegesis*, ed. Johannes C. de Moor, 98–114. Leiden: Brill, 1995.

Holquist, Michael. "Bakhtin and Beautiful Science: The Paradox of Cultural Relativity Revisited." In *Dialogue and Critical Discourse: Language, Culture, Critical Theory*, ed. M. Macovski, 215–36. New York: Oxfrod University Press, 1997.

Ibn Abī Yaʿlā, al-Qāḍī ibn al-Ḥusayn Muḥammad. *Ṭabaqāt al-Ḥanābila*. Vol. 1. Ed. Muḥammad Ḥāmid al-Fiqī. Cairo: Maṭbaʿat al-Sunna al-Muḥammadiyya, 1952.

Ibn al-Zubayr al-Gharnāṭī, Abū Jaʿfar Aḥmad ibn Ibrāhīm. *Al-Burhān fī tartīb suwar al-Qurʾān*. Ed. Muḥammad Shaʿbānī. Morocco: Wazārat al-Awqāf wa'l-Shuʾūn al-Islāmiyya, 1990.

Ibn Hishām, ʿAbd al-Malik. *Al-Sīra al-nabawiyya.* Vol. 2. Ed. Ṣidqī Jamīl al-ʿAṭṭār. Beirut: Dār al-Fikr, 1995.

Ibn Manẓūr al-Ifrīqī al-Miṣrī, Abū al-Faḍl Jamāl al-Dīn Muḥammad ibn Makram. *Lisān al-ʿarab*. Vol. 7. 3rd ed. Beirut: Dār Ṣādir, 1994.

Ibn Taymiyya, Ṭaqī al-Dīn Aḥmad ibn ʿAbd al-Ḥalīm. *Muqaddima fī uṣūl al-tafsīr.* Cairo: Maktabat al-Turāth al-Islāmī, 1988.

Ibn Wahb, ʿAbd Allāh. *Al-Jāmiʿ: Tafsīr al-Qurʾān*. 3 vols. Ed. Miklos Muranyi. Beirut: Dār al-Gharb al-Islāmī, 2003.

Ibrahim, M. Zakyi. "Oaths in the Qurʾan: Bint al-Shatʾ's Literary Contribution." *Islamic Studies* 48, no. 4 (2009): 475–98.

Inayatullah. "Reinhart Dozy, 1820–1883." *Journal of the Pakistan Historical Society* 8, no. 1 (1960): 19–24.

Iṣlāḥī, Amīn Aḥsan. *Tadabbur-ī Qurʾān*. 9 vols. Lahore: Faran Foundation, 1967–80.

Jāḥiẓ, Abū ʿUthmān ʿAmr ibn Baḥr al-, and Saʿd ʿAbd al-ʿAẓīm Muḥammad. *Naẓm al-Qurʾān: Jamʿ wa-tawthīq wa-dirāsa*. Cairo: Maktabat al-Zahrāʾ, 1995.

– *Rasāʾil al-Jāḥiẓ*. Vol. 2. Ed. ʿAbd al-Salām Muḥammad Hārūn. Beirut: Dār al-Kutub al-ʿIlmiyya, 2000.

Jajdelska, Elspeth. *Silent Reading and the Birth of the Narrator*. Toronto: University of Toronto Press, 2007.

Janssen, J.J.G. *The Interpretation of the Qurʾān in Modern Egypt*. Leiden: Brill, 1974.

Jindī, Darwīsh al-. *Al-Naẓm al-Qurʾānī fī kashshāf al-Zamakhsharī*. Cairo: Dār Nahḍat Miṣr, 1969.

– *Naẓariyyat ʿAbd al-Qāhir fī al-naẓm*. Al-Fajjāla, Cairo: Maktabat Nahḍat Miṣr, 1960.

Johns, A.H. "In Search of Common Ground: The Qurʾān as Literature?" *Islam and Christian-Muslim Relations* 4, no. 2 (1993): 191–209.

Jomier, Jaques. *The Great Themes of the Qurʾan*. Trans. Zoe Herzov. London: SCM Press, 1997.

Jung, Carl G. *The Collected Works of C.G. Jung*. Vol. 7. New York: Pantheon Books, 1953.

Jurjānī, ʿAbd al-Qāhir ibn ʿAbd al-Raḥmān ibn Muḥammad al-. *Asrār al-balāgha fī ʿilm al-bayān*. Ed. al-Sayyid Muḥammad Rashīd Riḍā. Cairo: Maṭbaʿat al-Manār, 1925.

– *Kitāb dalāʾil al-iʿjāz*. Ed. Abū Fihr Maḥmūd Muḥammad Shākir. Cairo: Maktabat al-Khānjī, [1984].

Kadi (al-Qāḍī), Wadad, and Mustansir Mir. "Literature and the

Qurʾān." In *Encyclopaedia of the Qurʾan*, vol. 3, ed. Jane Dammen McAuliffe, 205–27. Leiden: Brill Academic, 2006.

Kandil, Lamia. "Die Schwure in den Mekkanischen Suren." In *The Qurʾan as Text*, ed. Stefan Wild, 41–57. Leiden: Brill, 1996.

Kermānī, Navid. *Gott ist schön: Das ästhetische Erleben des Korans.* Munich: Verlag C.H. Beck, 1999.

Kessler, Martin. "Inclusio in the Hebrew Bible." In *Semitics*, vol. 6, ed. H.J. Dreyer and J.J. Glück, 44–9. Pretoria: University of South Africa, 1978.

Khaṭṭābī, Abū Sulaymān Ḥamd ibn Muḥammad al-. *Bayān fī iʿjāz al-Qurʾān* in *Thalāth rasāʾil fī iʿjāz al-Qurʾān.* Ed. Muḥammad Khalafallāh Aḥmad. Cairo: Dār al-Maʿārif, 1968.

Khūlī, Amīn al-. *Manāhij tajdīd fī al-naḥw wa'l-balāgha wa'l-tafsīr wa'l-adab.* Cairo: Al-Hayʾa al-Miṣriyya al-ʿĀmma li'l-Kitāb, 1995.

Kim, Ee Kon. "Who Is Yahweh? Based on a Contextual Reading of Exodus 3:14." *Asia Journal of Theology* 3, no. 1 (1989): 108–17.

Klar, Marianna. "Through the Lens of the Adam Narrative: A Reconsideration of *Sūrat al-Baqara*." *Journal of Qurʾanic Studies* 17, no. 2 (2015): 24–46.

Kohlberg, E. "Al-Rāfiḍa or al-Rawāfiḍ." In *Encyclopaedia of Islam*, vol. 8, 2nd ed., ed. P. Bearman, Th. Bianquis, C.E. Bosworth, E. van Donzel, and W.P. Heinrichs, 386. Leiden: Brill, 1960.

Lagarde, Michel. *Index du Grand Commentaire de Faẖr al-Dīn al-Rāzī.* Leiden: Brill, 1996.

Lane, Andrew. *A Traditional Muʿtazilite Qurʾān Commentary: The Kashshāf of Jār Allāh al-Zamakhsharī (d. 538/1144).* Brill: Leiden, 2006.

– "Working within Structure: Al-Zamakhsharī (d. 1144): A Late Muʿtazilite Qurʾan Commentator at Work." In *Ideas, Images, and Methods of Portrayal: Insights into Classical Arabic Literature and Islam*, ed. Sebastian Günther, 347–74. Leiden: Brill, 2005.

Laney, J. Carl. "God's Self-Revelation in Exodus 34:6–8." *Bibliotheca Sacra* 158, no. 629 (2001): 36–51.

Lawrence, Bruce. *The Qurʾan: A Biography.* Toronto: Douglas and McIntyre, 2006.

Lawson, Todd. "Duality, Opposition and Typology in the Qur'an: The Apocalyptic Substrate." *Journal of Qur'anic Studies* 10, no. 2 (2008): 23–49.

Leemhuis, Fred. "From Palm Leaves to the Internet." In *The Cambridge Companion to the Qur'an*, ed. Jane Dammen McAuliffe, 145–61. Cambridge, UK: Cambridge University Press, 2006.

Madigan, Daniel. "Themes and Topics." In *The Cambridge Companion to the Qur'an*, ed. Jane Dammen McAuliffe, 79–95. Cambridge, UK: Cambridge University Press, 2006.

Mahmood (Zafer), Hamza. "The Qur'ān's Communal Ideology: Rhetoric and Representation in Scripture and Early Historiography." PhD diss., Cornell University, 2014.

Martin, Richard C. "Inimitability." In *Encyclopaedia of the Qur'an*, vol. 2, ed. Jane Dammen McAuliffe, 526–36. Leiden: Brill Academic, 2006.

Mattson, Ingrid. *The Story of the Qur'an: Its History and Place in Muslim Life.* Malden, MA: Blackwell, 2008.

Mills, Mary E. *Images of God in the Old Testament.* London: Cassell, 1998.

Mir, Mustansir. *Coherence in the Qur'an: A Study of Islahi's Concept of Nazm in Tadabbur-i Qur'an.* Indianapolis, IN: American Trust, 1986.

– "The Qur'ān as Literature." *Religion and Literature* 20, no. 1 (1988): 49–64.

– "The Sūra as a Unity: A Twentieth Century Development in Qur'ān Exegesis." In *Approaches to the Qur'ān*, ed. G.R. Hawting and Abdul-Kader A. Shareef, 211–24. London: Routledge, 1993.

Moulton, Richard G. *The Literary Study of the Bible: An Account of the Leading Forms of Literature Represented in the Sacred Writings, Intended for English Readers.* London: Isbister, 1896.

Mubārakfūrī, Ṣafī al-Raḥmān. *Al-Miṣbāḥ al-munīr fī tahdhīb tafsīr Ibn Kathīr.* Riyadh: Darussalam, 2000.

– *Tafsīr Ibn Kathīr.* Riyadh: Darussalam, 2000.

Müller, David Heinrich. *Die Propheten in ihrer uhrsprünglichen Form.* Vienna: Alfred Hölder, 1896.

Murād, Walīd Muḥammad. *Naẓariyyat al-naẓm wa-qīmatuhā al-ʿilmiyya fī al-dirāsāt al-lughawiyya ʿinda ʿAbd al-Qāhir al-Jurjānī.* Damascus: Dār al-Fikr, 1983.

Muslim ibn al-Ḥajjāj, Abū al-Ḥusayn. *Ṣaḥīḥ Muslim.* Beirut: Dār al-Fikr, 1999.

Nahkola, Aulikki. *Double Narratives in the Old Testament: The Foundations of Method in Biblical Criticism.* Ed. Otto Kaiser. Berlin: Walter de Gruyter, 2001.

Nawas, John A. "The Miḥna of 218 A.H./833 A.D. Revisited: An Empirical Study." *Journal of the American Oriental Society* 116, no. 4 (1996): 698–708.

Nelson, Kristina. *The Art of Reciting the Qurʾan.* Austin: University of Texas Press, 1985.

Neuwirth, Angelika. "Images and Metaphors in the Introductory Sections of the Makkan *Sūras*." In *Approaches to the Qurʾān*, ed. G.R. Hawting and Abdul-Kader A. Shareef, 3–36. London: Routledge, 1993.

– "'Oral Scriptures' in Contact: The Qurʾānic Story of the Golden Calf and Its Biblical Subtext between Narrative, Cult and Inter-communal Debate." In *Scripture, Poetry and the Making of a Community: Reading the Qurʾan as a Literary Text*, 306–27. Oxford: Oxford University Press and the Institute of Ismaili Studies, 2014.

– "Referentiality and Textuality in *Sūrat al-Ḥidjr*: Some Observations on the Qurʾānic 'Canonical Process' and the Emergence of a Community." In *Literary Structures of Religious Meaning in the Qurʾān*, ed. Issa J. Boullata, 143–72. Richmond, UK: Curzon, 2000.

– "Some Remarks on the Special Linguistic and Literary Character of the Qurʾān." Trans. Gwendolin Goldbloom. 1977. Reprinted in *The Qurʾan: Style and Contents*, ed. Andrew Rippin, 253–7. Hampshire, UK: Ashgate, 2001.

– "Structural, Linguistic and Literary Features." In *The Cambridge Companion to the Qurʾan*, ed. Jane Dammen McAuliffe, 97–113. Cambridge, UK: Cambridge University Press, 2006.

– *Studien zur Komposition der mekkanischen Suren.* Berlin: Walter de Gruyter, 1981.

– "Sūra(s)." In *Encyclopaedia of the Qurʾan*, vol. 5, ed. Jane Dammen McAuliffe, 166–77. Leiden: Brill Academic, 2006.

– "*Sūrat al-Fātiḥa* (Q. 1): Opening of the Textual Corpus of the Qurʾan or Introit of the Prayer Service?" In *Scripture, Poetry and the Making of a Community: Reading the Qurʾan as a Literary Text*, 164–83. Oxford: Oxford University Press and the Institute of Ismaili Studies, 2014.

– "Vom Rezitationstext über die Liturgie zum Kanon: Zur Entstehung und Wiederauflosung der Surenkomposition im Verlauf der Entwicklung eines Islamischen Kultus." In *The Qurʾan as Text*, ed. Stefan Wild, 69–105. Leiden: Brill, 1996.

Nicholson, Reynold Alleyne. *A Literary History of the Arabs.* New York: Charles Scribner's Sons, 1907.

Nöldeke, Theodor. *Geschichte des Qorans.* 3 vols. 2nd ed. Leipzig: Dieterich, 1909–38.

Olsen, Stein Haugum. "What Is Poetics?" *Philosophical Quarterly* 26, no. 105 (1976): 338–51.

Pannenberg, Wolfhart, ed. *Offenbarung als Geschichte*. 2nd ed. Göttingen: Vandenhoeck und Ruprecht, 1963.

Parunak, H. Van Dyke. "Oral Typesetting: Some Uses of Biblical Structure." *Biblica* 62, no. 2 (1981): 153–68.

– "Transitional Techniques in the Bible." *Journal of Biblical Literature* 102, no. 4 (1983): 525–48.

Peters, Heiner. "Epanalēpsis." In *Encyclopedia of Rhetoric*, ed. Thomas O. Sloane, 250–1. Oxford: Oxford University Press, 2006.

Peterson, Rick. "Social Memory and Ritual Performance." *Journal of Social Archaeology* 13, no. 2 (2013): 266–83.

Polzin, Robert. *Samuel and the Deuteronomist: A Literary Study of the Deuteronomistic History: Part Two, 1 Samuel*. Indianapolis: Indiana University Press, 1989.

Poole, Ross. "Memory, Responsibility, and Identity." *Social Research* 75, no. 1 (2008): 263–86.

Pope, Marvin H. *Song of Songs: A New Translation with Introduction and Commentary.* Garden City, NY: Doubleday, 1977.

Pregill, Michael. "The Hebrew Bible and the Quran: The Problem of the Jewish 'Influence' on Islam." *Religion Compass* 1, no. 6 (2007): 643–59.

Pulitano, Elvira. "Writing in the Oral Tradition: Reflections of the Indigenous Literatures of Australia, New Zealand and North America." In *Teaching World Literature*, ed. David Damrosch, 216–31. New York: Modern Language Association of America, 2009.

Quash, Ben. "Heavenly Semantics: Some Literary-Critical Approaches to Scriptural Reasoning." *Modern Theology* 22, no. 3 (2006): 403–20.

Quṭb, Sayyid. *Fī ẓilāl al-Qurʾān.* 6 vols. 25th ed. Cairo: Dār al-Shurūq, 1972.

Rahman, Fazlur. *Major Themes of the Qurʾan.* 2nd ed. Minneapolis, MN: Bibliotheca Islamica, 1994.

Rājiḥ, Muḥammad Kurayyim, ed. *Mukhtaṣar tafsīr Ibn Kathīr.* Beirut: Dār al-Maʿrifa, 1983.

Rasmussen, Anne K. "The Qurʾan in Indonesian Daily Life: The Public Project of Musical Oratory." *Ethnomusicology* 45, no. 1 (2001): 30–57.

– *Women, the Recited Qurʾan, and Islamic Music in Indonesia.* Berkeley: University of California Press, 2010.

Rāzī, Fakhr al-Dīn al-. *Al-Tafsīr al-kabīr.* Vol. 2. Cairo: Al-Maṭbaʿa al-Bahiyya al-Miṣriyya, n.d.

Reda, Nevin. "Al-Niswiyya al-islāmiyya wa-uṣūl al-fiqh: Ruʾya muʿāṣira li'l-ijmāʿ min khilāl masʾalat taʿaddud al-zawjāt." Paper presented at the conference "Women's Issues: Toward a Contemporary *Ijtihad* (Islamic Reasoning)," Bibliotheca Alexandrina, Alexandria, 10 March 2014.

– "From the Canadian Sharia Debates to the Arab World: Developing a Quran-Based Theology of Democracy." In *Religion and Democracy: Islam and Representation*, ed. Ingrid Mattson, Paul Nesbitt-Larking, and Nawaz Tahir, 78–100. Newcastle upon Tyne, UK: Cambridge Scholars, 2015.

– "From Where Do We Derive 'God's Law'? The Case of Women's

Political Leadership: A Modern Expression of an Ancient Debate." In *Feminism and Islamic Perspectives: New Horizons of Knowledge and Reform*, ed. Omaima Abou Bakr, 119–35. Cairo: Women and Memory Forum, 2013.

– "The 'Good' Muslim, 'Bad' Muslim Puzzle? The Assertion of Muslim Women's Islamic Identity in the Sharia Debates in Canada." In *Debating Sharia: Islam, Gender Politics, and Family Law Arbitration*, ed. Anna C. Korteweg and Jennifer Selby, 231–56. Toronto: University of Toronto Press, 2012.

– "Holistic Approaches to the Qur'an: A Historical Background." *Religion Compass* 4, no. 8 (2010): 495–506.

– "The Qur'ānic Ṭālūt and the Rise of the Ancient Israelite Monarchy: An Intertextual Reading." *American Journal of Islamic Social Sciences* 25, no. 3 (2008): 31–51.

Rendsburg, Gary A. "Literary Devices in the Story of the Shipwrecked Sailor." *Journal of the American Oriental Society* 120, no. 1 (2000): 13–23.

Rendtorff, Rolf. "Directions in Pentateuchal Studies." *Currents in Research: Biblical Studies* 5 (1997): 43–65.

Ricoeur, Paul. *Essays on Biblical Interpretation.* Philadelphia: Fortress, 1980.

– *Hermeneutics and the Human Sciences*. Ed. and trans. John B. Thompson. Cambridge, UK: Cambridge University Press, 1981.

Rippin, Andrew. "Literary Analysis of the Qur'ān, Tafsīr and Sīra: The Methodologies of John Wansbrough." In *The Qur'ān and Its Interpretative Tradition*, 151–63. Aldershot, UK: Ashgate, 2001.

– "The Qur'ān as Literature: Perils, Pitfalls and Prospects." In *The Qur'ān and Its Interpretative Tradition*, 38–47. Aldershot, UK: Ashgate, 2001.

Robbins, Vernon K. *Exploring the Texture of Texts: A Guide to Socio-rhetorical Interpretation.* Valley Forge, PA: Trinity Press International, 1996.

Robbins, Vernon K., and Gordon D. Newby. "The Relation of the

Qurʾān and the Bible." In *Bible and Qurʾān: Essays in Scriptural Intertextuality*, ed. John Reeves, 23–42. Atlanta: Society of Biblical Literature, 2003.

Robinson, Neal. *Discovering the Qurʾan: A Contemporary Approach to a Veiled Text.* London: SCM Press, 1996.

Rowling, J.K. *Harry Potter and the Order of the Phoenix.* London: Bloomsbury, 2003.

Ṣaʿīdī, ʿAbd al-Mutaʿāl. *Al-Naẓm al-fannī fī al-Qurʾān.* Cairo: Maktabat al-Ādāb, n.d.

Ṣābūnī, Muḥammad ʿAlī al-, ed. *Mukhtaṣar tafsīr Ibn Kathīr.* Beirut: Dār al-Qurʾān al-Karīm, c. 1973.

Sadeghi, Behnam, and Mohsen Goudarzi. "Ṣanʿāʾ 1 and the Origins of the Qurʾān." *Der Islam* 87, no. 1 (2012): 1–36.

Saleh, Walid. *The Formation of the Classical Tafsir Tradition: The Qurʾan Commentary of al-Thaʿlabi (d. 427/1035)*. Leiden: Brill, 2004.

– "Ibn Taymiyya and the Rise of Radical Hermeneutics: An Analysis of *An Introduction to the Foundations of Qurʾānic Exegesis*." In *Ibn Taymiyya and His Times*, ed. Yossef Rapoport and Shahab Ahmed, 123–62. Karachi: Oxford University Press, 2010.

– *In Defense of the Bible: A Critical Edition and an Introduction to al-Biqaʿi's Bible Treatise*. Leiden: Brill, 2008.

– "A Muslim Hebraist: Al-Biqaʿi's (d. 885/1480) Bible Treatise and His Defense of Using the Bible to Interpret the Qurʾan." *Speculum* 83, no. 3 (2008): 629–54.

– "'Sublime in Its Style, Exquisite in Its Tenderness': The Hebrew Bible Quotations in al-Biqaʿi's Qurʾan Commentary." In *Adaptations and Innovations: Studies on the Interaction between Jewish and Islamic Thought and Literature from the Early Middle Ages to the Late Twentieth Century*, ed. Tzvi Langermann and Josef Stern, 331–48. Paris and Louvain: Peeters, 2007.

Sandmel, Samuel. *The Hebrew Scriptures.* New York: Oxford University Press, 1978.

Segal, Moses Hirsch. *The Pentateuch: Its Composition and Its Author-*

ship, and Other Biblical Studies. Jerusalem: Magnes Press, Hebrew University, 1967.

Sells, Michael. "A Literary Approach to the Hymnic Sūras of the Qurʾan: Spirit, Gender and Aural Intertextuality." In *Literary Structures of Religious Meaning in the Qurʾan*, ed. Issa J. Boullata, 3–25. Richmond, UK: Curzon, 2000.

Shahid, Irfan. "The Sūra of the Poets Revisited." *Journal of Arabic Literature* 39, no. 3 (2008): 398–423.

Sharqāwī, Nadya al- (Nadia Charkaoui). "Usus al-ʿilāqa bayna al-marʾa wa'l-rajul min manẓūr qurʾānī (The Basis for the Relationship between Women and Men from a Qurʾanic Perspective)." Paper presented at the conference "Women's Issues: Toward a Contemporary *Ijtihad* (Islamic Reasoning)," Bibliotheca Alexandrina, Alexandria, 10 March 2014.

Sherif, Faruq. *A Guide to the Contents of the Qurʾan*. Reading, UK: Garnet, 1995.

Simon, Richard. *Histoire Critique du Vieux Testament.* Rotterdam: Reinier Leers, 1685.

Smith, David E. "The Structure of Surat al-Baqarah." *Muslim World* 91, nos 1–2 (2001): 121–36.

Smith, James K.A. "How Religious Practices Matter: Peter Ochs' 'Alternative Nurturance' of Philosophy of Religion." *Modern Theology* 24, no. 3 (2008): 469–78.

Soroush, Abdol Karim. *Qabz o bast-e teutik-e shariat – nazariye-ye takamol-e marefat-e dini.* 3rd ed. Tehran: Sarat, 1994.

Spinoza, Baruch. *Tractatus Theologico-Politicus.* Hamburg: Apud Henricum Künraht, 1670.

Sternberg, Meir. *The Poetics of Biblical Narrative.* Bloomington: Indiana University Press, 1985.

Stewart, Devin J. "Sajʿ in the Qurʾān: Prosody and Structure." *Journal of Arabic Literature* 21, no. 2 (1990): 101–39.

Suyūṭī, Jalāl al-Dīn ʿAbd al-Raḥmān al-. *Al-Itqān fī ʿulūm al-Qurʾān*. Ed. Muḥammad Abū al-Faḍl Ibrāhīm. 4 vols. Cairo: Dār al-Turāth, n.d.

– *Tanāsuq al-durar fī tanāsub al-suwar*. Ed. ʿAbd Allāh Muḥammad al-Darwīsh. 2nd ed. Beirut: ʿĀlam al-Kutub, 1987.

Ṭabarī, Abū Jaʿfar Muḥammad ibn Jarīr al-. *Jāmiʿ al-bayān ʿan taʾwīl āy al-Qurʾān.* Ed. Maḥmūd Muḥammad Shākir. Vol. 1. Cairo: Dār al-Maʿārif, 1958.

Ṭabarsī, Abū ʿAlī al-Faḍl ibn al-Ḥasan al-. *Majmaʿ al-bayān fī tafsīr al-Qurʾān.* Vol. 1. Qom: Maktabat Āyat Allah al-ʿUẓmā al-Marʿashī al-Najafī, 1914.

Ṭabāṭabāʾī, Muḥammad Ḥusayn al-. *Al-Mīzān fī tafsīr al-Qurʾān*. 21 vols. Beirut: Al-Maṭbaʿa al-Tujāriyya, 1970-85.

Talmon, Shemaryahu. "Revelation in Biblical Times." *Hebrew Studies* 26, no. 1 (1985): 53–70.

Ṭanṭāwī, Muḥammad Sayyid. *Al-Tafsīr al-wasīṭ li'l-Qurʾān al-karīm.* Vol. 1. Madīnat al-Sādis min Uktūbar: Nahḍat Miṣr, 1997.

Thanwī, Ashraf ʿAlī. *Bayān al-Qurʾān.* 12 vols. 1908. Reprint, Delhi: Tāj Publishers, 1974.

Thomas, David. "Ibn al-Ikhshīd." In *Christian-Muslim Relations: A Biographical History,* vol. 2, *900–1050*, ed. David Thomas, Alexander Mallett, and Barbara Roggema, 221–3. Leiden: Brill, 2010.

Tirmidhī, Abū ʿĪsā Muḥammad ibn ʿĪsā ibn Sūra al-. *Al-Jāmiʿ al-ṣaḥīḥ wa-huwa sunan al-Tirmidhī*. Ed. Muṣṭafa Ḥusayn Ḥusayn al-Dhahabī. Cairo: Dār al-Ḥadīth, 1999.

Tull, Patricia. "Intertextuality and the Hebrew Scriptures." *Currents in Research: Biblical Studies* 8 (2000): 59–90.

Ṭūsī, Abū Jaʿfar Muḥammad ibn al-Ḥasan al-. *Al-Tibyān fī tafsīr al-Qurʾān.* Vol. 1. Ed. Aḥmad Ḥabīb Quṣayr al-ʿĀmilī. Najaf: Al-Maṭbaʿa al-ʿIlmiyya, 1957.

Useem, Andrea. "In Islam, a Vocal Exercise of Faith." *Chronicle of Higher Education* 47, no. 13 (2000): A72.

Vadet, J.C. "Ibn al-Ikhshīd." In *Encyclopaedia of Islam*, vol. 4, 2nd ed., ed. P. Bearman, Th. Bianquis, C.E. Bosworth, E. van Donzel, and W.P. Heinrichs, 807. Leiden: Brill, 1960.

van Ess, Joseph. "Verbal Inspiration?" In *The Qurʾan as Text*, ed. Stefan Wild, 177–94. Leiden: Brill, 1996.

Wadud, Amina. *Qur'an and Woman: Rereading the Sacred Text from a Woman's Perspective*. 2nd ed. New York: Oxford University Press, 1999.

Wansbrough, John. *Qur'anic Studies: Sources and Methods of Scriptural Interpretation.* Oxford: Oxford University Press, 1977.

Wehr, Hans. *The Hans Wehr Dictionary of Modern Arabic*. 4th ed. Ed. J.M. Cowan. Ithaca, NY: Spoken Languages Services, 1994.

Wellhausen, Julius. *Daṣ arabische Reich und seinen Sturz.* Berlin: Reimer, 1902.

– *Prolegomena zur ältesten Geschichte des Islams.* Berlin: Walter de Gruyter, 1899.

– *Prolegomena zur Geschichte Israels.* 5th ed. Berlin: Reimer, 1899.

Whybray, Robert Norman. *The Making of the Pentateuch: A Methodological Study*. Sheffield, UK: JSOT Press, 1987.

Wild, Stefan, ed. *Self-Referentiality in the Qur'an*. Wiesbaden: Harrassowitz Verlag, 2006.

Yāsīn, ʿAbd al-ʿAzīz Abū Sarīʿ. *Dirāsat al-Bāqillānī li'l-naẓm al-Qur'ānī fī kitābih iʿjāz al-Qur'ān: Taḥlīl wa-naqd.* [Cairo]: n.p., 1991.

Zabīdī, Muḥammad Murtaḍā al-. *Tāj al-ʿarūs min jawāhir al-qāmūs.* Vol. 9. Beirut: Dār al-Fikr, 1994.

Ẓahhār, Najāḥ Aḥmad ʿAbd al-Karīm al-. *Athar istikhdām naẓariyyat al-naẓm ʿinda al-shaykh ʿAbd al-Qāhir al-Jurjānī fī tanmiyat al-tadhawwuq al-balāghī ladā ṭālibāt al-lugha al-ʿArabiyya fī Kullīyat al-Tarbiyya fī al-Madīna al-Munawwara farʿ Jāmiʿat al-Malik ʿAbd al-ʿAzīz.* Riyadh: ʿUbaykān, 2006.

Zahniser, Matthias. "Major Transitions and Thematic Borders in Two Long Sūras: Al-Baqara and al-Nisāʾ." In *Literary Structures of Religious Meaning in the Qur'ān*, ed. Issa J. Boullata, 26–55. Richmond, UK: Curzon, 2000.

Zamakhsharī, Abū al-Qāsim Jār Allāh Maḥmūd ibn ʿUmar al-. *Al-Kashshāf ʿan ḥaqā'iq al-tanzīl wa-ʿuyūn al-aqāwīl fī wujūh al-ta'wīl.* Ed. Yūsuf al-Ḥammādī. 4 vols. Al-Fajjāla, Cairo: Maktabat Miṣr, n.d.

Zarkashī, Badr al-Dīn Muḥammad ibn ʿAbd Allāh al-. *Al-Baḥr al-muḥīṭ.* Cairo: Dār al-Kutub, 1994.

– *Al-Burhān fī ʿulūm al-Qurʾān*. Ed. Muḥammad Abū al-Faḍl Ibrāhīm. 4 vols. Cairo: Dār al-Turāth, n.d.

Zayn, Muḥammad Fārūq al-. *Bayān al-naẓm fī al-Qurʾān al-karīm.* 4 vols. Damascus: Dār al-Fikr, 2003–04.

Zwettler, Michael. "A Mantic Manifesto: The Sūra of 'The Poets' and the Qurʾānic Foundations of Prophetic Authority." In *Poetry and Prophecy: The Beginnings of a Literary Tradition*, ed. James Kugel, 75–119. Ithaca, NY: Cornell University Press, 1990.

Index